Corpus

John D. Caputo, *series editor*

PERSPECTIVES IN
CONTINENTAL
PHILOSOPHY

JEAN-LUC NANCY

Corpus

Translated by Richard A. Rand

Fordham University Press
New York ■ 2008

The text of "Corpus" reproduces and translates the French text of the second edition, © Éditions Métailié, Paris, 2006. That edition followed this English edition, then already in preparation, by including the French originals of "On the Soul," "The Extension of the Soul," and "Fifty-eight Indices on the Body," under the titles "De l'âme," "Extension de l'âme," and "58 indices sur le corps." The first and third essays © Éditions Galilée, 2006. "Extension de l'âme" and "Exister, c'est sortir du point," the original French version of "To Exist Is to Exit the Point," by Antonia Birnbaum, first appeared in a book by those titles, © 2003, Le Portique. "The Intruder" was first published in French as L'Intrus, © 2000, Éditions Galilée.

This work has been published with the assistance of the French Ministry of Culture—National Center for the Book.

Ouvrage publié avec le concours du Ministère français chargé de la culture—Centre National du Livre.

Library of Congress Cataloging-in-Publication Data

Nancy, Jean-Luc.
   [Corpus. English]
   Corpus / Jean-Luc Nancy ; translated by Richard A. Rand.
   p. cm.
   Includes bibliographical references.
   ISBN 978-0-8232-2961-1 (cloth : alk. paper)—
   ISBN 978-0-8232-2962-8 (pbk. : alk. paper)
   1. Body, Human (Philosophy)   I. Title.
   B105.B64N3613   2008
   128′.6—dc22
                        2008029151

Printed in the United States of America
12   5   4
First edition

Contents

Translator's Note

Jean-Luc Nancy wrote "Corpus," the title essay of this volume, between 1990 and 1992. It can be taken as a *summa* of his work in the decades preceding and a formulation for the work in the decades to follow. It sweeps, like the torch of a lighthouse, over the points of its author's compass.

The four other pieces by Nancy included here, all very different from each other in form and idiom, revisit some of the complex questions at work in "Corpus." To these have been added an exceptionally lucid article by Antonia Birnbaum, commenting on the most closely argued of the four essays.

There are no "translator's notes" to this volume. Since every sentence by Jean-Luc Nancy, however elastic or surprising, follows the train of its argument with all due justice and rigor, the translation can only succeed or fail to reflect this. Has the experiment actually worked? Given the exceptional richness and density of the title essay—bound on occasion to baffle the formulations of the most ingenious translator—the original French is here presented on the facing pages. Thus the reader can see what the translation has tried to capture.

Long in the making, this translation has undergone two very careful reviews. They could, in all fairness, be taken as revisions of the given drafts. First and foremost is the work that was done by Danielle Memoire, a superb novelist, bilingual, and expertly trained in philosophy. Danielle

made sense of the French and the English where none was yet to be found. And William Bishop, reviewing the manuscript at a later phase, transformed many a passage from "translationese" into legible English. Finally, a word of warmest thanks to Ann Smock for assistance on the opening pages.

Corpus

Corpus

Corpus

Hoc est enim corpus meum: nous provenons d'une culture dans laquelle cette parole rituelle aura été prononcée, inlassablement, par des millions d'officiants de millions de cultes. Dans cette culture, tous la (re)connaissent, qu'ils soient ou non chrétiens. Parmi les chrétiens, les uns lui donnent valeur de consécration réelle—le *corps* de Dieu est *là*—, les autres, de symbole—où communient ceux qui font *corps* en Dieu. Elle est aussi parmi nous *la* répétition la plus visible d'un paganisme obstiné, ou sublimé: pain et vin, autres corps d'autres dieux, mystères de la certitude sensible. Elle est peut-être, dans l'espace de nos phrases, la répétition par excellence, jusqu'à l'obsession—et jusqu'à faire que «ceci est mon corps» est aussitôt disponible pour une foule de plaisanteries.

C'est notre *Om mani padne* . . . , notre *Allah ill'allah* . . . , notre *Schema Israël* . . . Mais l'écart de notre formule mesure aussitôt notre différence la plus propre: nous sommes obsédés de montrer un *ceci*, et de (nous) convaincre que ce ceci, ici, *est* ce qu'on ne peut ni voir, ni toucher, ni ici, ni ailleurs—et que ceci est *cela* non pas de n'importe quelle manière, mais *comme son corps*. Le corps de *ça* (Dieu, absolu, comme on voudra), et que ça *a un corps* ou que ça *est* un corps (et donc, peut-on penser, que ça est *le* corps, absolument), voilà notre hantise. Le ceci présentifié de l'Absent par excellence: sans relâche, nous l'aurons appelé, convoqué, consacré, arraisonné, capté, voulu, absolument voulu. Nous aurons voulu l'assurance,

Corpus

Corpus

Hoc est enim corpus meum: we come from a culture where this cult phrase will have been tirelessly uttered by millions of people officiating in millions of rites. Everyone in this culture, Christian or otherwise, (re)cognizes it. Among Christians, some value it as a real consecration—God's *body* is *there*—others, as a symbol—thanks to which those who form a *body* with God can commune. For us, it's also the most visible repetition of an obstinate or sublimated paganism: bread and wine, other bodies of other gods, mysteries of sensory certitude. In the realm of our sentences, it's perhaps *the* repetition par excellence, to the point of obsession—to the point that "this is my body" immediately lends itself to more than a few jokes.

It's our *Om mani padne . . .* , our *Allah ill'allah*, our *Schema Israel*. But the twist of our formula promptly defines our own most distinctive difference: we're obsessed with showing a *this*, and with showing (ourselves) that this *this*, here, *is* the thing we can't see or touch, either here or anywhere else—and that *this* is *that*, not just in any way, but *as its body*. The body of *that* (God, or the absolute, if you prefer)—and the fact that "that" *has a body*, or that "that" *is* a body (and so we might think that "that" is *the* body, absolutely): that's our obsession. The presentified "this" of the Absentee par excellence: incessantly, we shall have called, convoked, consecrated, policed, captured, wanted, absolutely wanted it. We shall have wanted the assurance,

la certitude sans mélange d'un *VOICI*: *voici*, sans plus, absolument, voici, ici, ceci, *la même chose*.

Hoc est enim . . . défie, apaise tous nos doutes sur les apparences, et donne au réel la vraie dernière touche de son Idée pure: sa réalité, son existence. De cette parole, on n'en finirait pas de moduler les variantes (au hasard: *ego sum*, le nu en peinture, le *Contrat social*, la folie de Nietzsche, les *Essais*, le *Pèse-nerfs*, «Madame Bovary, c'est moi», la tête de Louis XVI, les planches de Vésale ou de Léonard, la voix—de castrat, de soprano, etc.—, le roseau pensant, l'hystérique, en vérité, c'est toute la texture dont nous sommes tissés . . .). *Hoc est enim* . . . peut générer le *corpus* entier d'une Encyclopédie Générale des Sciences, des Arts et des Pensées de l'Occident.

Le *corps*: voilà comment nous l'avons inventé. Qui d'autre au monde le connaît?

Mais bien sûr, on devine l'angoisse formidable: «voici» n'est donc pas sûr, il faut s'en assurer. Il n'est pas certain que *la chose même* puisse être là. *Là*, où nous sommes, n'est peut-être jamais que reflet, ombres flottantes. Il faut insister: «hoc est *enim*, je vous le dis, *en vérité*, et *je* vous le dis: qui serait plus certain de ma présence *en chair et en sang*? Ainsi, cette certitude sera la vôtre, avec ce corps que vous aurez incorporé.» Mais l'angoisse n'en finit pas: qu'est *ceci*, qui est le corps? Ceci, que je vous montre, mais *tout* «ceci»? tout l'indéterminé du «ceci» et des «ceci»? *Tout ça*? Sitôt touchée, la certitude sensible vire au chaos, à la tempête, tous les sens s'y dérèglent.

Corps est la certitude sidérée, mise en éclats. Rien de plus propre, rien de plus étranger à notre vieux monde.

Corps propre, corps étranger: c'est le corps *propre* que montre, fait toucher, donne à manger *hoc est enim*. Le corps propre, ou la Propriété même, l'Être-à-Soi *en corps*. Mais à l'instant, toujours, c'est un corps étranger qui se montre, monstre impossible à avaler. On n'en sort pas, empêtré dans un vaste gâchis d'images qui vont d'un Christ rêvant sur son pain azyme jusqu'à un Christ s'extirpant un Sacré-Cœur pantelant, sanguinolent. Ceci, ceci . . . *ceci* est toujours trop ou pas assez, pour être *ça*.

Et toutes les pensées du «corps propre», laborieux efforts pour réapproprier ce qu'on croyait fâcheusement «objectivé», ou «réifié», toutes ces pensées du corps propre sont des contorsions comparables: elles n'aboutissent qu'à l'expulsion de cela qu'on désirait.

L'angoisse, le désir de voir, de toucher et manger le corps de Dieu, *d'être* ce corps et *de n'être que ça* font le principe de (dé)raison de l'Occident. Du coup, le corps, du corps, *n'y a jamais lieu, et surtout pas quand on l'y nomme et l'y convoque*. Le corps, pour nous, est toujours sacrifié: hostie.

the unconditional certainty of a *THIS IS: here it is*, nothing more, absolutely, here it is, here, this one, *the same thing*.

Hoc est enim . . . challenges, allays all our doubts about appearances, conferring, on the real, the true final touch of its pure Idea: its reality, its existence. We could never finish modulating the variants of this phrase (at random: *ego sum*, the nude in painting, the *Social Contract*, Nietzsche's madness, the *Essays*, the *Nerve-scale*, "Madame Bovary, c'est moi," the head of Louis XVI, engravings by Vesalius or Leonardo, the voice—of a soprano, a castrato, etc.—a thinking reed, a hysteric, the whole fabric, finally, from which we've been woven . . .). *Hoc est enim* . . . can generate the whole *corpus* of a General Encyclopedia of Western Sciences, Arts, and Ideas.

The *body*: that's how we invented it. Who else in the world knows about it?

But we certainly feel some formidable anxiety: "here it is" is in fact not so sure, we have to seek assurance for it. That *the thing itself* would be there isn't certain. *Here*, where we are, amounts to nothing more, perhaps, than a reflection, or floating shadows. We have to insist: "I'm telling you *truly* that hoc est *enim*, and that *I*'m the one saying this: who else would be so sure of my presence *in flesh and blood*? And so this certainty will be yours, along with this body that you'll have incorporated." But the anxiety doesn't stop there: what's this *this*, who is the body? This, the one I show you, but *every* "this"? All the uncertainty of a "this," of "thises"? *All that?* Sensory certitude, as soon as it is touched, turns into chaos, a storm where all senses run wild.

Body is certitude shattered and blown to bits. Nothing's more proper, nothing's more foreign to our old world.

The body proper, the foreign body: *hoc est enim* displays the body *proper*, makes it present to the touch, serves it up as a meal. The body proper, or Property itself, Being-to-itself *embodied*. But instantly, always, the body on display is foreign, a monster that can't be swallowed. We never get past it, caught in a vast tangle of images stretching from Christ musing over his unleavened bread to Christ tearing open his throbbing, blood-soaked Sacred Heart. This, this . . . *this* is always too much, or too little, to be *that*.

And all thoughts of the "body proper," laborious efforts at reappropriating what we used to consider, impatiently, as "objectified" or "reified," all such thoughts about the body proper are comparably contorted: in the end, they only expel the thing we desired.

The anxiety, the desire to see, touch, and eat the body of God, to *be* that body and *be nothing but that*, forms the principle of Western (un)reason. That's why the body, bodily, *never happens, least of all when it's named and convoked*. For us, the body is always sacrificed: eucharist.

Si *hoc est enim corpus meum* dit quelque chose, c'est hors de parole, ce n'est pas dit, c'est excrit—à corps perdu.

Étranges corps étrangers

Qui d'autre au monde connaît quelque chose comme «le corps»? C'est le produit le plus tardif, le plus longuement décanté, raffiné, démonté et remonté de notre vieille culture. Si l'Occident est une chute, comme le veut son nom, le corps est le dernier poids, l'extrémité du poids qui bascule dans cette chute. Le corps *est* la pesanteur. Les lois de la gravitation concernent les *corps* dans l'espace. Mais tout d'abord, le corps pèse en lui-même: il est descendu en lui-même, sous la loi de cette gravité propre qui l'a poussé jusqu'en ce point où il se confond avec sa charge. C'est-à-dire, avec son épaisseur de mur de prison, ou avec sa masse de terre tassée dans le tombeau, ou bien avec sa lourdeur poisseuse de défroque, et pour finir, avec son poids spécifique d'eau et d'os—mais toujours, mais d'abord en charge de sa chute, tombé de quelque éther, cheval noir, mauvais cheval.

Précipité de très haut, par le Très-Haut lui-même, dans la fausseté des sens, dans la malignité du péché. Corps immanquablement *désastreux*: éclipse et tombée froide des corps célestes. Aurions-nous inventé le ciel dans le seul but d'en faire déchoir les corps?

Ne croyons surtout pas en avoir fini avec ça. Nous ne parlons plus de péché, nous avons des corps sauvés, des corps de santé, de sport, de plaisir. Mais qui ne voit que le désastre s'en aggrave: le corps est toujours plus tombé, plus bas, puisque sa chute est toujours plus imminente, plus angoissante. «Le corps» est notre angoisse mise à nu.

Oui, quelle civilisation a su inventer ça? Le corps si *nu*: le corps, enfin . . .

Étranges corps étrangers, doués de Yin et de Yang, de Troisième Œil, de Champs de Cinabre et d'Océan des Souffles, corps incisés, gravés, marqués, taillés en microcosmes, en constellations: ignorants du désastre. Étranges corps étrangers soustraits à la pesée de leur nudité, et voués à se concentrer en eux-mêmes, sous leurs peaux saturées de signes, jusqu'à la rétraction de tous les sens en un sens insensible et blanc, corps délivré-vivants, points purs d'une lumière toute en soi éjaculée.

Certes, pas un de *leurs* mots ne nous parle de *notre* corps. Le corps des Blancs, le corps qu'*ils* trouvent blafard, toujours au bord de se répandre au lieu de se resserrer, tenu par aucune marque, ni entaille, ni incrustation—ce corps leur est plus étranger qu'une chose étrange. A peine quelque *chose* . . .

If *hoc est enim corpus meum* says anything, it's beyond speech. It isn't spoken, it's exscribed—with bodily abandon.

Strange Foreign Bodies

Does anyone else in the world know anything like "the body"? It's our old culture's latest, most worked over, sifted, refined, dismantled, and reconstructed product. If, as its name suggests, the Occident is a fall, then the body is the ultimate weight, the extremity of the weight sinking from this fall. The body *is* weight. Laws of gravity involve *bodies* in space. But first and foremost, the body itself weighs: it is sunk into itself, according to a specific law of gravity that has pulled the body so far down that it can't be distinguished from its own weight. From its prison-wall thickness, say, or its earthy mass piled up in a tomb, or its clingy burden of cast-off clothing, or, finally, its own weight of water and bone—but always, first and foremost, sinking under the weight of its fall, dropping out of some ether, a black horse, a bad horse.

Flung from on high, by the Highest himself, in the falsehood of senses, the evil of sin. A unfailingly *disastrous* body: an eclipse, a cold shower of heavenly bodies. Did we invent the sky for the sole purpose of making bodies fall from it?

Above all, don't suppose that we're through with this. Sin is no longer a topic; we have saved our bodies, bodies of health, sports, and pleasure. But this only aggravates the disaster, as we all know: because the body is ever more fallen, the fall being further inward, more agonizing. "The body" is our agony stripped bare.

Yes, what civilization could have invented it? Such a *naked* body: the body, therefore . . .

Strange foreign bodies, endowed with Yin and Yang, with the Third Eye, the Cinnabar Field and the Ocean of Qi, bodies incised, engraved, marked, shaped into microcosms, constellations: unacquainted with disaster. Strange foreign bodies protected from the weight of their nudity, devoted to finding their center inside, under skins saturated with signs, in effect confining their senses to a single, empty, unfeeling sense, bodies liberated-alive, pure points of light emitted entirely from within.

Certainly, not a single one of *their* words tells us anything about *our* body. The White Man's body, which *they* find pallid, always almost scattered instead of tightened up, unlinked by any mark, carving, or incrustation—for them, this body's *stranger* than anything foreign. It's almost not a *thing* . . .

Nous n'avons pas mis le corps à nu: nous l'avons inventé, et il est la nudité, et il n'y en a pas d'autre, et ce qu'elle est, c'est d'être *plus étrangère* que tous les étranges corps étrangers.

Que «le corps» nomme l'Étranger, absolument, telle est la pensée que nous avons menée à bien. Je le dis sans ironie, je n'abaisse pas l'Occident. J'ai plutôt peur de mal estimer l'extrémité de cette pensée, sa force d'arrachement, et qu'il faut la traverser. Surtout, ne pas faire comme si elle n'avait pas eu lieu, et comme si le corps nu et blafard de Dieu, de l'Étranger, n'était pas jeté pour longtemps en travers du tableau.

(Qu'on ne se demande pas, en tout cas, pourquoi le corps suscite tant de haine.)

(Qu'on ne se demande pas pourquoi c'est un mot pincé, étroit, mesquin, distant, dégoûté—mais aussi bien dégoûtant, gras, louche, obscène, pornoscopique.)

(Ce mot, il vient à l'idée qu'on ne le sauve qu'avec de belles épures de géométrie à trois ou à n dimensions, avec d'élégantes axonométries: mais alors, tout flotte suspendu en l'air, et le corps *doit* toucher terre.)

Soit à écrire le corps

Soit à écrire, non pas *du* corps, mais le corps même. Non pas la corporéité, mais le corps. Non pas les signes, les images, les chiffres du corps, mais encore le corps. Cela fut, et sans doute cela n'est déjà plus, un programme de la modernité.

Désormais, il ne s'agit plus que d'être *résolument moderne*, et il n'y a pas programme, mais nécessité, urgence. Le motif, il suffit d'allumer la télévision pour l'avoir, chaque jour: il y a un quart ou un tiers du monde où fort peu de corps circulent (mais des chairs, des peaux, des visages, des muscles—les corps sont plus ou moins cachés: hôpitaux, cimetières, usines, lits parfois), et dans le reste du monde, il n'y a que ça, des corps toujours plus nombreux, le corps toujours multiplié (souvent affamé, abattu, meurtri, inquiet, et parfois rieur, danseur).

De cette manière encore, le corps est en limite, en extrémité: il nous vient du plus loin, l'horizon est sa multitude qui vient.

Écrire: toucher à l'extrémité. Comment donc toucher au corps, au lieu de le signifier ou de le faire signifier? On est tenté de répondre à la hâte, ou bien que cela est impossible, que le corps, c'est l'ininscriptible, ou bien qu'il s'agit de mimer ou d'épouser le corps à même l'écriture (danser, saigner . . .). Réponses sans doute inévitables—pourtant rapides, convenues, insuffisantes: l'une comme l'autre parlent au fond de *signifier* le corps, directement ou

We didn't lay the body bare: we invented the body, and nudity is what it is; there isn't anything else, and what it is is something *stranger* than any strange foreign body.

That "the body" might serve as a name for the Stranger, absolutely, is an idea we've pursued to its successful conclusion. I say so without irony, without slighting the West. Rather, I'm concerned with misjudging the radicality of this thought and the force of its uprooting, and the fact that we can't get around it. Above all, let's not act as if this thought hadn't happened, and as if the pale naked body of God, of the Stranger, hadn't been projected across the picture for a long time.

(In any case, it's no wonder the body inspires so much hatred.)

(It's no wonder the word's so pinched, narrow, wretched, distant, and disgusted—but also disgusting, fat, squinting, obscene, pornoscopic.)

(Maybe—maybe this word could be saved by beautiful geometrical designs in three or *n* dimensions, with elegant axonometries: but then everything would have to float, hanging in mid-air, and bodies *must* touch the ground.)

Either Writing the Body

Let there be writing, not *about* the body, but the body itself. Not bodihood, but the actual body. Not signs, images, or ciphers of the body, but still the body. This was once a program for modernity, no doubt already it no longer is.

From now on, it is no longer a question of anything but being *resolutely modern*, and there's no program, just necessity, urgency. Why? Just turn on the television, and you'll get the answer every day: in a quarter or a third of the world very few bodies circulate (only flesh, skin, faces, muscles—bodies there are more or less hidden: in hospitals, cemeteries, factories, beds from time to time), while everywhere else in the world bodies multiply more and more, the body endlessly multiplied (frequently starved, beaten, murdered, restless, sometimes even laughing or dancing).

In this way, too, the body's on edge, at an extreme limit: it comes toward us from the greatest distance; the horizon is the body's multitude, approaching.

Writing: touching upon extremity. How, then, are we to touch upon the body, rather than signify it or make it signify? It's tempting to reply, rashly, either that it's impossible, that the body's uninscribable, or that it's a question of mimicking or merging the body with writing (dancing, bleeding . . .). Unavoidable answers, no doubt, but hasty, conventional, and inadequate:

indirectement, comme absence ou comme présence. Écrire n'est pas signifier. On a demandé: comment toucher au corps? Il n'est peut-être pas possible de répondre à ce «comment»? comme à une demande technique. Mais ce qu'il faut dire, c'est que cela—*toucher* au corps, toucher le corps, toucher enfin—arrive tout le temps dans l'écriture.

Cela n'arrive peut-être pas exactement *dans* l'écriture, si celle-ci a un «dedans». Mais en bordure, en limite, en pointe, en extrémité d'écriture, *il n'arrive que ça*. Or l'écriture a son lieu sur la limite. Il n'arrive donc rien d'autre à l'écriture, s'il lui arrive quelque chose, que de *toucher*. Plus précisément: de toucher le corps (ou plutôt, tel et tel corps singulier) *avec l'incorporel* du «sens». Et par conséquent, de *rendre l'incorporel touchant*, ou de faire du *sens* une touche.

(Je n'essaierai même pas de protester que je ne fais pas l'éloge d'une douteuse «littérature touchante». Car je sais distinguer l'écriture de l'eau de roses, mais *je ne sache pas d'écriture qui ne touche pas*. Ou bien, ce n'est pas de l'écriture, c'est du rapport, de l'exposé, comme on voudra dire. Écrire touche au corps, par essence.)

Mais il ne s'agit pas du tout de trafiquer avec les limites, et d'évoquer on ne sait quels tracés qui viendraient s'inscrire sur les corps, ou quels improbables corps qui viendraient se tresser aux lettres. L'écriture touche aux corps *selon la limite absolue* qui sépare le sens de l'une de la peau et des nerfs de l'autre. Rien ne *passe*, et c'est là que ça touche. (Je déteste l'histoire kafkaïenne de *La colonie pénitentiaire*, fausse, facile et grandiloquente de bout en bout.)

Les «corps écrits»—incisés, gravés, tatoués, cicatrisés—sont des corps précieux, préservés, réservés comme les codes dont ils sont les glorieux engrammes: mais enfin, ce n'est pas le corps moderne, ce n'est pas ce corps que nous avons jeté, là, devant nous, et qui vient à nous, nu, seulement nu, et d'avance *excrit* de toute écriture.

L'*excription* de notre corps, voilà par où il faut d'abord passer. Son inscription-dehors, sa mise *hors-texte* comme le plus *propre* mouvement de son texte: le texte *même* abandonné, laissé sur sa limite. Ce n'est plus une «chute», ça n'a plus ni haut, ni bas, le corps n'est pas déchu, mais tout en limite, en bord externe, extrême, et que rien ne referme. Je dirais: l'anneau des circoncisions est rompu, il n'y a plus qu'une ligne in-finie, le trait de l'écriture elle-même excrite, à suivre infiniment brisé, partagé à travers la multitude des corps, ligne de partage avec tous ses lieux: points de tangence, touches, intersections, dislocations.

Nous ignorons quelles «écritures» ou quelles «excriptions» se préparent à venir de ces lieux. Quels diagrammes, quels réticules, quelles greffes topologiques, quelles géographies des multitudes.

in fact, answers end up, directly or indirectly, *signifying* the body as absence or presence. Writing isn't signifying. We ask: How are we to touch upon the body? Perhaps we can't answer this "How?" as we'd answer a technical question. But, finally, it has to be said that touching upon the body, touching the body, *touching*—happens in writing all the time.

Maybe it doesn't happen exactly *in* writing, if writing in fact has an "inside." But along the border, at the limit, the tip, the furthest edge of writing nothing *but* that happens. Now, writing takes its place at the limit. So if anything at all happens to writing, nothing happens to it but *touch*. More precisely: touching the body (or some singular body) *with the incorporeality* of "sense." And consequently, *to make the incorporeal touching*, to make of meaning a touch.

(I won't bother arguing that I'm not praising some dubious "touching literature." I know the difference between writing and flowery prose, but I *know of no writing that doesn't touch*. Because then it wouldn't be writing, just reporting or summarizing. Writing in its essence touches upon the body.)

But it's not at all a matter of playing with limits, of evoking some kind of pattern for inscribing bodies, or some kind of improbable bodies to be woven into letters. Writing touches upon bodies *along the absolute limit* separating the sense of the one from the skin and nerves of the other. Nothing *gets through*, which is why it touches. (I hate the story of Kafka's "Penal Colony," false, facile, and grandiloquent from beginning to end.)

"Written bodies"—incised, engraved, tattooed, scarred—are precious bodies, preserved and protected like the codes for which they act as glorious engrams: but this isn't really the modern body, this isn't the body we've projected, there, ahead of us, approaching us, naked, merely naked, and *exscribed* in advance from all writing.

We have to begin by getting through, and by means of, the *exscription* of our body: its being inscribed-outside, its being placed *outside the text* as the most *proper* movement of its text; the text *itself* being abandoned, left at its limit. Having no high or low, it's no longer a "fall"; the body isn't cast out but completely at the limit, at an extreme, outward edge that nothing closes up. I would say: the ring of circumcision is broken, the only thing left is an in-finite line, the tracing of writing, which is itself exscribed, to be followed, infinitely broken, distributed among the multitude of bodies, a line of separation imparted to all its sites—tangential points, touches, intersections, dislocations.

We know nothing about the "writings" or "exscriptions" preparing to come from these sites. What diagrams, networks, topological graftings, mass geographies.

Le temps vient en effet d'écrire et de penser ce corps dans l'éloignement infini qui le fait *nôtre*, qui le fait nous venir de plus loin que toutes nos pensées: le corps exposé de la *population* du monde.

(D'où cette nécessité, qui nous reste pour le moment tout à fait indéchiffrable: *ce corps exige une écriture, une pensée populaire.*)

Aphalle et acéphale

Platon veut qu'un discours ait le corps bien constitué d'un grand animal, avec tête, ventre et queue. C'est pourquoi nous autres, bons et vieux platoniciens, nous savons et nous ne savons pas ce que c'est qu'un discours *sans queue ni tête*, aphalle et acéphale. Nous savons: c'est du non-sens. Mais nous ne savons pas: nous ne savons quoi faire du «non-sens», nous n'y voyons pas plus loin que le bout du sens.

Toujous nous faisons signe au sens: au-delà, nous lâchons pied (Platon nous lâche, sacré corps de Dieu !).

«Le corps», c'est où on lâche pied. «Non-sens» ne veut pas dire ici quelque chose comme l'absurde, ni comme du sens à l'envers, ou comme on voudra contorsionné (ce n'est pas chez Lewis Carroll qu'on touchera aux corps). Mais cela veut dire: pas de sens, ou encore, du *sens* qu'il est absolument exclu d'approcher sous aucune figure de «sens». Du sens qui fait sens là où c'est, pour le sens, limite. Du sens muet, fermé, autistique: mais jutement, il n'y a pas d'*autos*, pas de «soi-même». L'autisme sans *autos* du corps, ce qui le fait infiniment moins qu'un «sujet», mais aussi infiniment autre chose, *jeté* non «sub-jeté», mais aussi dur, aussi intense, aussi inévitable, aussi singulier qu'un sujet.

Ni queue, ni tête, donc, puisque rien ne fait support ni substance à cette matière. Je dis «aphalle et acéphale», je ne dis pas «anoure», qui est bon pour les batraciens. Corps impuissant et inintelligent. Ses possibles sont ailleurs, ses forces, ses pensées.

Mais «impuissant» et «inintelligent» sont ici des mots impuissants et inintelligents. Le corps n'est ni bête, ni impotent. Il lui faut d'autres catégories de force et de pensée.

Que seraient les forces, les pensées, qui tiendraient tout d'abord à cet être-jeté-là qu'*est* le corps? Cet être-abandonné, répandu et resserré sur la limite du «là», de l' «ici-maintenant» et du «ceci»? Quelles forces, quelles pensées du *hoc est enim*? Il n'y a là ni action, ni passion, ni concept, ni intuition. Quelles forces et quelles pensées—quelles forces-pensées, peut-être—exprimeraient l'étrangeté si familière de cet être-là, de cet être-ça?

On dira que pour répondre, il faut au plus vite quitter la page d'écriture et le discours, que les corps n'auront jamais leur place ici. Mais ainsi, on se

Finally, it's time to write and think this body across the infinite distance that makes it *ours*, that brings it to come from a site more remote than any of our thoughts: the exposed body of the world's *population*.

(Whence a necessity still completely indecipherable: *this body calls for popular writing, popular thinking.*)

Aphallus and Acephale

Plato wants discourse to have the well-constituted body of a big animal, with a head, stomach, and tail. So all of us, good Platonists of long standing, know and don't know what a discourse *lacking a head and tail* would be, acephalic and aphallic. We know it's nonsense, but we don't know what to make of this "non-sense"; we don't see past the tip of sense.

We always assent to sense: beyond sense, we lose our footing. (Plato deserts us, sacred body of God!)

We lose our footing at "the body." Here, "non-sense" doesn't mean something absurd, or upside-down, or somehow contorted. (We won't be touching on the body in the work of Lewis Carroll.) It means, instead: no sense, or a *sense* whose approach through any figure of "sense" is absolutely ruled out. Sense making sense where sense meets its limit. Mute, closed, autistic sense: but, strictly speaking, there's no *autos*, no "self." Autism without an *autos* for the body, making the body infinitely less than a "subject," but also infinitely other, *thrown*, not "subjected," but just as hard, intense, inevitable, and singular as a subject.

No head or tail, then, since nothing provides support or substance for this material. I say "acephalic and aphallic," not "anurous," which is fine for batrachians. An impotent, unintelligent body. Its possibilities, forces, and thoughts lie elsewhere.

But the words *impotent* and *unintelligent* are impotent and unintelligent in this context. The body's not stupid or impotent. It demands other categories of force and thought.

What forces and thoughts pertain, first of all, to the being-thrown-there that the body *is*? This abandoned-being, spread out and pulled back at the limit of the "there," the "here and now," the "this"? What forces and thoughts about the *hoc est enim*? No action, passion, concept, or intuition will be found there. What forces and thoughts—force-thoughts, perhaps— *could express* the very familiar strangeness of this being-there, this being-that?

As we look for answers, we'll hear that we must immediately give up discourse and the written page, since bodies will never belong there. This would be wrong for the following reason. What we call "writing" and "ontology"

tromperait. Ce qu'on appelle «écriture» et ce qu'on appelle «ontologie» n'ont à faire qu'à ceci: de la place pour ce qui reste, ici, sans place. Artaud pourrait nous crier que nous ne devrions pas être ici, mais à nous tordre, suppliciés, sur des bûchers: je réponds qu'il n'est pas très différent de s'efforcer à écarter, dans le présent et dans le plein du discours et de l'espace que nous occupons, la place, l'ouverture des corps.

Les corps ne sont pas du «plein», de l'espace rempli (l'espace est partout rempli): ils sont l'espace *ouvert*, c'est-à-dire en un sens l'espace proprement *spacieux* plutôt que spatial, ou ce qu'on peut encore nommer le *lieu*. Les corps sont des lieux d'existence, et il n'y a pas d'existence sans lieu, sans *là*, sans un «ici», «voici», pour le *ceci*. Le corps-lieu n'est ni plein, ni vide, il n'a ni dehors, ni dedans, pas plus qu'il n'a ni parties, ni totalité, ni fonctions, ni finalité. Aphalle et acéphale dans tous les sens, si l'on peut dire. Mais c'est une peau diversement pliée, repliée, dépliée, multipliée, invaginée, exogastrulée, orificée, évasive, invasie, tendue, relâchée, excitée, sidérée, liée, déliée. Sous ces modes et sous mille autres (il n'y a pas ici de «formes *a priori* de l'intuition», ni de «table des catégories»: le transcendantal est dans l'indéfinie modification et modulation spacieuse de la peau), le corps *donne lieu* à l'existence.

Et très précisément, il donne lieu à ceci que l'existence a pour essence de n'avoir point d'essence. C'est bien pourquoi *l'ontologie du corps* est l'ontologie même: l'être n'y est rien de préalable ou de sous-jacent au phénomène. Le corps *est* l'être de l'existence. *Comment mieux prendre la mort au sérieux?* Mais aussi: *comment dire que l'existence n'est pas «pour» la mort*, mais que «la mort» est son corps, ce qui est bien différent. Il n'y a pas «la mort», comme une essence à laquelle nous serions voués: il y a le corps, l'espacement mortel du corps, qui inscrit que l'existence n'a pas d'essence (pas même «*la* mort»), mais ex-iste seulement.

Toute sa vie, le corps est aussi un corps mort, le corps d'un mort, de ce mort que je suis vivant. Mort ou vif, ni mort, ni vif, je *suis* l'ouverture, la tombe ou la bouche, l'une dans l'autre.

Le corps ontologique n'est pas encore pensé.

L'ontologie n'est pas encore pensée, en tant que fondamentalement elle est ontologie du corps = du lieu d'existence, ou de *l'existence locale*.

(«Local» n'est pas à prendre, ici, au sens du coin de terre, de la province ou du territoire réservé. Mais au sens pictural de *la couleur locale*: la vibration, l'intensité singulière—elle-même changeante, mobile, multiple—d'un événement de peau, ou d'une peau comme lieu d'événement d'existence.)

(On peut y ajouter ceci: la peinture est l'art des corps, parce qu'elle ne connaît que la peau, elle est peau de part en part. Et un autre nom pour la couleur locale est la *carnation*. La carnation est le grand défi jeté par ces millions de

are concerned with just one thing: the place for what remains, here, without place. Artaud might protest that we shouldn't be here; we should be tortured and sacrificed at the stake. I'd answer that it's not so very different, straining to dislocate the place and the opening of bodies, in the present, and in the midst of the very discourse and space that we occupy.

Bodies aren't some kind of fullness or filled space (space is filled everywhere): they are *open* space, implying, in some sense, a space more properly *spacious* than spatial, what could also be called a *place*. Bodies are places of existence, and nothing exists without a place, a *there*, a "here," a "here is," for a *this*. The body-place isn't full or empty, since it doesn't have an outside or an inside, any more than it has parts, a totality, functions, or finality. It's acephalic and aphallic in every sense, as it were. Yet it is a skin, variously folded, refolded, unfolded, multiplied, invaginated, exogastrulated, orificed, evasive, invaded, stretched, relaxed, excited, distressed, tied, untied. In these and thousands of other ways, the body *makes room* for existence (no "a priori forms of intuition" here, no "table of categories": the transcendental resides in an indefinite modification and spacious modulation of skin).

More precisely, it makes room for the fact that the essence of existence is to be without any essence. That's why the *ontology of the body* is ontology itself: being's in no way prior or subjacent to the phenomenon here. The body *is* the being of existence. *How best to take death seriously?* But also: *How are we to explain that existence isn't "for" death*, but that "death" is the body of existence, a very different thing. There's no "death," taken as an essence to which we've been consigned: there's the body, the mortal spacing of the body, registering the fact that existence has no essence (not even "death"), but only ex-ists.

In the span of its lifetime, the body is also a dead body, the body of a dead person, this dead person I am when alive. Dead or alive, neither dead nor alive, I *am* the opening, the tomb or the mouth, the one inside the other.

The ontological body has yet to be thought.

Ontology has yet to be thought out, to the extent that it's basically an ontology where the body = the place of existence, or *local existence.*

(Here "local" shouldn't be taken as a piece of ground, a province or a reservation. It should be taken, rather, in the pictorial sense of *local color*: the vibration and the singular intensity—itself changing, mobile, multiple—of a skin-event or of skin as the place for an event of existence.)

(We could add the following: painting is the art of bodies, in that it only knows about skin, being skin through and through. Another name for local color is *carnation*. Carnation is the great challenge posed by those millions of

corps de la peinture: non pas l'*incarnation*, où le corps est insufflé d'Esprit, mais la simple carnation, comme le battement, couleur, fréquence et nuance, d'un lieu, d'un événement d'existence. Ainsi Diderot disait envier le peintre capable d'approcher en couleurs ce que lui, l'écrivain, ne pouvait approcher: le plaisir d'une femme.)

Mais peut-être cette ontologie n'est-elle plus exactement à penser. Ou bien: *qu'appelle-t-on penser, si penser c'est penser les corps?* Quel rapport, par exemple, de cette pensée à la peinture? Et au toucher? Et à la jouissance (et à la souffrance)?

Peut-être le «corps ontologique» n'est à penser que là où la pensée *touche* à la dure étrangeté, à l'extériorité non- pensante et non-pensable de ce *corps*. Mais seul un tel toucher, ou une telle touche, est la condition d'une pensée véritable.

Ce qui a queue et tête ne relève pas du lieu, mais de la *place*: queue et tête sont placées le long d'un *sens*, et l'ensemble lui-même fait une place de sens, et toutes les places sont comprises dans le grand tête-à-queue de l'Animal Universel. Mais le sans-queue-ni-tête ne rentre pas dans cette organisation, ni dans cette épaisseur compacte. *Les corps n'ont lieu, ni dans le discours, ni dans la matière.* Ils n'habitent ni «l'esprit», ni «le corps». Ils ont lieu à la limite, *en tant que la limite*: limite—bord externe, fracture et intersection de l'étranger dans le continu du sens, dans le continu de la matière. Ouverture, *discrétion*.

Queue et tête, pour finir, ils le *sont* aussi bien: ils sont *la discrétion même des places du sens, des moments de l'organisme, des éléments de la matière.* Un corps est le lieu qui ouvre, qui écarte, qui espace phalle et céphale: leur *donnant lieu* de faire événement (jouir, souffrir, penser, naître, mourir, faire sexe, rire, éternuer, trembler, pleurer, oublier . . .).

Soit à écrire au corps

C'est ainsi que l'ontologie s'avère comme écriture. «Écriture» veut dire: non la monstration, ni la démonstration, d'une signification, mais un geste pour *toucher* au *sens*. Un toucher, un tact qui est comme une adresse: celui qui écrit ne touche pas sur le mode de la saisie, de la prise en main (du *begreifen* = saisir, s'emparer de, qui est le mot allemand pour «concevoir»), mais il touche sur le mode de s'adresser, de s'envoyer *à* la touche d'un dehors, d'un dérobé, d'un écarté, d'un espacé. Sa touche même, et qui est bien *sa* touche, lui est dans le principe retirée, espacée, écartée. Elle *est*: qu'advienne le contact étranger, l'étranger restant étranger dans le con-

bodies in paintings: not *in*carnation, where Spirit infuses the body, but carnation plain and simple, referring to the vibration, color, frequency, and nuance of a place, of an event of existence. This is why Diderot claimed to envy painters, who could approximate, in colors, something he couldn't approximate in writing: a woman's pleasure.)

But maybe we shouldn't be thinking this ontology any more. Or rather: *If thinking is thinking bodies, what is called thinking?* What, for instance, is the link of such thinking to painting? And touching? And pleasure (and suffering)?

Perhaps we shouldn't think the "ontological body" except where thinking *touches* on the hard strangeness of this *body*, on its un-thinking, unthinkable, exteriority. But such touching, or such a touch, is the sole condition for true thought.

Something with a head and a tail rises up from a *site*, not a place: head and tail are placed alongside a *sense* (direction, meaning), the ensemble itself placing a setting for sense, and all the sets are included in the great head-to-tail of the Universal Animal. But something-without-head-or-tail isn't a part of this organization, or this compact thickness. *Bodies don't take place in discourse or in matter.* They don't inhabit "mind" or "body." They take place at the limit, *qua limit*: limit—external border, the fracture and intersection of anything foreign in a continuum of sense, a continuum of matter. An opening, discreteness.

Bodies, in the end, *are* also that—head and tail: *the very discreteness of the sites of sense, of the moments of an organism, of the elements of matter.* The body is a place that opens, displaces and spaces phallus and cephale: *making room for them* to create an event (rejoicing, suffering, thinking, being born, dying, sexing, laughing, sneezing, trembling, weeping, forgetting . . .).

Or Writing by the Body

Ontology, then, is affirmed as writing. "Writing" means: not the monstration, the demonstration, of a signification but a gesture toward *touching* upon *sense*. A touching, a tact, like an address: a writer doesn't touch by grasping, by taking in hand (from *begreifen* = seizing, taking over, German for "conceiving") but touches by way of addressing himself, sending himself *to* the touch of something outside, hidden, displaced, spaced. His very touch, which is certainly *his* touch, is in principle withdrawn, spaced, displaced. It *is*: may the foreign contact draw near, with the foreigner remaining foreign

tact (restant *dans* le contact étranger *au* contact: c'est toute l'affaire du tact, de la touche des corps).

Écrire s'adresse ainsi. Écrire est la pensée adressée, envoyée au corps, c'est-à-dire à ce qui l'écarte, à ce qui l'étrange.

Ce n'est pas tout. Car c'est *depuis mon corps* que je suis adressé *à* mon corps—ou bien, c'est depuis les corps que le «je» d'écriture est envoyé aux corps. C'est depuis mon corps que *j'ai* mon corps comme à moi étranger, exproprié. Le corps est l'étranger «là-bas» (c'est le lieu de tout étranger) *parce qu'il est ici*. Ici, dans le «là» de l'ici, le corps ouvre, coupe, écarte le «là»-bas.

L'écriture s'adresse (nous adresse) de là à là-bas, dans l'ici-même. C'est aussi bien ce qui est écrit dans *hoc est enim*: si ce n'est pas la transsubstantiation (c'est-à-dire l'incarnation généralisée, l'immanence de la transcendance absolument médiatisée), c'est au contraire cet écart des substances ou des sujets qui seul leur laisse leurs chances singulières, ni immanentes, ni transcendantes, mais dans la dimension, ou dans le geste, de l'adresse, de l'espacement. Ainsi, les corps des amants: ils ne se livrent pas à la transsubstantiation, ils se touchent, ils se renouvellent infiniment leur espacement, ils s'écartent, ils s'adressent l'un (à) l'autre.

(«Écriture» est encore un mot trompeur. Ce qui s'adresse ainsi au corps-dehors *s'excrit*, comme j'essaie de l'écrire, à même ce dehors, ou comme ce dehors.)

«Ontologie du corps» = excription de l'être. Existence adressée au-dehors (*là*, il n'y a pas d'adresse, pas de destination; et pourtant (mais comment?) il y a destinataire: moi, toi, nous, les corps enfin). Ex-istence: les corps sont l'exister, l'acte même de l'ex-istence, *l'être*.

Écrivez aux corps (que fait d'autre l'écrivain?): ça sera envoyé à l'être, ou bien encore, l'être s'envoyant (que pense d'autre la pensée?).

C'est depuis les corps que nous avons, à nous, les corps comme nos étrangers. Rien à voir avec dualismes, monismes ou phénoménologies du corps. Le corps n'est ni substance, ni phénomène, ni chair, ni signification. Mais l'être-excrit.

(Si j'écris, je fais des effets de sens—je place tête, ventre et queue—et je m'écarte donc des corps. *Mais justement*: il faut ça, il faut une mesure infinie, toujours retracée de cet écart. L'excription passe par l'écriture—et certainement pas par des extases de la chair ou du sens. Il faut donc écrire, depuis ce corps que nous n'avons pas, et que nous ne sommes pas non plus: mais où l'être est excrit.—Si j'écris, cette main étrangère est déjà glissée dans ma main qui écrit.)

De là qu'il n'est pas possible d'écrire «au» corps, ou d'écrire «le» corps, sans ruptures, volte-faces, discontinuités (discrétion), ni même sans inconséquences, contradictions, écarts du discours en lui-même. Il faut se jeter

in that contact (remaining a stranger *to* contact *in* contact: that's the whole point about touching, the touch of bodies).

This is how writing is addressed. Writing is thinking addressed, thinking sent to the body, sent, that is, to the very thing that displaces, estranges it.

That's not all. I am addressed *to* my body *from my body*—or rather, the writing "I" is being sent from bodies to bodies. It is from my body that *I have* my body as a stranger to me—expropriated. The body is the stranger "out there" (the place for all strange things) *because it is here*. Here, in the "there" of the here, the body opens, cuts, displaces the *out*-"there."

Writing is addressed (it addresses us) from a there to an out-there, in the right-here. This, too, is inscribed in *hoc est enim*: if it's not transubstantiation (meaning a generalized incarnation, the immanence of an absolutely mediated transcendence), then it's the separation of substances or subjects that alone allows them their singular chance. Their chance is neither immanent nor transcendent but lies in the dimension, or the gesture, of an address, a spacing. Thus the bodies of lovers: they do not give themselves over to transubstantiation, they touch one another, they renew one another's spacing forever, they displace themselves, they address themselves (to) one another.

("Writing" remains a deceptive word. Anything so addressed to the body-outside is *exscribed*, as I try to write it, right alongside this outside, or as this outside.)

"Ontology of the body" = exscription of being. Existence addressed to an out-side (*there*, where there's no address, no destination; and yet (but how?) someone does the receiving: myself, you, us, bodies, finally). Existence: bodies are existence, the very act of ex-istence, *being*.

Writing to bodies (what else do writers do?): something's being sent to being, or better yet, being's sending itself. (What else does thinking think?)

It's from bodies that we have, for ourselves, bodies as our strangers. Nothing to do with a dualism, a monism, or a phenomenology of the body. The body's neither substance, phenomenon, flesh, nor signification. Just being-exscribed.

(If I write, I create sense-effects—I place the head, the tail, the stomach—and I thereby displace myself from bodies. *But rightly so*: this has to happen, we need an infinite measure, always retraced from this displacement. Exscription passes through writing—and certainly not through the ecstasies of flesh or meaning. And so we have to write from a body that we neither have nor are, but where being is exscribed. If I write, this strange hand has already slipped into my writing hand.)

Hence the impossibility of writing "to" the body, or of writing "the" body without ruptures, reversals, discontinuities (discreteness), or trivialities,

au travers de ce «sujet», et de ce «sujet», le mot *corps*, à lui seul, impose une dureté sèche, nerveuse, qui claque les phrases où on l'emploie.

Peut-être *corps* est-il le mot sans emploi par excellence. Peut-être est-il, de tout langage, le mot *en trop*.

Mais cet «en trop», en même temps, n'est rien. Il ne se signale pas par des déchaînements hurlants ou chantants d'outre-langue, ni par des abîmes de silence. Non; *corps* excède le langage de rien, de «trois fois rien», un mot comme un autre, tout à fait à sa place (et même, à beaucoup de places possibles), faisant seulement une infime saillie, une excroissance minuscule mais jamais résorbée.

Avec cette excroissance il y a l'imminence toujours possible d'une fracture, et d'un épanchement du *mot* tout seul hors des veines de sens où il circulait avec les autres. *Corps* comme un bout d'os, comme un caillou, un grave, un gravier qui tombe à pic.

Quelque chose en appelle donc au fragment, ici plus que partout ailleurs. En fait, la fragmentation de l'écriture, depuis qu'elle a lieu et là où elle a lieu (que ce soit toujours et partout, ou bien sous l'exigence d'un «genre»), répond à une instance répétée des corps dans—contre—l'écriture. Une intersection, une interruption, *cette effraction de tout langage où le langage touche au sens.*

Psyche ist ausgedehnt

Le mot le plus fascinant, et peut-être (je le dis sans forcer) le plus décisif de Freud est dans cette note posthume: *«Psyche ist ausgedehnt: weiss nichts davon.»* «La psyché est étendue: n'en sait rien.» C'est-à-dire que la «psyché» est *corps*, et que c'est précisément ce qui lui échappe, et dont (peut-on penser) l'échappée ou l'échappement la constitue en tant que «psyché», et dans la dimension d'un ne-pas-(pouvoir/vouloir)-se-savoir.

Le corps, ou les corps, qu'il s'agit de toucher par la pensée sont cela même: corps de «psyché», être-étendu et hors-de-soi de la présence-au-monde. Naissance: espacement, sortie de la ponctualité, extension par réseaux dans des ectopies multiples (pas seulement le sein), dehors/dedans, *fort/da*, géographie du *ça*, sans carte ni territoire, zones (le plaisir a lieu *par lieux*). Ce n'est pas un hasard si le *topique* a hanté Freud: l'«inconscient» est l'être-étendu de Psyché, et ce qu'après Lacan d'aucuns nomment *sujet*, c'est le singulier d'une *couleur locale* ou d'une *carnation*.

Il n'en est que plus surprenant qu'un certain discours de la psychanalyse semble s'obstiner, au déni de son objet, à rendre le corps «signifiant», au lieu de débusquer la signification comme ce qui partout fait écran aux espacements des corps. Cette analyse «ectopise» (ou «utopise») le corps *hors-lieu*:

contradictions, and displacements of discourse within itself. We have to throw ourselves across this "subject," and the word *body*, of itself, when used with reference to this "subject," imposes a dry and edgy hardness that makes our sentences clatter.

Perhaps *body* is the word without employment par excellence. Perhaps, in any language, it's the word *in excess*.

At the same time, however, this "in excess" is nothing. It isn't announced by shouts or songs from beyond language, or by chasms of silence. No: *body* does not exceed language by anything, anything whatsoever, being a word like any other, entirely in its place (in many possible places, even), sticking out ever so slightly, a minuscule excrescence, but never reabsorbed.

Along with this excrescence comes the always possible imminence of a fracture and of a spontaneous outpouring of the *word* itself from veins of sense, where it was circulating with other words. *Body*, like a piece of bone, a pebble, a stone, a granule, falls right where we need it.

Which is why fragments are necessary, here more than anywhere else. In fact, the fragmentation of writing, wherever it occurs (either always and everywhere, or according to a "genre"), responds to the ongoing protest of bodies in—against—writing. An intersection, an interruption: *this breaking into any language, where language touches on sense.*

Psyche ist ausgedehnt

Freud's most fascinating and perhaps (I say this without exaggerating) most decisive statement is in this posthumous note: *Psyche ist ausgedehnt: weiss nichts davon.* "The psyche's extended: knows nothing about it." The "psyche," in other words, is *body*, and this is precisely what escapes it, and its escape (we may suppose), or its process of escape, constitutes it as "psyche," in a dimension of not (being able/wanting)-to-know-itself.

So, too, the body, or bodies, that we try to touch through thought: "psyche's" body, the being-extended and outside-itself of presence-to-the-world. Birth: a spacing, an escape from punctuality, an extension through networks into multiple ectopias (not just the breast), outside/inside, *fort/da*, a geography of the *id*, with no map and no terrain, zones (pleasure happens *in places*). It's not an accident that Freud was obsessed with the *topical*: the "unconscious" is the being-extended of Psyche, and the thing that some, following Lacan, have called the *subject* is the uniqueness of *local color* or *carnation*.

It's even more surprising, then, that a certain psychoanalytic discourse would seem to insist, while denying its object, on making the body "signify," rather than flushing out signification as something that always screens off the spacings of bodies. This kind of analysis "ectopizes" (or "utopizes") the

elle le volatilise et l'indexe sur l'incorporel du sens. C'est ainsi, semble-t-il, que l'hystérie est instituée comme exemplaire: un corps saturé de signification. Et donc, plus de corps . . . Je voudrais au contraire voir dans l'hystérie un parasitage complet de l'incorporel du sens par le corps, jusqu'à rendre l'incorporel muet, pour exhiber à sa place un morceau, une zone d'*a*-signifiance. (Car enfin, il faudrait savoir si l'hystérique tout d'abord s'engage dans de la traduction, de l'interprétation, ou bien au contraire, et au plus profond, dans un blocage résolu de la transmission du sens. Discours incarné, ou corps bloquant: qui ne voit que sans corps bloquant il n'y a même plus d'hystérie?)

Le corps hystérique est exemplaire en ce qu'il affirme, sur une limite intenable, une *pure* concentration en soi, un pur être-à-soi de son étendue, qui en dénie et qui en catatonise l'extension, l'espacement. Corps qui ne peut pas se desserrer, s'ouvrir. Sujet, substance absolue, absolument a-signifiant. Cette limite expose la vérité du corps, sous la forme de son implosion. (Mais peut-être, en revanche, ce qui s'ouvre au lieu de se concentrer, dans la souffrance ou dans la jouissance, ce qui *donne lieu* au passage de la limite, et non à son durcissement, peut-être cela est-il de *l'hystérie joyeuse*, et le corps même du sens?)

Il n'y a pas d'abord la signification, la traduction, l'interprétation: il y a cette *limite*, ce bord, ce contour, cette extrémité, ce plan d'exposition, cette couleur-sujet locale, qui peut simultanément se contracter, se concentrer, tendre à l'inextension d'un point, d'un centre-de-soi, et se détendre, s'étendre, être traversée de passages, de partages. Cela seulement peut fermer ou dégager de l'espace pour des «interprétations».

Sans doute, on me dira que la concentration ou l'extension, l'en-topie ou l'ec-topie *sont déjà des interprétations*. Et que, par conséquent, il n'y a pas de corps qui ne soit déjà noué au réseau de la signification, il n'y a pas de «corps libre», flottant hors-sens. Je réponds que *c'est le sens lui-même qui va flotter, pour finir ou pour commencer, sur sa limite*: et cette limite *est le corps*, non pas comme une pure et simple extériorité au sens, non pas comme on ne sait quelle «matière» intacte, intouchable, enfoncée dans une invraisemblable transcendance close dans l'immédiateté la plus épaisse (cela, c'est l'extrémité caricaturale du «sensible» de tous les idéalismes et de tous les matérialismes), *non pas donc, pour finir comme «le corps», mais bien comme LE CORPS DU SENS.*

Le *corps du sens* n'est en rien l'incarnation de l'idéalité du «sens»: c'est au contraire la fin de cette idéalité, la fin du sens, par conséquent, en ce qu'il cesse de *se* renvoyer et de *se* rapporter à soi (à l'idéalité qui le fait «sens»), et se suspend, *sur cette limite qui fait son «sens» le plus propre*, et qui l'expose comme tel. Le corps du sens *expose* ce suspens «fondamental» du sens (il

body *beyond-place*: it volatilizes it, indexing it to the incorporeality of sense. Hence, it would seem, hysteria is instituted as exemplary: a body saturated with signification. And hence no more body . . . I would prefer to take hysteria as the body's becoming totally parasitical upon the incorporeality of sense, to the point that it silences incorporeality, thereby showing, in its stead, a piece, a zone, of *a*-significance. (Because, ultimately, we would have to know whether the hysteric is engaging mainly in translation and interpretation or in something contrary and much deeper, namely, a resolute blockage of the transmission of sense. Discourse incarnate, or a blocking body: Who doesn't see that there is no hysteria without a blocking body?)

The hysterical body is exemplary in its affirmation—at an unattainable limit—of a *pure* concentration in itself, the pure being-in-itself of its extension, which in turn denies and renders catatonic its extendedness and its spacing. A body that cannot be unfolded or opened up. A subject, an absolute substance, absolutely a-signifying. This limit manifests the truth of the body, in the form of its implosion. (But perhaps something that opens up in pain or pleasure, and does not withdraw, something that *makes room* for a passage through the limit, rather than hardening it—is this not, perhaps, a kind of *joyful hysteria*, and the very body of sense?)

At the outset, there is no signification, translation, or interpretation: there is this *limit*, this edge, this contour, this extremity, this outline, this local subject-color, which can be withdrawn, concentrated, and pulled into the nonextension of a point or self-center, simultaneously distending or extending itself through passages and partitions. This alone can close or release a space for "interpretations."

I'll undoubtedly be told that concentration or extension, the en-topic or ec-topic, *are already interpretations.* And that therefore all bodies are caught up in a network of signification, and that no "free body" floats beyond sense. I say in reply that *sense itself will float, in order to stop or start at its limit*: and that this limit *is the body*, and not as a pure and simple exteriority of sense, or as some unknown, intact, untouchable matter, thrust into some improbable transcendence closed in the densest immediacy (such, indeed, is the extreme caricature of "the sensory" in all idealisms and materialisms)—*not then, finally, as "the body," but instead as THE BODY OF SENSE.*

In no way is the *body of sense* the incarnation of an ideality of "sense": on the contrary, it is the end of such an ideality—and thus the end of sense as well, since it no longer returns to itself or refers to itself (to an ideality making "sense" of it)—suspending itself *at a limit that makes its own most proper "sense"* and exposes it as such. The body of sense *exposes* this "fundamental" suspension of sense (exposes *existence*), what we might indeed call

expose l'*existence*)—qu'on peut aussi bien nommer l'*effraction* qu'*est* le sens dans l'ordre même du «sens», des «significations» et des «interprétations».

Le corps expose l'effraction de sens que l'existence constitue, absolument et simplement.

C'est pourquoi on ne le dira, ni antérieur, ni postérieur, ni extérieur, ni intérieur à l'ordre signifiant—mais en limite. Et pour finir, on ne dira pas «le corps du sens», comme si «le sens» pouvait encore, sur cette limite, être support ou sujet de quoi que ce soit: mais on dira le corps, absolument, *comme l'absolu du sens même proprement exposé.*

Le corps n'est ni «signifiant», ni «signifié». Il est exposant/exposé: *ausgedehnt*, extension de l'effraction qu'est l'existence. Extension du *là*, du lieu d'effraction par où *ça* peut *venir du monde*. Extension mobile, espacements, écartements géologiques et cosmologiques, dérives, sutures et fractures des archi-continents du sens, des plaques tectoniques immémoriales qui remuent sous nos pieds, sous notre histoire. *Le corps est l'archi-tectonique du sens.*

(C'est ainsi que sont tressés l'un dans l'autre deux «hoc est enim . . . »: celui qui approprie *hoc* en «corps du sens», opère la transsubstantiation, égale le sens à la totalité achevée du monde; et celui qui s'expose à l'enfouissement et au déplacement archi-tectoniques du même *hoc*.)

Ego

Non pas «mon corps», mais: *corpus ego*. «Ego» n'a de sens qu'à être prononcé, proféré (et dans sa profération, son sens est simplement identique à l'existence: «ego sum, ego existo»). Descartes dit fort bien que la vérité de cet énoncé tient à la circonstance, au «chaque fois» de son énonciation: «chaque fois que je le prononce, ou que je le conçois» (où il est clair que la «conception», «dans mon esprit» comme le précise Descartes, est équivalente à la profération parce qu'elle en est un mode: c'est la même articulation). Il faut une *fois*, une quantité discrète qui donne *l'espace de temps* de l'articulation, ou qui lui donne *lieu* (que cette «fois», sans doute, ait lieu sans cesse, à toutes les fois, à tout espace de temps de l'exister, à tout moment, cela n'est en rien contradictoire: cela indique simplement que l'exister existe selon cette discrétion, cette discontinuité continue, c'est-à-dire, son corps). Ainsi, dans l'articulation de l'*ego* cartésien, la bouche ou l'esprit c'est tout un: c'est toujours le corps. Non pas le corps *de* l' «ego», mais *corpus ego*, «ego» qui n'est «ego» qu'articulé, s'articulant comme l'espacement, la flexion, voire l'inflexion d'un *lieu*. L'énonciation d' «ego» n'*a* pas seulement lieu. Bien plutôt, elle *est* lieu. Elle n'est que localisée: *ego = ici* (du coup, dislocation: *ego* s'est aussi

a *breakthrough*—the sense in the very order of "sense," of "significations," of "interpretations."

The body exposes a breakthrough of sense, constituted absolutely and simply by existence.

Which is why we will not speak of it as anterior or posterior, exterior or interior to the signifying order—but at the limit. And finally, we will not call it "the body of sense," as if "sense" at this limit could still be the support or subject of anything at all: instead, and absolutely so, we will call it *the body, as the absolute of sense itself, properly exposed.*

The body is neither a "signifier" nor a "signified." It's exposing/exposed: *ausgedehnt*, an extension of the breakthrough that existence is. An extension of the *there*, the site of a breakthrough through which *it* can *come in from the world*. A mobile extension, spacings, geological and cosmological displacements, drifts, sutures and fractures in archi-continents of sense, in immemorial tectonic plates shifting under our feet, under our history. *The body is the architectonics of sense.*

(This is how two kinds of "hoc est enim . . ." get interwoven: the one that appropriates *hoc* into a "body of sense" effects a transubstantiation and equates sense with the achieved totality of the world; the other is exposed to the archi-tectonic burial and displacement of that very *hoc*.)

Ego

Not "my body," but: *corpus ego.* "Ego" makes sense only when it is declared, proffered (and when proffered, its sense is exactly identical to existence: *ego sum, ego existo*). Descartes keenly remarks that this declaration owes its truth to the circumstance, the "each time," of its statement: "each time I declare it, or conceive it" (where "conception," "in my mind," as Descartes specifies, clearly amounts to the act of proffering as one of its modes: it's the same articulation). It needs *one time*, a discrete quantity providing articulation with *a space of time*, or a *place* (it's not a contradiction, certainly, that this "once" happens unceasingly, every time, in every space of time, in every moment of existing: this simply indicates that existing exists along with this discreteness, or continuous discontinuity, in other words, with its body). In the Cartesian *ego's* articulation, therefore, mouth and mind are the same: it's always the body. Not the body *of* the ego, but *corpus ego*, "ego" being "ego" only when articulated, articulating itself as spacing or flexion, even the inflection of a *site*. The enunciation of "ego" doesn't just *take* place. To the contrary, it *is place*. Unless localized, it is not: ego = *here* (in effect, a dislocation: *ego*, moreover, is posed *there*, deposed *over* there, at a remove from

bien posé *là*, déposé *là-bas*, à distance d'articulation). Tous les lieux se valent, pour pro-férer «ego» (pour se le pousser hors de soi, afin qu'il y ait «soi») mais seulement en tant que lieux. Il n'y a ni atopie, ni utopie d'*ego*. Mais seulement l'ec-topie articulatoire, constitutive de la topique absolue, chaque fois absolue d'ego. *Hic et nunc, hoc est enim* . . . Ici, maintenant, c'est-à-dire, selon cet espace, ce battement, cette effraction de la substance qu'est le corps existant, l'existence absolument corporelle. *Je* suis, chaque fois que je suis, la flexion d'un lieu, le pli ou le jeu par où ça (se) pro-fère. *Ego sum* cette inflexion locale, telle et telle chaque fois, singulièrement (et combien de fois en «une» fois? combien d'articulations en «une»?), voire cet accent ou ce *ton*.

L'axiome matériel, ou l'archi-tectonique absolue, du *corpus ego* implique ainsi qu'il n'y a pas «ego» en général, mais seulement la *fois*, l'occurrence et l'occasion d'un *ton*: tension, vibration, modulation, couleur, cri ou chant. En tout cas, toujours *voix*, et non pas «*vox significativa*», non pas l'ordre signifiant, mais *ce timbre du lieu où un corps s'expose et se profère*. Il ne lui faut pas moins qu'une extension qui n'est pas celle de deux lèvres au bout d'un agencement d'organes, mais qui est l'extension même, le corps *partes extra partes*. C'est de tête en queue, et fût-ce sans queue ni tête, que ça doit s'écarter pour qu'*ego* soit prononcé.

Corpus ego est sans propriété, sans «égoïté» (et combien plus sans égoïsme). L'égoïté est une signification (nécessaire) d'*ego*: ego se liant à soi, liant la déliaison de sa profération, liant le corps, serrant sur lui le lacet de *soi*. L'égoïté instaure l'espace continu, l'indistinction des *fois* d'existence (avec elle, l'horreur de la mort . . .), la boucle du sens ou le sens en tant que bouclé.

Corpus ego fait le sens débouclé, ou fait sa boucle indéfinie, discrète traversée de lieu en lieu, de tous les lieux. Un corps traverse tous les corps, autant qu'il est à travers de lui-même: c'est l'exact revers d'un monde de monades closes, à moins que ce ne soit, enfin *en corps*, la vérité de l'intersection et de la compénétration des monades en totalité.

Ego toujours s'articulant—*hoc, et hoc, et hic, et illic* . . . —, allée-venue des corps: voix, nourriture, excrément, sexe, enfant, air, eau, son, couleur, dureté, odeur, chaleur, poids, piqûre, caresse, conscience, souvenir, syncope, regard, paraître, enfin toute les *touches* infiniment multipliées, tous les *tons* proliférant.

Le monde des corps est le monde non-impénétrable, le monde qui n'est pas d'abord soumis à la compacité de l'espace (lequel, comme tel, n'est que remplissement, au moins virtuel), mais où *les corps articulent d'abord l'espace*. Lorsque les corps ne sont pas dans l'espace, mais l'espace dans les corps, alors il est espacement, tension du lieu.

articulation). For prof-fering "ego" (for thrusting it outside the self, so that there might be a "self"), all places are equally effective, but only as places. There is no atopia, no utopia, for *ego*. But only an articulatory ec-topia, constituting the absolute topic of *ego*, absolute every time. *Hic et nunc, hoc est enim . . .* In other words, here and now according to this space—this pulse, this breakthrough of substance that the existing body is, absolutely corporeal existence. *I* am, every time I am, the flexion of a place, a fold or motion through which it prof-fers (itself). *Ego sum* this local inflection, singularly, such and such each time (and how many times in "one" time? how many articulations in "one?"), even this accent, or this *tone*.

Thus the *corpus ego*'s material axiom, or absolute archi-tectonic, implies that there's no "ego" in general, only the one *time*, the occurrence and occasion for a *tone*: a tension, vibration, modulation, color, cry, or song. Always, in any case, a *voice*, and not a *vox significativa*, not a signifying order, but *the timbre of the place where a body exposes and proffers itself.* It calls for nothing less than an extension that is not as two lips at the end of an organic assemblage but extension as such, the body *partes extra partes*. In order that *ego* be declared, this thing has to be displaced from head to tail—even without head or tail.

Corpus ego has no propriety, no "ego-ness" (still less any "egotism"). Ego-ness is a (necessary) signification of *ego*: ego binding itself to itself, binding the unbinding of its proffering, binding the body, tightening the lace of the *self* around it. Ego-ness installs continuous space, the indistinctness of the *times* of existence (and with it, the horror of death . . .), the closure of sense, or sense as closed.

Corpus ego forces sense to unbuckle, or makes its closure indefinite, a discrete crossing from place to place, in all places. Insofar as it is across itself, a body crosses all bodies: it is the exact opposite of a world of closed monads—unless, finally, *as a body*, it is the truth of the intersection and co-penetration of monads in their totality.

Ego forever articulating itself—*hoc, et hoc, et hic, et illic . . .*—the coming-and-going of bodies: voice, food, excrement, sex, child, air, water, sound, color, hardness, odor, heat, weight, sting, caress, consciousness, memory, swoon, look, appearing—all *touches* infinitely multiplied, all *tones* finally proliferating.

The world of bodies is the nonimpenetrable world, a world that is not initially subject to the compactness of space (space, as such, being only a filling-up, or at least virtually so); rather, it is a world where *bodies initially articulate space*. The world is spacing, a tension of place, where bodies are not in space, but space in bodies.

Partes extra partes: ce qui est impénétrable, ici, ce n'est pas l'épaisseur massive de la *pars*, c'est au contraire l'écartement de l'*extra*. Jamais un corps ne «pénètre» l'ouverture d'un autre corps *sauf en le tuant* (c'est pourquoi il y a tout un pauvre lexique sexuel qui n'est qu'un lexique de meurtre et de mort . . .). Mais un corps «dans» un corps, ego «dans» ego, ça n' «ouvre» rien: c'est à *même* l'ouvert que le corps est déjà, infiniment, plus qu'originellement; c'est à même *ça* qu'a lieu cette traversée sans pénétration, cette mêlée sans mélange. L'amour est le toucher de l'ouvert.

Mais «l'ouvert» n'est pas et ne peut pas être un «substantif». L' «extra» n'est pas une autre «pars» entre les «partes», mais seulement le partage des parts. Partage, partition, départ.

Alter

Ego forme aussi bien l'obstacle absolu au corps, à la venue d'un corps. Le *point d'ego* d'un corps qui (s')énonce, c'est-à-dire qui, (s')étend, forme aussi, identiquement, non contradictoirement, et pourtant avec contrariété, un point de concentration extrême où *se* qui *s*'étend et qui *s*'énonce offusque aussi l'étendue, le corps qu'il est. *Ego* énoncé se retranche à l'instant d'*ego* énonçant, et précisément parce qu'il est le *même*, et que c'est ainsi qu'il est *ego*: identité retranchée, identifié retranché, identique à son retranchement. Il se retranche en un point, le point de sa propre contrariété: là où *corpus* (s')énonce «ego», *ego* entre dans la contrariété, il se contrarie d'un *soi* en face de soi-*même*, et *corpus* devient la matière-obstacle de cette contrariété (et le lieu même de l'énonciation). La matière ob-jetée du sub-jet. C'est pourquoi il n'y a pas de «corps propre», c'est une reconstruction. Ou bien le corps est encore seulement le «s'étendre», et il est trop tôt pour le «propre», ou bien il est déjà pris dans cette contrariété, et il est trop tard. *Mais corpus n'est jamais proprement moi.*

Il est toujours «objet», corps ob-jecté précisément *à la prétention d'être corps-sujet*, ou sujet-en-corps. Descartes est véridique aussi de cette manière: je m'objecte mon corps, chose étrangère, étrange, extériorité à mon énonciation («ego») *de* cette énonciation elle-*même*. Ou bien, Hegel: «l'esprit est un os», dit-il à propos de la conformation du crâne humain, c'est-à-dire que l'os échappe à l'esprit, lui résiste, le contrarie d'une objection impénétrable. (*Hoc est enim corpus meum*: c'est une appropriation impossible, c'est l'impossibilité même de l'appropriation en général. Du «moi», il n'y en a pas *étendu*: dès que *je* est étendu, il est aussi livré aux autres. Ou bien, l'étendu que *je* suis, je le suis m'étant retranché, soustrait, ôté et objecté.

Un corps est toujours objecté du dehors, à «moi» ou à autrui. Les corps sont d'abord et sont toujours autres—de même que les autres sont d'abord

Partes extra partes: here, what is impenetrable is not the massive thickness of the *pars*, but the displacement of the *extra*. A body only ever "penetrates" the opening of another body *when killing it* (which is why the sexual lexicon is completely meager, a lexicon of nothing less than murder and death . . .). But a body "in" a body, ego "in" ego, doesn't "open" anything: it is *at the very* opening that the body already is, infinitely, and more than originally so; this crossing takes place *right there*, without penetration, this melee occurs without mingling. Love is the touch of the open.

But "the open" is not, and cannot be, "substantive." The "extra" is not a "pars" among other "partes," but an imparting of parts. Imparting, partition, departure.

Alter

Ego also forms an absolute obstacle to the body, to the coming of a body. The *ego-point* of a body enunciating or extending (itself) also forms, identically and without contradiction, even when contrary, a point of extreme concentration where the *self* extending or enunciating (itself) also obscures the extension, or the body, that it is. *Ego* enunciated is instantly detached from *ego* enunciating, precisely because it's the *same*, and hence *ego*: it's an identity withdrawn, identified as withdrawn, identical to its withdrawal. It withdraws at the point of its own contrariety: wherever *corpus* declares (itself) as "ego," *ego* enters into contrariety, being countered by a *self* that confronts its *self*, with *corpus* becoming the matter-obstacle of this contrariety (and the very site of its declaration). The ob-jected matter of the sub-ject. This is why there is no "proper body," just a reconstruction. Either it's just an "extending of itself," and too early for the "proper," or it's already caught in this contrariety, already too late. *But* corpus *is never properly me.*

It's always an "object," a body ob-jected precisely *against the claim of being a body-subject*, or a subject-in-a-body. Here, again, Descartes is correct, and in the following way: I ob-ject my body against myself, as something foreign, something strange, the exteriority *to* my enunciation ("ego") *from* this enunciation it-*self*. Or, again, Hegel: "the mind is a bone," he says, referring to the conformation of the human skull, meaning that the bone eludes the mind, resists it, counters it with an impenetrable objection. (*Hoc est enim corpus meum*: it's an impossible appropriation, it's the very impossibility of appropriation in general.) Nothing of the "me" is *extended*: as soon as *I* is extended, it's also delivered to others. Or again, I'm the extension that *I am* by being withdrawn, subtracted, removed, and ob-jected.

A body's always ob-jected from the outside, to "me" or to someone else. Bodies are first and always other—just as others are first and always bodies.

et sont toujours corps. J'ignorerai toujours mon corps, je m'ignorerai toujours comme corps *la même* où «corpus ego» est une certitude sans réserves. Les autres, au contraire, je les saurai toujours en tant que corps. *Un autre est un corps* parce que seul *un corps est un autre*. Il a ce nez, ce teint de peau, ce grain, il a cette taille, ce creusement, ce pincement. Il pèse ce poids. Il sent cette odeur. Pourquoi ce corps est-il tel, et non pas autre? *Parce qu'il est autre*—et que l'altérité consiste dans l'être-*tel*, dans le sans-fin de l'être tel et tel et tel de *ce* corps, exposé jusqu'aux extrémités. Le *corpus* inépuisable des traits d'un corps.

L'ob-jection touche. *Ce* corps, *ce* trait, *cette* zone de *ce* corps me touche (touche «mon» corps). Ça me plaît ou ça me déplaît, ça me contrarie ou non, ça m'intrigue ou non, ça me frappe ou ça me laisse indifférent, ça m'excite ou ça me révulse. Mais ça sera toujours venu de plus loin que toute autre chose de l'autre. Ça sera venu *dans la venue* même de l'autre. Autrui sera d'abord venu, du plus loin, du plus écarté, dans un corpus de traits qui finit par s'identifier à «lui»—et qui pourtant reste en lui-même inidentifiable: car ces traits sont tous étrangers les uns aux autres, ce bras avec ce menton, ces poils avec ces hanches, et cette voix, et cet . . . . tous faisant corps *et* disloqués ensemble.

Et ainsi jusqu'au point où il devient clair que «autre», «autrui» ne sont même pas les mots justes, mais seulement «corps». Le monde auquel *je* nais, je meurs, j'existe, n'est pas le monde «des autres», puisqu'il est tout autant le «mien». C'est le monde des corps. Le monde du dehors. Le monde des dehors. Le monde sens dedans-dehors, dessus-dessous. Le monde de la contrariété. Le monde de l'encontre. Une encontre immense, interminable: chaque corps, chaque masse prélevée sur un corps est immense, c'est-à-dire sans mesure, infinie à parcourir, à toucher, soupeser, regarder, à laisser se poser, diffuser, infuser, à laisser peser, à soutenir, à résister, à soutenir comme un poids et comme un regard, comme le regard d'un poids.

Pourquoi y a-t-il cela, la vue, et non pas plutôt quelque chose qui mêlerait le voir et l'entendre? Mais d'un tel mélange, y a-t-il seulement du *sens* à parler? En quel sens? Pourquoi y a-t-il *cette* vue, qui ne voit pas les infrarouges? Cette ouïe qui n'entend pas les ultrasons? Pourquoi y a-t-il, à chaque sens, des seuils, et entre tous les sens, des murs. Plus encore: les sens ne sont-ils pas des univers séparés? Ou bien: la dislocation de tout univers possible? Qu'est-ce que l'écartement des sens? Et pourquoi cinq doigts? Pourquoi ce grain de beauté? Pourquoi ce pli au coin des lèvres? Pourquoi ce sillon, là? Pourquoi cet air, cette allure, cette mesure, cette démesure? Pourquoi *ce* corps, pourquoi *ce* monde, pourquoi absolument et exclusivement lui?

I'll never know my body, never know myself as a body *right there* where "corpus ego" is an unqualified certainty. By contrast, I'll always know others as bodies. *An other is a body* because only *a body is an other.* It has this nose, that skin color, this texture, that size, this fold, tightness. It weighs this weight. It smells that way. Why is this body thus, and not otherwise? *Because it is other*—and alterity consists in being-*thus*, in being the thus and thus and thus of *this* body, exposed all the way into its extremities. The inexhaustible *corpus* of a body's features.

The ob-jection touches. *This* body, *this* feature, *this* zone of *this* body touches me (touches "my" body). This pleases or displeases me, does or does not oppose me, does or does not interest me, strikes me or leaves me cold, excites or repels me. This will always have come, however, from farther than anything else belonging to the other. This will have come *in the very coming* of the other. The other will have come first, from the farthest, most displaced place, a corpus of features finally identified with "him"—yet remaining in itself unidentifiable: because these features are all foreign to each other, this arm and that chin, those hairs and these hips, and this voice, and this . . . .
all coming together *and* being dislocated at one and the same time.

And so on, until it becomes clear that *other* is not even the right word, just *body.* The world where *I'*m born, die, and exist isn't the world "of others," since it's "mine" as much as anyone's. It's the world of bodies. The world of the outside. The world of outsides. The world inside-outside, upside-down. The world of contrariety. The world of being countered. An immense, unending encounter: each body, each mass taken from a body, is immense, which means immeasurable, an infinity offered to reach, touch, weigh, watch, to be left resting, dispersing, infusing, left to weigh, support, resist, sustain like a weight and a look, like the look of a weight.

Why is there this thing, sight, rather than sight blended with hearing? And would it make any *sense* to discuss such a blend? In what sense? Why *this* sight, which doesn't see infrared? This hearing, which doesn't hear ultrasound? Why should every sense have a threshold, and why are senses walled off from each other? Further still: aren't senses separate universes? Or else the dislocation of every possible universe? What's the disjunction of senses? And why five fingers? Why that beauty spot? Why this fold at the corner of the lips? That crease, there? That appearance, this gait, that restraint, this excess? Why *this* body, *this* world, absolutely and exclusively this one?

Hoc est enim: ce monde-*ci*, ci-gisant, avec sa chlorophylle, sa galaxie solaire, ses roches métamorphiques, ses protons, sa double hélice désoxyribonucléique, son nombre d'Avogadro, sa dérive des continents, ses dinausaures, sa couche d'ozone, les rayures de son zèbre, sa bête humaine, le nez de Cléopâtre, le nombre des pétales de la marguerite, le spectre de l'arc-en-ciel, la manière de Rubens, la peau du serpent python, la figure que fait André sur cette photo du 16 janvier, ce brin d'herbe et cette vache qui le broute, et la nuance de l'iris de l'œil de qui lit ce mot, ici et maintenant? Et pourquoi pas aussi des sens qu'on ne nomme pas, des sens qu'on ne sent pas, ou pas comme des sens, un sens de la durée, du temps qui passe? Et même un sens de l'espacement des sens? Et un sens de l'ex-tension pure? Ou de l'ex-istence?

Expeausition

Les corps toujours sur le départ, dans l'imminence d'un mouvement, d'une chute, d'un écart, d'une dislocation. (Ce que c'est qu'un *départ*, même le plus simple: cet instant où tel corps n'est plus *là*, *ici* même où il était. Cet instant où il fait place à la seule béance de l'espacement qu'il est lui-même. Le corps qui s'en va emporte son espacement, il s'emporte comme espacement, et en quelque sorte il se met à part, il se retranche en lui—mais en même temps, il laisse ce même espacement «derrière lui»—comme on dit—, c'est-à-dire *à sa place*, et cette place reste la sienne, absolument intacte et absolument abandonnée, à la fois. *Hoc est enim absentia corporis et tamen corpus ipse*.)

Cet espacement, ce départ, c'est son intimité même, c'est l'extrémité de son retranchement (ou si l'on veut, de sa distinction, ou de sa singularité, voire de sa subjectivité). Le corps est *soi* dans le départ, en tant qu'il part— qu'il s'écarte ici même de l' *ici*. L'intimité du corps *expose* l'aséité pure comme l'écart et le départ qu'elle *est*. L'aséité—l'à-soi, le par soi du Sujet— n'*existe* que comme l'écart et le départ de cet *a*—(de cet *à part soi*) qui est le lieu, l'instance propre de sa présence, de son authenticité, de son sens. *L'a part soi en tant que départ*, voilà ce qui est exposé.

L' «exposition» ne signifie pas que l'intimité est extraite de son retranchement, et portée au-dehors, mise en vue. Le corps serait alors une exposition du «soi», au sens d'une traduction, d'une interprétation, d'une mise en scène. L' «exposition» signifie au contraire que l'expression est elle-même l'intimité et le retranchement. L'*à part soi* ne s'y traduit pas, ne s'y incarne pas, il y est ce qu'il est: ce vertigineux retranchement *de* soi qu'il faut pour ouvrir l'infini du retranchement *jusqu'à* soi. Le corps est ce départ de soi, à soi.

Hoc est enim: this world-*here*, stretched out here, with its chlorophyll, its solar galaxy, its metamorphic rocks, its protons, its deoxyribonucleic double helix, its Avogadro number, its continental drift, its dinosaurs, its ozone layer, the stripes of its zebra, its human beast, Cleopatra's nose, the number of petals on a daisy, the ghost of a rainbow, the style of Rubens, a python's skin, André's face in this photo taken on January 16, this blade of grass and the cow that grazes on it, the nuance of an iris in the eye of the one reading this very word, here and now? And why not senses, also, without names, senses we don't sense, or not as senses, like the sense of duration, or of time passing? Or even the sense of the spacing of senses? Or the sense of pure ex-ten-sion? Of ex-istence?

Expeausition (Skin-Show)

Bodies always about to leave, on the verge of a movement, a fall, a gap, a dislocation. (Even the simplest *departure* is just this: the moment when some body's no longer *there*, right *here* where he was. The moment he makes room for a lone gulf in the spacing that he himself *is*. A departing body carries its spacing away, itself gets carried away as spacing, and somehow it sets itself aside, withdraws into itself—while leaving its very spacing "behind"—as one says—*in its place*, with this place remaining its own, at once absolutely intact and absolutely abandoned. *Hoc est enim absentia corporis et tamen corpus ipse.*)

This spacing, this departure, is its very intimacy, the extremity of its separation (or, if we prefer, of its distinction, its singularity, even its sub-jectivity). The body is *self* in departure, insofar as it parts—displaces itself right here from the *here*. The intimacy of the body *exposes* pure a-seity as the swerve and departure that it *is*. Aseity—the *a-se(lf)*, the to-itself, the by-itself of the Subject—*exists* only as the swerve and departure of this *a*—(of this *a-part-self*), which is the place, the moment proper of its presence, its authenticity, its sense. The *a-part-self, as departure*, is what's exposed.

"Exposition" doesn't mean that intimacy is extracted from its withdrawal, and carried outside, put on display. Because then the body would be an ex-position of the "self," in the sense of a translation, an interpretation, or a staging. "Exposition," on the contrary, means that expression itself is an in-timacy and a withdrawal. The *a-part-self* is not translated or incarnated into exposition, it is what it is there: this vertiginous withdrawal *of* the self *from* the self that is needed to open the infinity of that withdrawal *all the way up to* self. The body is this departure of self to self.

Exposé, donc: mais ce n'est pas la mise en vue de ce qui, tout d'abord, eût été caché, renfermé. Ici, l'exposition est l'être même (cela se dit: l'exister). Ou mieux encore: si l'être, en tant que le sujet, a pour essence l'autoposition, ici l'autoposition est elle-même, en tant que telle, par essence et par structure, l'exposition. *Auto = ex* = corps. Le corps est l'être-exposé de l'être.

C'est pourquoi l'exposition est bien loin de n'avoir lieu que comme l'extension d'une surface. Cette extension elle-même en expose d'autres—et par exemple, ce mode du *partes extra partes* qu'est le singulier désassemblement des «cinq sens». Un corps n'est corps sentant que dans cet écart, ce partage des sens qui n'est ni le phénomène, ni le résidu d'une «auto-esthésie» profonde, mais qui fait au contraire toute la propriété du *corps esthétique*, cette simple tautologie.

L'une sur l'autre, dans l'autre, à même l'autre s'exposent ainsi toutes les esthétiques dont le corps est rassemblement discret, multiple, foisonnant. Ses membres—phalles et céphales—, ses parties—cellules, membranes, tissus, excroissances, parasites—, ses téguments, ses sueurs, ses traits, ses couleurs, toutes ses couleurs locales (rien ne sera fini avec le racisme, tant qu'on lui opposera une fraternité générique des hommes, au lieu de lui renvoyer, affirmée, confirmée, la dis-location de nos races et de nos traits, noirs, jaunes, blancs, crépus, camus, lippus, obtus, poilus, graisseux, bridés, épatés, rauques, fluets, prognathes, busqués, plissés, musqués . . .). Partout de corps en corps, de lieu en lieu, de lieux où sont les corps en zones et points du corps, partout le capricieux désassemblement de ce qui ferait l'assomption d'*un* corps. Partout une décomposition, qui ne se referme pas sur un *soi* pur et non exposé (la mort), mais qui propage *jusque dans la dernière pourriture*, oui, qui propage encore là—insupportable comme elle l'est—une invraisemblable *liberté* matérielle, qui ne laisse de place à aucun *continuum*, de teintes, d'éclats, de tons, de lignes, qui en est au contraire l'effraction disséminée, renouvelée sans fin du tout initial assemblement/découplement de cellules par quoi vient à naître «un corps».

De cette effraction, de ce départ des corps en tous les corps, tous les corps font *partie*, et la liberté matérielle—la matière comme liberté—n'est pas celle d'un geste, encore moins d'une action volontaire, sans être aussi celle de deux nuances de mica, de millions de coquilles dissemblables, et de l'extension indéfinie d'un *principium individuationis* tel que les individus eux-mêmes *ne cessent pas de s'in-dividuer*, toujours plus différents d'eux-mêmes, toujours donc plus semblableset plus substituables entre eux, jamais pourtant confondus en substances sans que la substance, avant que de rien soutenir, ni soi, ni autre, ne vienne à être exposée *ici*: au monde.

Exposed, therefore: but this does not mean putting something on view that would have previously been hidden or shut in. Exposition, here, is the very being (what's called "existing"). Or better yet: where the being, as a subject, has for its essence self-positing; self-positing here is exposition itself, in and of itself, in essence and structure. *Auto* = *ex* = body. The body is the being-exposed of the being.

This is why "exposition" is very far from simply taking place as the extension of a surface. This very extension exposes other kinds—such as, for instance, the *partes extra partes* that is the singular dis-assembly of the "five senses." A body is a feeling body only in this displacement or division of senses, which is neither the phenomenon nor the residue of a deep "auto-aesthesia" but yields, on the contrary, the entire property belonging to that simple tautology, the *aesthetic body*.

One on top of the other, inside the other, right at the other, thus exposed are all those aesthetics whose assembly—discrete, multiple, and swarming—is the body. Its members—phallus and cephale—its parts—cells, membranes, tissues, excrescences, parasites—its teguments, its sweatings, features, colors, all its local colors (we'll never get past racism unless we stop saying generic human brotherhood is its contrary instead of linking it to the dis-location, affirmed and confirmed, of our races and characteristics, black, yellow, white, thick-lipped, snub-nosed, frizzy, thick, shaggy, oily, braided, flat-nosed, coarse, fine, prognathous, hook-nosed, creased, musky . . .). Everywhere, from bodies to bodies, from place to place, from places where bodies are in zones and body-points, everywhere the random disassembly of what might allow *a* body to be assumed. Decomposition everywhere, not confined to a pure and unexposed *self* (death), but propagating *all the way to the worst rotting*, yes, even there—unbearable as it is—propagating an unlikely material *freedom*, leaving no place for any *continuum*, whether of tints, highlights, tones, or lines, being, on the contrary, a disseminated and endlessly renewed break-up of the utterly initial assemblage/uncoupling of cells whereby "the body" is born.

All bodies are *part* of this breakthrough, of this departure of bodies in all bodies; which is why material freedom—matter as freedom—is not a freedom of gesture, still less of voluntary action, without also being the freedom of two shades of mica, of millions of dissimilar shells, and of the indefinite extension of the *principium individuationis*, such that individuals in themselves *never stop being in-dividuated*, differing ever more from themselves, hence being ever more alike, interchangeable with themselves, but never reduced to substances, unless the substance, prior to sustaining something (self or other), comes to be exposed *here*: in the world.

(Il faut bien l'avouer: toute la «philosophie de la nature» est à refaire, si la «nature» doit être pensée comme l'exposition des corps.)

(C'est-à-dire: la liberté.)

Pensée

Dans la pensée du corps, le corps force la pensée toujours plus loin, toujours *trop* loin: trop loin pour qu'elle soit encore pensée, mais jamais assez pour qu'elle soit corps.

C'est pourquoi il n'y a pas sens à parler de corps et de pensée à part l'un de l'autre, comme s'ils pouvaient avoir quelque subsistance chacun pour soi: ils ne *sont* que leur toucher l'un de l'autre, la touche de leur effraction l'un par l'autre et l'un en l'autre. Cette touche est la limite, l'espacement de l'existence. Pourtant, elle a un nom, elle s'appelle «joie» et «douleur» ou «peine». Ce nom ne signifie, sans doute, que la limite de toute signification—et le bord même, l'abord de l'espacement. Il ne signifie rien, il expose la combinatoire de ces quatre termes: corps-pensée-joie-peine. Toutes leurs figures touchent au même écart qui distribue les quatre.

Il y a encore un nom de la combinatoire, ou de la distribution: «sexe». Ce n'est pas le nom de quoi que ce soit qui serait exposé: c'est le nom de toucher à l'exposition elle-même.

«Sexe» touche à l'intouchable. C'est le *nom-éclat* du corps, le nom qui ne nomme qu'en espaçant d'abord les corps selon les éclats de cette esthésie supplémentaire: *des sexes*. Ces sexes eux-mêmes, on ne peut ni les nombrer, ni les nommer. Ici, «deux» n'est que l'index d'un écart polymorphe. «Mon» sexe n'est pas un de part en part, il est contact discret, aléatoire, événementiel de zones de «mon» corps tout autant que d'autres—mon corps devenant autre à s'y toucher, à y être touché, devenant donc *le même*, plus absolu, plus retranché que jamais, plus identifié en tant qu'être-lieu du toucher (de l'étendue). D'(a)phalle en (a)céphale, un corps étal, égal, pluriel, zoné, ombré, touché. On ne le nommera ni «femme», ni «homme»: ces noms, quoi que nous en ayons, nous laissent trop entre fantasmes et fonctions, là où précisément il ne s'agit ni des uns, ni des autres. On dira donc plutôt: *un* corps indistinct/distinct, indiscret/discret, est le corps-éclat sexué glissé d'un corps à l'autre jusqu'à l'intimité, éclatante en effet, de la limite où ils touchent leur écart.

Il s'ensuit quelques conséquences: la loi du moindre attouchement, ou du clin d'œil comme intensité déjà maximale de jouissance; la loi de la plus grande superficialité, celle où le corps vaut absolument comme *peau*, sans plus aucune épaisseur d'organe ni de pénétration (les corps sexués sont invulnérables, sont éternels); la loi, connexe, selon laquelle il n'y a pas de sexe

(One thing has to be admitted: if "nature" is to be thought as the exposition of bodies, all of the "philosophy of nature" has to be reworked.)

(In other words: as freedom.)

Thought

With thoughts about the body, the body always forces us to think farther, always *too* far: too far to carry on as thought, but never far enough to become a body.

Which is why it makes no sense to talk about body and thought apart from each other, as if each could somehow subsist on its own: they *are* only their touching each other, the touch of their breaking down, and into, each other. This touching is the limit and spacing of existence. But it has a name, it is called "joy" and "sorrow" or "pain." No doubt this name only signifies the limit of all signification—and the very edge, the approach, of spacing. It signifies nothing, exposing instead the combination of those four terms: body-thought-joy-pain. Their figures touch upon a swerve common to all four, which distributes them.

There's even a name for this combination, or distribution: "sex." It doesn't name anything that would be exposed: it names the process of touching upon exposition itself.

"Sex" touches upon the untouchable. It's the body's *flash-name*, a name that only designates, to begin with, by spacing bodies according to the flashes of that supplementary aesthesia: *sexes*. We can neither number nor name those sexes in themselves. Here "two" is only an index for a polymorphous swerve. "My" sex isn't one thing throughout; it's a discrete, random, eventful contact of the zones of "my" body, as much as of others—my body becoming other, by touching itself there, by being touched there, becoming thereby *the same*, more absolute, more separated than ever, more identified as a taking place of touching (of extension). From (a)phallic to (a)cephalic, a level, smooth, plural, zoned, shaded, touched body. We won't call it "woman" or "man": those names, for good or ill, leave us too much among fantasies and functions, when it is precisely not about them. Therefore let us instead say: that *one* indistinct/distinct, indiscrete/discrete body is a sexed body-flash, sliding from body to body, right at the intimacy—the flashing, in effect—of the limit at which they touch their swerve.

Various consequences follow from this: the law of least contact, or of winking as an already maximal intensity of pleasure; the law of the highest superficiality, where the body counts absolutely as *skin*, with no deeper organ or penetration (sexed bodies are invulnerable, eternal); a related law according to which there's no sex without a minimum, even an infinitesimal

(sauf à en exclure des opérations finalisées de laboratoire) sans un minimum d'amour, même infinitésimal (et volontiers dénié), ni d'amour sans sexe, fût-il imperceptible; enfin, le sexe comme loi, cet impératif de toucher, de baiser, dont ni la poussée de l'espèce, ni même la «libido» ne rendent compte. Car cet impératif ne vise aucun objet, ni grand, ni petit, ni soi, ni enfant, mais seulement la joie/la peine d'un *se*-toucher. (Ou bien encore: d'un rester-soi, ou d'un devenir-soi *sans* revenir à soi. Jouir est au *cœur* de la dialectique une diastole sans systole: ce cœur, c'est le corps.)

Se toucher toi (et non «soi»)—ou encore, identiquement, *se toucher peau* (et non «soi»): telle est la pensée que le corps force toujours plus loin, toujours trop loin. En vérité, c'est la pensée elle-même qui s'y force, qui s'y disloque: car tout le poids, toute la gravité de la pensée—qui est elle-même une *pesée*—, ne va pour finir à rien d'autre qu'à *consentir aux corps*. (Consentement exaspéré.)

Vient le monde des corps

Il y a eu *cosmos*, le monde des places distribuées, lieux donnés par les dieux et aux dieux. Il y a eu *res extensa*, cartographie naturelle des espaces infinis et de leur maître, l'ingénieur conquistador, lieu-tenant des dieux disparus. Vient à présent *mundus corpus*, le monde comme le peuplement proliférant des lieux (du) corps.

Ce qui vient n'est en rien ce que prétend le discours faible du semblant et du spectacle (un monde d' apparences, de simulacres, de fantasmes, sans chair et sans présence). Ce discours faible n'est pas autre chose que le discours chrétien de la transsubstantiation, simplement vidé de substance (et sans doute de christianisme . . .). Discours foutu: les corps ont commencé à lui passer dessus. Ce qui vient est une tout autre version, une tout autre articulation de *hoc est enim* . . .

Et tout d'abord, ce n'est peut-être rien d'autre, rien de plus que *ceci*: il vient *ce que nous montrent les images*. Nos milliards d'images nous montrent des milliards de corps—comme jamais corps ne furent montrés. Des foules, des amas, des mêlées, des paquets, des colonnes, des attroupements, des pullulements, des armées, des bandes, des débandades, des paniques, des gradins, des processions, des collisions, des massacres, des charniers, des communions, des dispersions, un trop-plein, un débordement de corps toujours à la fois en masses compactes et en divagations pulvérulentes, toujours collectés (dans des rues, des ensembles, des mégapoles, des banlieues, des lieux de transit, de surveillance, de commerce, de soins, d'oubli) et toujours abandonnés à un brouillage stochastique des mêmes lieux, à l'agitation, qui

(and willfully denied) measure of love (finalized laboratory operations excepted), just as there's no love without sex, even when imperceptible; finally, sex as a law, an imperative to touch, to fuck—something that neither instinct nor "libido" as such can account for. Because this imperative has no object as its aim—no adult, child, self, or infant—just the joy/pain of *self-touching*. (Or yet again: of remaining-oneself or becoming-oneself *without* coming back to oneself. An orgasm is the diastole without systole at the *heart* of the dialectic: this heart is the body).

Feeling oneself touching you (and not "oneself")—or else, identically, *feeling oneself touching skin* (and not "oneself"): the body is always forcing this thought farther forward, always too far. Thought itself, at this point, is really forcing itself, dislocating itself: because the whole weight, the gravity, of thought—in itself a *weighing*—amounts to nothing more than a *consenting to bodies*. (An exasperated consenting.)

Comes the World of Bodies

There was *cosmos*, a world of distributed places, given by, and to, the gods. There was *res extensa*, a natural cartography of infinite spaces with their master, the conquistador-engineer, a place-taking lieutenant for vanished gods. Now comes *mundus corpus*, the world as a proliferating peopling of (the) body('s) places.

What is coming is not at all what a weak discourse about appearance and spectacle would have us presume (a world of appearances, simulacra, and phantasms, lacking flesh and presence). This kind of weak discourse is only a Christian discourse on transubstantiation, but lacking substance (and also Christianity, no doubt . . .). A ruined discourse: bodies are starting to pass right over it. What's coming is an entirely different version, an entirely different articulation of *hoc est enim* . . .

And, to begin with, perhaps it's nothing other, or more, than *this*: what's coming is *whatever images show us*. Our billions of images show billions of bodies—as bodies have never been shown before. Crowds, piles, melees, bundles, columns, troops, swarms, armies, bands, stampedes, panics, tiers, processions, collisions, massacres, mass graves, communions, dispersions, a sur-plus, always an overflowing of bodies, all at one and the same time, compacted in masses and pulverizing dispersals, always collected (in streets, housing-projects, megapolises, suburbs, points of passage, of surveillance, of commerce, care, and oblivion), always abandoned to the stochastic confusion of the same places, to the structuring agitation of their endless, generalized, *departure*. This is the world of world-wide departure: the spacing

les structure, d'un incessant *départ* généralisé. Voici le monde du départ mondial: l'espacement du *partes extra partes*, sans rien qui le surplombe ni le soutienne, sans Sujet de son destin, ayant seulement lieu comme une prodigieuse *presse* des corps.

Ce monde—le nôtre, déjà—est le monde des corps parce qu'il a, parce qu'il *est* la *densité même de l'espacement*, ou la densité, et l'intensité, du *lieu*. Cette densité le distingue d'un univers de l'étalement (atomes, structures, plaques, espaces publics privés de public), aussi bien que d'une économie de la déchirure (âmes, destins, besoins, espaces publics privés d'espace). L'étalement et la déchirure paraissent être les formes reconnues, et du reste combinées, de l'agencement humain général (ou de l'«homme» en tant que généralité, généricité). Ces formes bordent et traversent le monde dense des corps. En un sens, il leur appartient. Pourtant, il est ce qui leur reste inappropriable, hors de prise, hors de vue, hors de torture. Il est, lui, le monde de l'appropriation du propre: monde de la non-généralité, monde qui n'est pas offert à l'«humanité», mais à ses corps singuliers. Non général: mondial.

Ce qui nous vient, c'est ce monde dense et grave, ce monde *mondial* qui ne réfère ni à autre, ni à outre-monde, qui n'est plus «international», mais déjà autre chose, et qui n'est pas non plus monde des apparences, ni des espérances. Mais il est *monde* enfin, c'est-à-dire *lieu propre* des extensions réelles, de l'espacement de nos corps, des partitions de leurs existences, des partages de leurs résistances. Lieu propre, ou bien encore, *propriété du lieu* enfin donnée à l'étendue des corps. Peut-être jusqu'ici n'y avait-il pas de *corps*, ou bien ne leur avait-on pas consenti la propriété du lieu (la propriété d'être, absolument, l'avoir-lieu de l' existence). Et peut-être fallait-il atteindre cette extrémité de l'Occident, cette tension et cette extension ultimes—planétaire, galactique, cosmique: notre espacement a gagné, traversé le cosmos—pour en venir ainsi au *lieu*. (Pour que le non-lieu, ou le sous-lieu, de la caverne platonicienne vienne à s'approprier le caractère *local*, et à l'approprier absolument.)

(Je dis: «enfin», «jusqu'ici», «il fallait atteindre», et j'implique ainsi une histoire, un processus et même une finalité. Il faudrait l'éviter, il faudrait dire seulement: à présent, c'est ainsi, voici l'ici-maintenant. D'autant plus qu'une *fin* est une concentration ponctuelle—et qu'en ce sens l'espacement des corps ne saurait faire une fin. Il fait fin autrement: en tant que bord, tracé des corps. Cependant, il reste vrai que quelque chose s'accomplit *aussi*: car il reste vrai que la caverne de Platon est *déjà* l'unique et exclusive «localité»— ou «dis-location»—du monde que présente l'Occident naissant. Nous ne pourrons pas ne pas penser, ne pas expérimenter, que *nous nous sommes*

of *partes extra partes*, with nothing to oversee it or sustain it, no Subject for its destiny, taking place only as a prodigious *press* of bodies.

This world—already our own—is the world of bodies, because it has, because it *is*, the *very density of spacing*, or the density, intensity, of *a place*. This density distinguishes it from a leveled universe (atoms, structures, plates, public spaces lacking a public), and from a shattered economy (souls, destinies, needs, public spaces that lack space). Leveling and shattering would seem to be the known, conjoint, forms of general human agency (or of man as a generality, a genericity). These forms line up alongside, and cross, the dense world of bodies. In a sense, the world belongs to them. And yet for them the world remains inappropriable, beyond their grasp, out of sight, beyond their pain. It, this world, is the world of the appropriation of the proper: a world of nongenerality, a world offered not to "humanity" but to its singular bodies. Not general: world-wide.

What is coming to us is a dense and serious world, a *world-wide* world, one that doesn't refer to another world, or to an other-world, that is no longer "international" but already something else, and that is no longer a world of appearances or aspirations. But it's still a *world*, a *proper place* for real extensions, for the spacing of our bodies, for the partitions of their existences, for the sharing of their resistances. A proper place, or more precisely, a *propriety of place*, that's being granted, at last, to the body's extension. Perhaps up until now there haven't been any bodies, or perhaps no one had granted them the propriety of place (the propriety of being, absolutely, existence's taking-place). And maybe we had to reach this Western extremity, this ultimate tension and extension—planetary, galactic, cosmic, because our spacing has attained, has traversed, the cosmos—to arrive thereby at the *place*. (So that the non-place, or the nether-place, of Plato's cave would be able to appropriate a *local* character for itself, and appropriate it absolutely.)

(I say: "at last," "until now," "we had to wait," thereby implying a history, a process, even a finality. This should be avoided, and we should only say: for now, this is how it is, here's the here-and-now. Especially because an *ending* is a punctual concentration—and no spacing of bodies could ever furnish an end in this sense. It provides a different end: as an edge, a tracing, of bodies. And yet it remains the case that there is *also* something coming to completion: because it's still true today that Plato's cave is *already* the unique and exclusive "locality"—or "dis-location"—of the world presented by an emerging West. We won't be able to stop thinking or experiencing the fact that *we destined ourselves to the place*. But neither can

destinés au lieu. Et pourtant, nous ne pouvons pas non plis ignorer que l'histoire qui vient, en tant qu'elle *vient*, déjoue, défie les destins et les fins. En tant qu'elle *vient*, elle *espace* aussi. Nous aurons à penser l'espacement du temps, c'est-à-dire *le temps comme corps . . .*).

Aréalité

«Aréalité» est un mot vieilli, qui signifie la nature ou la propriété d'*aire* (*area*). Par accident, le mot se prête aussi à suggérer un manque de réalité, ou bien une réalité ténue, légère, suspendue: celle de l'écart qui localise un corps, ou dans un corps. Peu de réalité du «fond», en effet, de la substance, de la matière ou du sujet. Mais ce peu de réalité fait tout le *réel aréal* où s'articule et se joue ce qui a été nommé l' archi-tectonique des corps. En ce sens, l'aréalité est l'*ens realissimum*, la puissance maximale de l'exister, dans l'extension totale de son horizon. Simplement, le réel en tant qu'*aréal* réunit l'*infini* du maximum d'existence («quo magis cogitari non potest») à l'absolu *fini* de l'horizon aréal.

Cette «réunion» n'est pas une médiation: et ce que veut dire *corps*, ce que veut dire ou ce que donne à penser *corps*, c'est précisément *ça*, qu'il n'y a pas *ici* de médiation. Le fini et l'infini ne *passent* pas l'un en l'autre, ils ne se dialectisent pas, ils ne subliment pas le lieu en point, ils ne concentrent pas l'aréalité en substrat. C'est ce que veut dire *corps*, mais d'un vouloir-dire qu'il faut dès lors retirer lui-même à la dialectique signifiante: *corps ne peut vouloir dire un sens réel du corps hors de son horizon réel.* «Corps» doit donc avoir sens *à même* l'étendue (y compris l'étendue du *mot* «corps» . . .). Cette condition «signifiante» (si on peut encore la nommer ainsi) est inacceptable, impraticable pour notre discours. *Mais elle est la condition réelle/aréale de tout sens possible pour un monde des corps.*

C'est bien pourquoi une «pensée» du corps doit en être, avec ou sans étymologie, une *pesée* réelle, et pour cela, un *toucher*, ployé-déployé selon l'aréalité.

Mystère?

On l'a déjà dit: le «toucher» de cette pensée—ce *pèse-nerfs* qu'il faut qu'elle soit, ou rien—n'appartient pas à une immédiateté antérieure et extérieure au sens. Du sens, au contraire, il est la limite même—et la limite du sens se prend dans tous les sens, dont chacun fait effraction de l'autre . . .

Mais il ne faut donc pas faire au «toucher» un crédit trop simple, et surtout pas croire qu'on viendrait à toucher *le* sens de «toucher» en tant qu'il fait limite au(x) sens. C'est une tendance assez ordinaire des idéologies du «corps»

we ignore the fact that history yet to come—because it is *coming*—also un-ravels, and challenges, destinies along with endings. Because it *is coming*, it also *spaces*. We will have to ponder the spacing of time—of *time*, that is, *as a body. . . .*)

Areality

Areality is an antique word, signifying the nature or specificity of an *aire* ("area"). By chance, this word also serves to suggest a lack of reality, or rather a slight, faint, suspended reality: the reality of a swerve localizing the body, or a displacement within the body. In effect, a faint reality of "ground," sub-stance, matter, or subject. But this faint reality makes the whole *areal real*, where the so-called archi-tectonics of bodies is played out and articulated. In this sense, areality, in the total extension of its horizon, is the *ens realis-simum*, the greatest power of existing. The real, as *areal*, merely reunites the *infinity* of maximal existence ("quo magis cogitari non potest") with the *fi-nite* absolute of an areal horizon.

This "reunion" is not a mediation: and what *body* means, what body means and provides for thought, is only *this*, that there's no mediation *here*. The finite and the infinite do not *pass* into one another, they do not dialecticize each other, or sublimate the place to a point, or concentrate areality into a substratum. *Body* has this sense, but this sense must, in turn, be subtracted from a signifying dialectic: *body cannot mean body's real sense beyond body's reality horizon.* "Body" must therefore make sense *right at* ex-tension (including the extension of the *word body . . .*). For our discourse, this "signifying" condition (if we can still call it that) is not receivable, not feasible. *But it's the real/areal condition for every possible sense of a world of bodies.*

This is why a "thought" about the body should really *ponder* the body, be a feeling of its weight, and, in that, a *touching*, played-displayed in ac-cord with areality.

Mystery?

It has been said before: the "touch" of this thought—the *nerve-meter* which this thought has to be, if it is going to be anything—does not refer to an immediacy preceding or exceeding sense. On the contrary, it is the very limit of sense—and the limit of sense taken in every sense, each producing a breakthrough into the other . . .

But then we must not credit "touch" too quickly or, still less, suppose that we could eventually touch upon *the* sense of "touch" as a setting of limits for

les plus robustes, c'est-à-dire les plus grossières (le genre «pensée musclée», ou «pensée sacré-cœur», le fascisme vitalo-spiritualiste—avec, sans doute, sa réelle et secrète horreur des corps).

Exposant l'espacement des corps, fixant les yeux sur cet écart, je n'éviterais pas de finir par proposer quelque vision dernière: l'œil planté dans l'écart de l'être. Cette vision répond au plus puissant modèle visionnaire de la métaphysique en son fond mystique. Elle est la Vision des Mystères, telle que Platon la relève et la transmet. L'*epopteia*, la vue accomplie, c'est-à-dire la vue où se dépasse l'initiation (qui ne fait que «comprendre») pour accéder à la «contemplation», à un «sur-voir» qui est un «dévorer des yeux» (l'œil lui-même se dévorant), qui est une *prise* et pour finir un *toucher*: l'absolu même du toucher, le toucher-l'autre comme se-toucher, l'un dans l'autre absorbé, dévoré. Telle est, pour toute la tradition, la *consommation* du Mystère de la Certitude Sensible: voyez, ici, sorti du panier de Cybèle, phalle et céphale, *hoc est enim corpus meum*.

Mais l'aréalité ne peut sortir d'un panier, fût-il celui des Mystères. L'aréalité n'est pas à voir—pas comme veut voir l'*epopteia*. Elle n'est à voir d'aucune manière: ni en tant qu'elle est l'extension ou l'ex-tensivité pure du corps, le hors-soi qui comme tel ne (se) donne pas à voir (ce que la logique du Mystère pose comme «imprésentable» *pour* le présenter à sa sur-optique), *ni* en tant qu'elle est aussi bien, et identiquement, le présentable même: la configuration déterminée, le *trait* de ce corps-ci. Car de ce corps-ci, on ne verrait rien, à ne voir que lui dans la pure visibilité de sa présentation. Voir *un corps* n'est précisément pas le saisir d'*une* vision: la vue elle-même s'y distend, s'y espace, elle n'embrasse pas la totalité des *aspects*. L'«aspect» lui-même est un fragment du tracé aréal, la vue est fragmentaire, fractale, à éclipses. Du reste, c'est un corps qui voit un corps . . .

L'*epopteia* mystérique, en revanche, ne connaît qu'un aspect et qu'une vision: elle est l'œil planté en pleine face, en plein centre de l'aréalité, dans la fente ou dans le trou de l'*ex*. Elle est proprement et absolument vision de la mort, désir mystérique absolu qui ne peut se décharger sans foudroyer les corps (foudroyant donc aussi sa propre vue . . .). Tout est ici lourd et morbide, comme cet érotisme qui se plaît à fixer la fente de la vulve, voyant s'y présenter la tête de Méduse. L'érotisme métaphysique de la médusation est un sûr témoin du déni des corps. Méduse en arrête le trait, en paralyse l'extension: il reste une masturbation de l'œil.

Mais les fentes, les trous, les zones ne donnent rien à voir, ne révèlent rien: la vision ne pénètre pas, elle glisse le long des écarts, elle suit les départs. Elle est toucher qui n'absorbe pas, qui se déplace le long des traits et des retraits qui inscrivent et qui excrivent un corps. Caresse mobile, instable, voyant au

(the) sense(s). This tendency is very typical of the crudest and most robust ideologies (a vitalist-spiritualist fascism in the style of "muscled thought," or "sacred-heart thought"—with, undoubtedly, its real and secret horror of bodies).

Exposing the spacing of bodies, and fixing my eyes on this swerve, I will not be able to avoid having to propose a final vision: an eye planted in the swerve of being. This vision corresponds to the most potent visionary model of metaphysics in its mystical grounds. It is the Vision of the Mysteries as expounded and transmitted by Plato. *Epopteia*, completed sight—meaning the sight that brings us beyond initiation (which only "understands") to "contemplation," a "super-sight" that is a "devouring of the eyes" (the eye devouring its very self), a *grasping* and finally a *touching*: the very absolute of touching, touching-the-other as being-touched, each being absorbed and devoured in the other. In the whole tradition, this is the *consummation* of the Mystery of Sensory Certainty: behold, arising here from Cybele's basket, phallus and cephale, *hoc est enim corpus meum.*

But areality cannot come from a basket, not even one that belongs to the Mysteries. Areality is not to be seen—not as the *epopteia* wants us to see. There is no way to see it: *neither* as the extension or pure ex-tensiveness of the body, something beyond-the-self that, as such, cannot lend (itself) to sight (being posed by the logic of Mystery as "unpresentable," *with the aim of* presenting it to its over-optics), *nor*, simultaneously and identically, as the presentable itself: the determinate configuration, or *characteristic*, of this body *here*. Because we would see nothing of this body here if we only saw it in the pure visibility of its presentation. To see *a body* is precisely not to grasp it with *a* vision: sight itself is distended and spaced by this body here, it does not embrace the totality of *aspects*. An "aspect" is itself a fragment of the areal trace, and sight is fragmentary, fractal, shadowy. And anyway, the body is seen by a body . . .

The mysterical *epopteia*, by contrast, knows only one aspect and one vision: it is an eye planted in the middle of the face, in the very center of areality, in the slit or hole of the *ex*. It is properly and absolutely a vision of death, an absolute, mysterical desire that cannot be fulfilled without blasting bodies apart (and thereby blasting apart its own sight as well . . .). Everything about it is heavy and morbid, like the eroticism that takes pleasure in staring at the slit of the vulva, seeing in it the presentation of the Medusa's head. A metaphysical eroticism of petrifaction is a sure sign of the denial of bodies. Medusa fixes the body's feature, paralyses its extension: it remains a masturbation of the eye.

But slits, holes, and zones do not present things to be seen, do not reveal anything: vision does not penetrate, but glides along swerves and follows along departures. It is a touching that does not absorb but moves along lines and recesses, inscribing and exscribing the body. A mobile, unstable

ralenti, à l'accéléré, à l'arrêt sur image, voyant aussi par *touches* d'autres sens, odeurs, goûts, timbres, et même, avec les sons, les sens des mots (le «oui» qui jouit).

Voir les corps n'est pas dévoiler un mystère, c'est voir ce qui s'offre à voir, l'image, la foule d'images qu'est le corps, *l'image nue*, mettant à nu l'aréalité. Cette image est étrangère à tout imaginaire, à toute apparence—et de même, à toute interprétation, à tout déchiffrement. Il n'y a rien, d'un corps, à déchiffrer—sinon ceci, que le chiffre d'un corps est ce corps même, non chiffré, étendu. La vue des corps ne pénètre rien d'invisible: elle est complice du visible, de l'ostension et de l'extension que le visible est. Complicité, consentement: celui qui voit *comparaît* avec ce qu'il voit. C'est ainsi qu'ils se discernent, selon la mesure infiniment finie d'une juste clarté.

Juste clarté

Juste la clarté: elle s'étend d'abord, avant toute étendue, elle est la substance et le sujet de l'étendue. Mais toute la matérialité et toute la subjectivité de la clarté tiennent au juste partage du clair-obscur: *là* commencent l'écart du trait et la couleur locale, ensemble, l'un dans l'autre, premier aspect, première vue, première peinture. Un corps, d'abord, s'expose comme sa photographie (l'espacement d'une clarté).

Cela seul, d'abord, rend justice au corps: à son *évidence*. Il n'y a pas d'autre évidence—claire et distincte ainsi que la veut Descartes—que celle du corps. Les corps sont évidents—et c'est pourquoi toute justesse et toute justice commencent et finissent à eux. L'injuste est de brouiller, casser, broyer, étouffer les corps, les rendre indistincts (ramassés sur un centre obscur, tasses à écraser l'espace entre eux, en eux—à leur assassiner même l'espace de leur juste mort).

Nous n'avons pas encore pratiqué le monde de la clarté. Nous en sommes encore à l'ordre solaire, dont le flamboiement souverain n'est pas plus la clarté que ne l'est son vis-à-vis, le gel lunaire. (La vision mystérique est toujours de midi ou de minuit). Mais la mise au monde des corps, leur photographie, se fait dans la clarté qui vient *après* la lune et *avant* le soleil. L'aube est le tracement du trait, la présentation du lieu. L'aube est le seul milieu des corps, qui ne subsistent ni dans le flamboiement, ni dans le gel (la pensée solaire sacrifie les corps, la pensée lunaire les fantasmagorise: l'une avec l'autre composent le Système Aztèque-Autrichien, qu'on appelle aussi, pour faire vite, la Métaphysique).

Aussi longtemps que les corps sont là, c'est la clarté de l'aube—elle-même labile dans son évidence, diverse, posée, déplacée par touches. L'aube est

caress, seeing the image in slow motion, fast-forwarded, or frozen, seeing as well with *touches* from other senses, smells, tastes, timbres, or even, with sounds, from the senses of words (the "sure" that yields "pleasure").

To see bodies is not to unveil a mystery; it is seeing what is there to be seen, an image, the crowd of images that the body is, *the naked image*, stripping areality bare. Images of this kind are foreign to any imagining and any appearance—and any interpretation as well, any deciphering. There is nothing to decipher in a body—except for the fact that the body's cipher is the body itself, not ciphered, just extended. The sight of bodies does not penetrate anything invisible: it is the accomplice of the visible—of the ostentation and extension that the visible *is*. Complicity, consent: the one who sees *compears* with what he sees. That is how they can be discerned, according to the infinitely finite measure of just clarity.

A Just Clarity

Just clarity: it extends itself in advance, before extension, it's the substance and subject of extension. But clarity's materiality and subjectivity belong entirely to the fair sharing of light and shade: displacements of feature and local color start together *there*, one within the other, the first aspect, the first view, the first painting. A body, first of all, is displayed as its photo-graphy (the spacing of clarity).

Only this, to begin with, does justice to the body: to its *evidence*. Beyond the body's there's no evidence—clear and distinct as Descartes would have it be. Bodies are evident—and that's why all justice and justness start and end with these. Injustice is the mixing, breaking, crushing, and stifling of bodies, making them indistinct (gathered up in a dark center, piled up to eliminate the space between them, within them—assassinating even the space of their just death).

We have yet to practice a world of clarity. We remain in a solar order whose sovereign blaze is no clearer than lunar ice, its opposite. (The mysterical vision is always of noon or midnight). But the bringing of bodies into the world, their photography, takes place in a clarity that comes *after* the moon and *before* the sun. Dawn is the drawing of a line, a presentation of place. Dawn is the sole medium for bodies, which subsist neither in fire nor in ice (solar thinking sacrifices bodies, lunar thinking phantasmagorizes them: taken together, they compose the Aztec-Austrian System—in a word, Metaphysics).

As long as bodies are there, there's the clarity of dawn—itself labile in its evidence, diverse, placed and displaced by touches. The dawn is areal: it

aréale: elle dispose les contours du paraître, la comparution des corps. Elle, la clarté, n'est que l'énoncé: voici, *hoc est enim . . .*

Ostension sans ostentation, la clarté montre un corps nu, dénué de chiffre et de mystère, étant infiniment le mystère évident, le mystère évidé de cette clarté même. Le monde est l'aube des corps: c'est tout son sens, jusqu'au plus secret.

Juste ce sens: c'est le sens juste.

Tant qu'il y a un corps, il y a l'aube et rien d'autre, ni astres, ni torches. Et' il y a, il a lieu chaque fois *l'aube propre* de tel corps, de ce corps tel ou tel. Ainsi, un corps souffrant a sa part de clarté, égale à toute autre, et distincte. La limite de la douleur offre une évidence intense, où bien loin de devenir «objet» le corps en peine s'expose absolument «sujet». Celui qui meurtrit un corps, s'acharnant sur l'évidence, ne peut pas ou ne veut pas savoir qu'il rend à chaque coup ce «sujet»—ce *hoc*—plus clair, plus impitoyablement clair.

L'aube est juste: elle s'étend égale d'un bord à l'autre. Sa demi-teinte n'est pas le clair-obscur du contraste ni de la contradiction. C'est la complicité des lieux à s'ouvrir et s'étendre. C'est une condition commune: non les espaces mesurés, mais les espacements sont tous égaux, tous de même lumière. L'égalité est la condition des corps. Quoi de plus commun que les corps? Avant toute autre chose, «communauté» veut dire l'exposition nue d'une égale, banale évidence souffrante, jouissante, tremblante. Et c'est d'abord *ça* que l'aube soustrait à tous les sacrifices et à tous les fantômes, pour l'offrir au monde des corps.

(Écrire, penser ainsi: seulement pour rendre justice à l'aube. *Fin de la philosophie.*)

L'aube, ou bien les projecteurs impeccables sur une scène large ouverte, toute en évidence, comme seule peut l'être une scène d'opéra italien. Bouches, corps grands ouverts campés pour clamer de purs morceaux d'espace—*dinanzi al re ! davanti a lui! venez, voici, allons, venons, partons, restons*—, les voix venues du ventre, les chœurs, nombreux, et le chant, populaire—*allons, voyons, je ris, je pleure, je vis, je meurs.* Écrire et penser ainsi, la bouche ouverte, opus-corpus.

Citation

«Tout étonné, Kazik a découvert qu'il était condamné pour la vie à traîner un peu le pied gauche, qu'un de ses yeux distinguait à grand-peine les formes et les couleurs, que, plus il vieillissait, plus se multipliaient sur le dos de ses mains de vilaines taches brunes, et qu'il perdait ses cheveux et ses dents. Il

distributes emerging contours, the compearance of bodies. Clarity itself is merely its statement: here, *hoc est enim . . .*

As ostension without ostentation, clarity shows the naked body denuded of cipher and mystery, always an evident mystery, hollowed out by this very clarity. The world is the dawn of bodies: such is the sum of its sense, including its deepest secret.

Just this sense: it's the just sense.

As long as there's a body, there's just dawn and nothing else—no stars, no torches. And there is, or occurs, *the proper dawn* of just that body every time, just that body such and such that it is. Thus the body in pain has its own portion of clarity, equal to everyone else's, and distinct. The limits of suffering provide intense evidence that a body in pain, far from becoming an "object," is an absolutely exposed "subject." Anyone who murders a body, relentlessly attacking the obvious, cannot know, or wishes not to know, that he only renders the "subject"—this *hoc*—more clear, more unmercifully clear, with each blow.

The dawn is just: it stretches equally from one edge to another. Its half-tone is not a chiaroscuro of contrast or contradiction. It's a complicity of places to be opened up and extended. It's a common condition: not of measured spaces, though all spacings are equal, all in the same light. Equality is the condition of bodies. What's more common than bodies? Before anything else, "community" means the naked display of equivalent and banal evidence, suffering, trembling, and joyous. And the dawn, above all else, withdraws *this* from every sacrifice and phantom, offering it to the world of bodies.

(Writing, thinking like this: just doing justice to dawn. *The end of philosophy.*)

Either the dawn, or immaculate spotlights on a large, open stage, everything in evidence, as only a scene from Italian opera could be. Mouths, large open bodies deployed to proclaim pure pieces of space—*dinanzi al re! davanti a lui! Come, here, let's go, let's come, let's leave, let's stay*—voices emerging from the belly, choruses numerous, a popular song—*let's go, let's see, I laugh, I cry, I live, I die.* Writing and thinking like this, mouth agape, opus-corpus.

Citation

"Completely astonished, Kazik discovered that he was condemned to a life of dragging his left foot slightly, that one of his eyes made out forms and colors with great difficulty, that the more he aged, ugly brown spots would proliferate on the backs of his hands, and that he was losing his hair and

observait ces changements comme s'il lisait l'histoire d'un étranger, mais le chagrin et la douleur se levaient en lui et le torturaient: le chagrin de la détérioration, la douleur de la séparation. Des varices bleues avaient rapidement couvert son mollet gauche—il se penchait et les regardait comme on regarde la carte d'une région inconnue. Ses yeux larmoyaient aussitôt qu'il s'approchait du foin fraîchement coupé, les cerises lui donnaient la diarrhée, la traversée des pelouses du zoo des démangeaisons, et sa paupière droite clignait toute seule dans les moments de grande émotion; ce n'étaient que des bagatelles, mais elles lui empoisonnaient peu à peu la vie. (. . .) Il a appris que, le plus souvent, quand quelqu'un dit "c'est mon lot," il pense, en fait, au tas de chair qu'il traîne avec lui. C'est Aharon Markus, le pharmacien, qui a émis la supposition qu'après des milliers d'années d'existence sur cette terre, l'homme était peut-être la seule créature vivante encore imparfaitement adaptée à son corps, dont il avait souvent honte. Et parfois, a remarqué le pharmacien, on dirait que l'homme attend naïvement l'étape suivante de l'évolution, au cours de laquelle son corps et lui seront séparés en deux créatures distinctes. (. . .) Il faut signaler que Neigel n'a pas compris grand-chose de ce qui était dit sur la relation entre l'homme et son corps: pour être admis dans les SS, le candidat devait être en parfaite santé; un seul plombage suffisait à disqualifier un aspirant.» (David Grossman)

Corpus: Autre départ

Un *corpus* n'est pas un discours, et ce n'est pas un récit. C'est un *corpus* qu'il faudrait donc ici. *Ici*, il y a comme une promesse qu'il doit s'agir du corps, qu'il *va* s'agir de lui, là, presque sans délai. Une espèce de promesse qui ne fera ni l'objet d'un traité, ni la matière de citationset de récitations, ni le personnage ou le décor d'une histoire. Il y a, pour tout dire, une sorte de promesse de *se taire*. Et même moins de se taire «au sujet» du corps, que de *se taire du corps*, de matériellement le soustraire aux empreintes signifiantes: et cela, *ici, à même la page d'écriture et de lecture*. Que nous le voulions ou non, des corps se touchent sur cette page, ou bien, elle est elle-même l'attouchement (de ma main qui écrit, des vôtres tenant le livre). Ce toucher est infiniment détourné, différé—des machines, des transports, des photocopies, des yeux, d'autres mains encore se sont interposées—, mais il reste l'infime grain têtu, ténu, la poussière infinitésimale d'un contact partout interrompu et partout poursuivi. A la fin, votre regard touche aux mêmes tracés de caractères que le mien touche à présent, et vous me lisez, et je vous écris. *Quelque part*, cela a lieu. Ce quelque part n'a pas le caractère de la transmission soudaine, celui que le télécopieur exemplifie. Plutôt que de FAX-similitude, il s'agit ici de détour et de dissemblance, de transposition et de

teeth. He observed these changes as one reads the life of a foreigner, but chagrin and sorrow rose up within him and tortured him: the chagrin of de-
teriorating, the sorrow of separating. Blue varicose veins had rapidly
covered his left calf—he leaned over and looked at them as one looks at the
map of some unknown territory. His eyes would fill up with tears when he
approached the new-mown hay, cherries would give him diarrhea, crossing
the lawns of a zoo would make him itch, and his right eyelid would blink
by itself during moments of great emotion: and while these were just triv-
ial things, they poisoned his life bit by bit. . . . He learned that when someone says 'that's my fate,' in fact he usually thinks of the pile of flesh he's
hauling around. Aharon Markus, the pharmacist, volunteered that
mankind, having existed on this earth for millions of years, was perhaps
the only creature alive still imperfectly adapted to his body, of which he
was often ashamed. And, as the pharmacist remarked on occasion, man
might be said to naively await the next stage of evolution, when he and
his body would be separated into two different creatures. . . . It has to be
noted that Neigel didn't understand much of what was being said about a
man's relationship to his body: to be admitted into the SS, a candidate had
to have perfect health; the filling of a single tooth was enough to disqual-
ify the candidate."[1]

Corpus: Another Departure

A *corpus* isn't a discourse, and it isn't a narrative. So a *corpus* is what we'd
need here. *Here*, there is something like the promise that this must *involve*
the body, *shall* involve it, almost immediately. A promise of the kind that's
not subject to a treatise, or something to be cited and recited, or the character or setting of a story. In effect, a kind of promise to *keep silent*. Silent
less "about" the body than *from the body*, subtracting it materially from its
signifying imprints: and doing so *here, on the read and written page*. Bodies,
for good or ill, are touching each other upon this page, or more precisely,
the page itself is a touching (of my hand while it writes, and your hands while
they hold the book). This touch is infinitely indirect, deferred—machines,
vehicles, photocopies, eyes, still other hands are all interposed—but it continues as a slight, resistant, fine texture, the infinitesimal dust of a contact,
everywhere interrupted and pursued. In the end, here and now, your own
gaze touches the same traces of characters as mine, and you read me, and I
write you. *Somewhere*, this takes place. This "somewhere" lacks the quality
of a sudden transmission, as exemplified by the telecopying machine. It's a
matter less of FAX-similitude than of detour and dissemblance, transposition and re-encoding: "somewhere" is distributed throughout some very

réencodage: «quelque part» se distribue sur de très longs circuits techniques, «quelque part» *est* la technique, notre *contact* discret, puissant, disséminé. Et comme un flash muet, le temps d'un suspens des circuits, la touche de la promesse: on se taira du corps, on lui laissera les lieux, on n'écrira, on ne lira que pour abandonner aux corps les lieux de leurs contacts.

A cause de cette promesse intenable et jamais faite—bien qu'elle insiste, là, quelque part—, il faudrait un *corpus*: un catalogue au lieu d'un logos, l'énumération d'un logos empirique, sans raison transcendantale, une liste glanée, aléatoire dans son ordre et dans sa complétude, un ânonnement successif de pièces et de morceaux, *partes extra partes*, une juxtaposition sans articulation, une variété, un mélange ni explosé, ni implosé, à l'ordonnance vague, toujours extensible . . .

Le modèle du *corpus* est le *Corpus Juris*, collection ou compilation des Institutiones, Digestes et autres Codices de tous les articles du droit romain. Ce n'est ni un chaos, ni un organisme: le *corpus* se tient, non pas exactement entre les deux, mais plutôt ailleurs. Il est la prose d'un autre espace, ni abyssal, ni systématique, ni effondré, ni fondé. Tel est l'espace du droit: son fondement s'y dérobe à sa place, le droit du droit lui-même est toujours sans droit. Le droit surplombe tous les cas, mais il est lui-même le *cas* de son institution, étranger à Dieu comme à la nature. Le *corpus* obéit à la règle qui va de cas en cas, continuité discrète du principe et de l'exception, de l'exigence et de la dérogation. La *juridiction* consiste moins à énoncer l'absolu du Droit, à en dérouler les raisons, qu'à dire *ce que* peut être le droit *ici*, là, maintenant, dans ce cas, en ce lieu. *Hoc est enim* . . . : diction locale, espacée, horizontale, et moins diction de l'être du droit que de son faire, de son savoir-faire et de son pouvoir-faire *dans ce cas*. Mais il n'y a pas d'essence du cas, ni de synthèse transcendantale: il n'y en a que des appréhensions successives, des contours occasionnels, des modifications. *Ici*, l'ontologie est *modale*—ou modifiable et modifiante—de manière essentielle, entière et exclusive. Et c'est de quoi un *corpus* est l'écriture.

Ainsi des corps: leur espace est juridique, tout autant que l'espace du droit est l'espace des corps configurés selon les cas. Le *corps* et le *cas* sont appropriés l'un à l'autre. A chaque corps convient une propre juridiction: «hoc est enim . . . ».

Il faudrait donc un *corpus*. Discours inquiet, syntaxe casuelle, déclinaison d'occurrences. *Clinamen*, prose inclinée vers l'accident, fragile, fractale. Non le corps-animal du sens, mais l'aréalité des corps: oui, des corps étendus jusqu'au corps mort. Non le cadavre, où le corps disparaît, mais ce corps *comme quoi le mort paraît*, dans la dernière discrétion de son espacement: non le corps mort, mais le mort comme corps—et il n'y en a pas d'autre.

long technical circuits; "somewhere" *is* technique—our discrete, potent, and disseminated *contact*. Like a silent flash, a momentary suspension of the circuits, the touch of a promise: we shall keep silent about the body, leaving it to its places, writing and reading only to abandon to bodies the places of their contact.

Because of this promise, which can never be made or kept—not that it doesn't, somewhere, insist—we'd need a *corpus*: a catalogue instead of a logos, the enumeration of an empirical logos, without transcendental reason, a list of gleanings, in random order and completeness, an ongoing stammer of bits and pieces, *partes extra partes*, a juxtaposition without articulation, a variety, a mix that won't explode or implode, vague in its ordering, always extendable . . .

The model of the *corpus* is the *Corpus Juris*, a collection, or compilation, of Institutions, Digests, and other Codices comprising all the articles of Roman law. The *corpus* is neither chaos nor organism: it doesn't fall in between the two, but lies somewhere else. It's prose from a different space, not abyssal, systematic, grounded, or ungrounded. This is the space of the law: its foundation slips away from its place—the law of the law itself being always unlawful. The law surveys every case, but itself is the *case* of its institution, as foreign to God as it is to Nature. The *corpus* obeys a law that passes from case to case, a discrete continuity of rules and exceptions, of demands and derogations. *Jurisdiction* consists less in enunciating the absolute of the Law, or in unfolding its reasons, than in saying *what* the law can be *here*, there, now, in this case, in this place. *Hoc est enim* . . . : its diction is local, spaced, horizontal, a diction less of the law's being than of its practice, competence, and capacity *in this case*. But the case has no essence or transcendental synthesis: there are only successive apprehensions, accidental contours, modifications. *Here*, in an essential, all-embracing and exclusive way, ontology is *modal*—or modifiable, or modifying. And the writing of this is a *corpus*.

So, too, with bodies: their space is juridical, just as the space of the law is a space of bodies configured according to cases. The *body* and the *case* fit each other. There is a jurisdiction proper to each body: "hoc est enim . . ."

And so we'd need a *corpus*. An uneasy discourse, with a casual syntax, a declension of occurrences. *Clinamen*, a fragile, fractal prose, inclining to accident. Not the body-animal of sense, but the areality of bodies: of bodies indeed, including the dead body. Not the cadaver, where the body disappears, but this body *as the dead one's apparition*, in the final discreteness of its spacing: not the dead body, but the dead one as a body—and there is no other.

Il faudrait un *corpus*: une écriture des morts qui n'ait rien à faire avec le discours de la Mort—et tout à faire avec ceci, que l'espace des corps ne connaît pas la Mort (le fantasme de l'espace aboli), mais connaît chaque corps comme un mort, comme *ce* mort qui nous partage l'étendue de son *ci-gît*. Non le discours d'un être-*pour*-la-Mort, mais l'écriture de l'horizontalité des morts comme naissance de l'étendue de tous nos corps—de tous nos corps *plus que* vivants. *Corpus*: il faudrait pouvoir seulement collecter et réciter un par un les corps, pas même leurs noms (ce ne serait pas exactement un mémorial), mais leurs lieux.

Corpus serait la topo-graphie du cimetière *d'où nous venons*, non de celui que remplit la fantasmagorie médusante de la Pourriture. Topographie, et photographie, d'une paix des cimetières, non dérisoire, mais puissante, donnant lieu à la communauté de nos corps, ouvrant l'espace *nôtre*. Ce qui ne voudrait pas dire écriture sans douleur—sans angoisse, peut-être, mais non sans douleur (ou sans peine), non plus que sans joie. *Corpus*: repères dispersés, difficiles, lieux-dits incertains, plaques effacées en pays inconnu, itinéraire qui ne peut rien anticiper de son tracé dans les lieux étrangers. Écriture du corps: du pays étranger. Non l'Étranger en tant que l'Être ou que l'Essence-Autre (avec sa vision mortifère), mais l'étranger comme *pays*: cet étrangement, cet écartement qu'est le pays, en tout pays et en tout lieu. Les pays: ni territoires, ni domaines, ni sols, ces étendues que l'on parcourt sans jamais les ramasser dans un synopsis, ni les subsumer sous un concept. Les pays toujours étrangers—et l'étranger en tant que pays, contrées, parages, passages, traversées, ouverture de paysages, reliefs inattendus, chemins menant à part, à nulle part, départs, retours. *Corpus*: une écriture qui verrait du pays, l'un après l'autre tous les pays du corps.

Entrées

Il nous faut un corpus des *entrées* du corps: entrées de dictionnaire, entrées de langue, entrées encyclopédiques, tous les *topoi* par où introduire le corps, les registes de tous ses articles, l'index de ses places, postures, plans et replis. Le corpus serait l'enregistrement de cette longue discontinuité des entrées (*ou* sorties: portes toujours battantes). Sismographe aux stylets impalpablement précis, littérature pure des corps en effraction, accès, excès, orifices, pores et portes de toutes les peaux, cicatrices, nombrils, blason, pièces et champs, corps par corps, lieu par lieu, entrée par entrée par sortie. Le corps est la topique de tous ses accès, de ses ici/là, ses *fort/da*, ses va-et-vient, avale-et-crache, inspire/expire, écarte et ferme.

We'd need a *corpus*: a writing of the dead having nothing to do with the discourse of Death—only with this fact, that the space of bodies knows no Death (the fantasy of abolished space), but knows each body as a dead one, as *this* dead one, sharing with us the extension of its *here lies*. Not the discourse of a being-*toward*-Death, but the writing of the horizontality of the dead as the birth of all our bodies' extension—of all our bodies being *more than* alive. *Corpus*: we'd need to be able merely to collect and recite bodies, one by one, not their names (this wouldn't be a memorial exactly), but their places.

Corpus would be the topo-graphy of the cemetery *whence we come*, which isn't filled with the petrifying medusa-phantasmagoria of Rot. A topography, a photography, of graveyard tranquility, not derisive, simply potent, making room for the community of our bodies, opening the space that is *ours*. Which wouldn't mean writing without sorrow—without anxiety, perhaps, but not without sorrow (or pain), and not without joy. *Corpus*: some dispersed, difficult points of reference, uncertain place names, plaques erased in an unknown country, an itinerary that can never anticipate its trace in foreign places. A writing of the body: of a strange land. Not the Strange as Being, or as Other-Essence (with its death-bearing vision), but the strange as *country*: such estrangement, such displacement, being the country in every land and place. Countries: not territories, domains, or lands, but extensions that we cross without ever gathering them into a synopsis or subsuming them under a concept. Countries always foreign—and the foreigner as countries, regions, surroundings, passages, crossings, the opening of countrysides, unexpected surfaces, pathways leading away, off to nowhere, departures, returns. *Corpus*: a writing that would get out and see some countryside, all the body's countries, one by one.

Entries

We need a corpus of *entries* into the body: dictionary entries, language entries, encyclopedia entries, all the body's introductory *topoi*, registers for all its articles, an index for all its places, postures, planes, and recesses. A corpus would be the registration of this long discontinuity of entries (*or* exits: the doors always swing both ways). A seismograph with impalpably precise styluses, a pure literature of breaching bodies, accesses, excesses, orifices, pores and portals of all skins, scars, navels, blazon, pieces, and fields, body by body, place by place, entry by entry by exit. A body is the topic of its every access, its every here/there, its *fort/da*, its coming-and-going, swallowing-and-spitting, breathing in / breathing out, displacing and closing.

Un *corpus* ne serait donc possible qu'à la condition qu'il y ait accès aux corps, et qu'ils ne soient pas impénétrables, ainsi que les définit la physique. Car s'il en est ainsi, le corpus se produit comme une combinatoire de chocs, comme une agitation brownienne de bonds et de rebonds particulaires, moléculaires. Or il en est ainsi. Les corps sont impénétrables aux langues— et celles-ci sont impénétrables aux corps, étant corps elles-mêmes. Les langues sont chacune un dur bloc étendu de signifiance, *partes extra partes*, *verba extra verba*, mots compacts impénétrables les uns aux autres et aux choses. Tel ce mot CORPS, qui dérobe à l'instant sa propre entrée, et l'incorpore à son opacité. *Corpus, corpse, Körper, corpo*, corps et cris, corps et âme, à corps perdu.

Deux corps ne peuvent occuper simultanément le même lieu. Et donc, pas vous et moi en même temps au lieu où j'écris, au lieu où vous lisez, où je parle, où vous écoutez. Pas de contact sans écart. Le fax va vite: mais la vitesse est de l'espacement. Nous n'avons, vous et moi, aucune chance de nous toucher, ni de toucher aux entrées des corps. Un discours se doit d'indiquer sa source, son point d'émission, et sa condition de possibilité, et son embrayeur. Mais je ne peux pas parler *d'où* vous écoutez, ni vous, écouter *d'où* je parle—ni chacun d'entre nous écouter d'où il parle (et *se* parle).

Corps impénétrables: n'est pénétrable que leur impénétrabilité. *L'accès* en tant que mur qui sonne plein. *Corpus*, cela pourrait-il être une écriture compacte, collection de coups sourds et de syncopes mates, à même la paroi d'un sens brut de coffrage? Mots ramenés à même la bouche, à même la page, l'encre ou l'écran, rentrés dès que sortis, sans propagation de signification. Il n'y a rien ici à discourir, rien à communiquer, *que corps, et corps et corps*. Communauté des corps, exaspérés par l'inscription, rassérénés dans l'excription. Communauté des corps étrangers.

Il faudrait un *corpus* d'une si infinie simplicité: nomenclature égrenée des corps, liste de leurs entrées, récitation elle-même énoncée de nulle part, et même pas énoncée, mais annoncée, enregistrée et répétée, comme si je dis: pied, ventre, bouche, ongle, plaie, frapper, sperme, sein, tatouage, manger, nerf, toucher, genou, fatigue . . .

Bien entendu, l'échec est donné avec l'intention.

Les corps sont absolument inviolables. Chacun est une vierge, une vestale sur sa couche: et ce n'est pas d'être fermée qu'elle est vierge, c'est d'être ouverte. C'est «l'ouvert» qui est vierge, et qui le reste à jamais. C'est l'abandon qui reste sans accès, l'étendue sans entrée.

Et c'est un double échec qui est donné: échec à parler du corps, échec à le taire. Double bind, psychose. La seule entrée du corps, le seul accès repris à chacune de ses entrées, c'est un accès de folie.

A *corpus* could only happen, then, by gaining access to bodies that are not impenetrable, as defined precisely by physics. If this is the case, then a corpus is produced as a combination of shocks, as a brownian agitation of molecular leaps and bounds. As indeed it is. Bodies are impenetrable to languages—and languages are impenetrable to bodies, themselves being bodies. Every language is a hard, extended block of significance, *partes extra partes, verba extra verba*, compact words impenetrable to one another and to things. Like this word *BODY*, which immediately conceals its own entry and incorporates it into its opacity. *Corpus, corpse, Körper, corpo*, bodies and cries, body and soul, with bodily abandon.

Two bodies can't occupy the same place simultaneously. Therefore you and I are not simultaneously in the place where I write, where you read, where I speak, where you listen. No contact without displacement. The fax goes fast: but speed is spacing. There is no way that we, you and I, will touch each other, or touch on entries into bodies. A discourse is obligated to indicate its source, its point of emission, its condition of possibility, and its point of departure. But I can't speak *from where* you listen, and you can't hear *from where* I speak—nor can we, either of us, hear where the discourse is speaking from (and *is spoken from*).

Impenetrable bodies: only their impenetrability is penetrable. The *access* as of a wall ringing aloud. Might a *corpus* be a compact writing, a collection of deaf blows and dull syncopes, directly on the packing-planks of raw sense? Words gathered right at the mouth, at the very page, ink, or screen, returning as soon as gone, not propagating signification. There's nothing here to discourse about or communicate *but bodies, bodies and bodies*. A community of bodies, exasperated by inscription, whose minds are at rest in exscription. A community of foreign bodies.

There would have to be a *corpus* of such infinite simplicity: a drop-by-drop nomenclature of bodies, a list of their entries, a recitation itself enunciated out of nowhere, and not even enunciated, but announced, recorded, and repeated, as if I say: foot, belly, mouth, nail, wound, hitting, sperm, breast, tattoo, eating, nerve, touching, knee, fatigue . . .

It goes without saying that failure is part of the intention.

Bodies are absolutely inviolable. Each is a virgin, a vestal on its bed: and virginal not because she is closed, but because she is open. "The open" is the virginal, and will always remain so. Abandon remains without access, and extension without entry.

And a twofold failure is given: a failure to speak about the body, a failure to keep silent about it. A double bind, a psychosis. The only entry into the body, the only access regained at each of its entries, is an access of madness.

Corps, corpus, corpus hoc est une intraitable folie. Non pas un désordre, ni un délire, ni une manie, ni une mélancolie, qui sont les très ordinaires folies de l'«esprit». Mais cette folie fière, plantée, tendue, toujours imminente en pleine présence, en plein «moi», en plein «nous», en plein «instant». Cette ouverture stridente en plein recueillement, au plein recueillement. Cette densité espacée, nerveuse, qui fuse au cœur de tout ce qu'il y a de *propre*, et *ne laisse pas s'approprier sans se distendre*, sans devenir *à soi* son pays étranger, ni sans faire du sens, de son sens, bien autre chose encore, une extension sans laquelle du sens pourrait bien être sensé, mais jamais, nulle part *avoir lieu*. Par cette folie, on entre au corps, et par toutes les entrées du corps—et par celle que chaque corps *est*—on accède à cette folie.

Mais il n'y pas d' «accès». La folie du corps n'est pas une crise, et n'est pas morbide. Elle est seulement l'infiniment délié et distendu de l'avoir-lieu à soi-même tendu. Elle est cette offrande du lieu.

Il n'y a pas de crise, pas de contorsion, pas d'écume, pas plus qu'il n'y a place pour vous et moi au même endroit en même temps. Pas de secret du corps à nous communiquer, et pas de corps secret à nous révéler. Ce qui est «révélé», c'est que les corps sont plus visibles que toute révélation.

Ainsi, j'ai déjà fini de parler des corps: je n'ai pas commencé. Je n'en finirai pas de dire ce non-commencement, mais lui, le corps même de cette parole, ma bouche, ma main, mon cerveau, n'en finira pas de le taire. Et de le taire dans une évidence à laquelle, pourtant, il n'y a pas d'accès—pas de vision. Je finirai par dire, lourdement: le corps *est* à l'écart, telle est la certitude qui lui revient, et qu'il ne nous permet pas de partager.

Ce pauvre programme est connu d'avance. Il est même le seul programme raisonnable d'un discours, quel qu'il soit, consacré au «corps». En mettant «le corps» au programme, on le met à l'écart. Qui peut savoir, ici même en ce moment, quel corps s'adresse, est adressé à quel autre? Qui peut, ici en cet instant, toucher le corps des mots, en dissipant l'incorporel qui les fait *mots*?

Pourtant, on ne prétendra pas que les corps sont ineffables, que leur accès se fait par l'ineffable. Le thème de l'ineffable sert toujours la cause d'une parole—d'une fable—plus haute, plus relevée, plus secrète, silencieuse et sublime: un pur trésor de sens auquel accède qui se joint à Dieu. Mais «Dieu est mort» veut dire: Dieu *n'a plus de corps*. Le monde n'est plus l'espacement de Dieu, ni l'espacement en Dieu: il devient le monde des corps. L'autre monde se dissout comme le corps de la Mort, comme la Mort en Personne: pourriture où s'abolit l'espace, pure concentration, broyat, lysat de corps dans le suave ineffable grouillant de *cette chose qui n'a de nom dans aucune langue*, cet au-delà du cadavre où Tertullien, Bossuet, combien d'autres, font

Corps, corpus, corpus hoc is an incurable madness. Not a disorder, delerium, mania, or melancholy, all very ordinary madnesses of the "mind." But a proud madness, planted, tense, always imminent, in the midst of presence, in the midst of "me," in the midst of "us," in the midst of the "instant." This strident opening in utter contemplation, *to* utter contemplation. This spaced and nervous density, launched from the heart of everything *proper*, which *cannot allow itself to be appropriated without being distended*, without becoming *to itself* its foreign land, or without making sense, its own sense, into something truly different, an extension in whose absence sense might indeed be sensible, yet never *take place* anywhere. With this madness, we enter the body, and through all the body's entries—and through the entry that each body *is*—we accede to this madness.

But there is no "access." The madness of the body isn't a crisis, and isn't morbid. It's just this endlessly untied and distended place-taking, tending toward itself. The body's madness is this offering of place.

There's no crisis, no contortion, no foam, any more than there's room for you and me in the same place at the same time. No secret of the body to be communicated to us, no secret body to be revealed to us. "Revealed" is the fact that bodies are more visible than any revelation.

And so I've already stopped talking about bodies: I haven't started. I won't stop stating this not-starting, though the actual body of this speech, itself—my mouth, my hand, my brain—won't stop being silent about it. But being silent about it with evidence to which there is still no access—no vision. I'll close by saying, ponderously: the body *is* set apart, such certainty is its due, and it won't let us share.

This poor program is known in advance. It's indeed the only reasonable program for any discourse, whatever it may be, devoted to the "body." And by putting "the body" into the program, we set it apart. Who can know, here and now in this moment, what body addresses, is addressed to, what other body? Who here, at this instant, can touch the body of words, while dissipating the incorporeality that makes them *words*?

And yet we won't claim that bodies are ineffable, that access to them is gained through the ineffable. The theme of the ineffable always serves the cause of a certain kind of speech—or a fable—more elevated, more refined, more secret, silent, and sublime: a pure treasure of sense, accessible to those connected to God. But "God is dead" means: God *no longer has a body*. The world is neither the spacing of God nor the spacing in God: it becomes the world of bodies. The other world is dissolved as the body of Death, as Death in Person: a rotting where space is abolished, a pure concentration, crushing, dissolving body into the suave ineffable, crawling with *this thing that*

voir l'issue du monde. Dieu innommé s'évanouit avec cette chose innommable: il disparaît *en elle*, il s'*y révèle mort*, et la Mort en Personne, c'est-à-dire *aucun corps*.

Il se peut qu'avec le corps de Dieu aient disparu toutes les entrées de tous les corps, toutes les idées, images, vérités, interprétations du corps—et qu'il ne nous reste plus que le *corpus* de l'anatomie, de la biologie et de la mécanique. Mais cela même, cela précisément veut dire: *ici*, le monde des corps, la mondialité du corps, et *là*, discours coupé, l'incorporel, le sens dont on ne déchiffre plus l'orientation, l'entrée ni la sortie.

Telle est désormais la condition du sens: sans entrée ni sortie, l'espacement, les corps.

Ce qu'on ne peut plus dire, il convient de ne pas cesser d'en parler. Il ne faut pas cesser de presser la parole, la langue et le discours contre ce corps au contact incertain, intermittent, dérobé, insistant pourtant. Ici ou là, on peut en être sûr, il s'en suivra un corps à corps avec la langue, un corps à corps de sens d'où pourra naître, ici ou là, l'exposition d'un corps, touché, nommé, excrit hors sens, *hoc enim*.

Corps glorieux

En vérité, le corps de Dieu était le corps de l'homme même: la chair de l'homme était le corps que Dieu s'étaitdonné. (L'homme est le corps, absolument, ou il n'est pas: le corps de Dieu, ou le monde des corps, mais rien d'autre. C'est pourquoi l'«homme» de l'«humanisme», voué à signifier, sursignifier, insignifier son corps, a lentement dissous et ce corps et lui-même.) Dieu s'était fait corps, il s'était étendu et pétri *ex limon terrae*: de l'extension grasse, lisse, déformable de la glaise, de la matière *première*, laquelle consiste tout entière, non en substance, mais en modalisation, ou en modification. Que Dieu crée le *limon*, et que du *limon* il façonne le *corps*, cela veut dire que Dieu *se* modalise ou *se* modifie, mais que son *soi* n'est lui-même rien d'autre que l'extension et l'expansion indéfinie des modes. Cela veut dire que la «création» n'est pas la production d'un monde à partir d'on ne sait quelle matière de néant, mais qu'elle est ceci que la matière (cela même qu'il y a) essentiellement *se modifie*: elle n'est pas une substance, elle est l'extension et l'expansion des «modes», ou bien, pour le dire de manière plus exacte, elle est l'exposition de ce qu'il y a. Les corps sont l'exposition de Dieu, et il n'y en a aucune autre—pour autant que Dieu s'expose.

C'est donc bien lui qui s'expose *mort* comme *le monde des corps*. D'une part, le corps divin pourri, putréfié, pétrifié, face de Méduse et de Mort—

has no name in any language, this beyond of the cadaver where Tertullian and Bossuet, and so many others, make us *see* the end of the world. An un-named God disappears with this unnameable thing: he disappears *into it*, he's *revealed dead there*, as Death in Person, in other words, *no body*.

It may be that all entries into all bodies, all ideas, images, truths, and in-terpretations of the body, have disappeared with the body of God—and per-haps we're left only with the *corpus* of anatomy, biology, and mechanics. But even this, and precisely this, means: *here*, the world of bodies, the worldliness of bodies, and *there*, a cut off, incorporeal discourse, the orientation, entry, or exit whose sense we no longer decipher.

Such, henceforth, is the condition of sense: lacking entry or exit, spacing, bodies.

Whereof we can no longer speak, thereof we must not stop talking. We have to keep pressing speech, language, and discourse against this body, whose con-tact is uncertain, intermittent, hidden, and yet insistent. Here and there, we can be sure that a body-to-body struggle with language is on the way, a body-to-body struggle of sense from which there might emerge, here and there, the exposition of a body—touched, named, exscribed outside sense, *hoc enim*.

Glorious Body

In truth, the body of God was the body of man himself: man's flesh was the body God gave himself. (Man is the body, absolutely, or he's not: the body of God, or the world of bodies, but nothing else. Which is why the "man" of "humanism," dedicated to signifying, oversignifying, unsignifying his body, has slowly dissolved this body along with himself.) God had made him-self body, he had been extended and molded *ex limon terrae*: out of the fat, smooth, deformable extension of clay, the *raw* matter, consisting entirely of modalizing, or modification, rather than substance. That God created *limon*, and that he made the *body* out of *limon*, means that God modalized or modified himself, but that his *self* in itself is only the extension and in-definite expansion of modes. This means that "creation" isn't the production of a world from some unknown matter of nothingness but consists in the fact that *the* matter (only that which there is) essentially *modifies itself*: it's not a substance, it's the extension and expansion of "modes" or, to put it more precisely, the exposition of what there is. Bodies are the exposition of God, and there is no other—to the extent that God exposes himself.

Thus, indeed, he's the one who's exposing himself *dead* like *the world of bodies*. On the one hand, the divine body rotting, putrified, petrified, the

et d'autre part, *comme l'autre part de la même mort de Dieu*, le corps divin exposé, étendue matérielle première du monde des corps, Dieu infiniment modifié. C'est-à-dire: pas de Dieu, même pas les dieux, seulement les *lieux*. Les lieux: ils sont divins *parce que débarrassés* du Corps de Dieu et de la Mort en Personne. Divins de l'ouverture par où tout le «divin» s'effondre et se retire, laissant à nu le inonde de nos corps. Lieux du dénudement, lieux du dénuement, lieux du *limon terrae*.

Tel est le partage de la gloire de Dieu: la Mort, le Monde. La pourriture comme Mystère, la boue comme façon, comme *ductus* des lieux. Toute l'ontothéologie est traversée, est travaillée par cette ambivalence de la vérité du corps comme *corps glorieux*. Un même geste, ou presque—un geste dont il est certain que nous n'en finirons pas de le dédoubler, ni de le redoubler—dresse Dieu comme Corps de la Mort; *et* livre l'espace à la multiplication des corps. Un même geste prononce le dégoût et le goût des corps.

Ou bien le corps glorieux est la transfiguration du corps étendu, ou bien il en est l'étendue même, la figuration dans le limon plastique. Ou bien, ou bien, à la fois.

Étendue de la gloire: «Tout le Cosmos étendu dans l'espace n'est que l'expansion du coeur de Dieu» (Schelling). Gloire de l'étendue: «Dans les yeux se trouve le feu; dans la langue, qui forme la parole, l'air; dans les mains, qui ont en propre le toucher, la terre; et l'eau dans les parties génitales» (Bernard de Clairvaux).

Avec le corps, qu'il se donne, de l'homme—avec cet homme, et femme, qu'il se donne pour corps—le créateur ne reproduit pas son image. La puissance du créateur tient à la déconstruction originelle de toute image reconnaissable. Le monde créé n'imite rien, que l'inimitable. Le corps est l'image—mais en ce qu'il est la visibilité de l'invisible, l'éclat plastique de l'espacement.

L'*idée* même de la «création» est l'idée, ou la pensée, d'une absence originaire d'Idée, de forme, de modèle, de tracé préalable. Et si le *corps* est le *créé* par excellence, si «corps créé» est une tautologie—ou plutôt «corps créés», car *le* corps *est* toujours au pluriel—, alors *le corps est la matière plastique de l'espacement* sans forme et sans Idée. Il est la plasticité même del' expansion, de l'extension selon laquelle ont lieu les existences. L'*image* qu'il est ainsi n'a pas rapport avec l'idée, ni en général avec une «présentation» visible (et/ou intelligible) *de* quoi que ce soit. Le corps n'est pas image-de. Mais il est *venue en présence*, à la manière de l'image qui vient à l'écran de la télévision, du cinéma, venant *de* nul fond de l'écran, *étant* l'espacement de cet écran, existant en tant que son étendue—exposant, étalant cette aréalité, non pas comme une idée donnée à ma vision de sujet ponctuel (encore moins comme

face of Medusa and Death—and on the other, *as the other side of the same death of God*, the divine body exposed, the first material extension of a world of bodies, God infinitely modified. In other words: no God, not even gods, just *places*. Places: these are divine *because rid* of God's Body, and of Death in Person. Places divine through an opening whereby the whole "divine" collapses and withdraws, leaving the world of our bodies bare. Places of bareness, of destitution, places of *limon terrae*.

This is the way God's glory is shared: Death, the World. Rotting as Mystery, mud as the manner and *ductus* of places. All ontotheology is traversed and worked through by this ambivalence about the truth of the body as a *glorious body*. A single gesture, or almost—a gesture whose doubling and redoubling we certainly won't ever be done with—erects God as the Body of Death: *and* delivers space to the multiplication of bodies. A single gesture betrays disgust with bodies as well as a taste for them.

The glorious body is either a transfiguration of the extended body or its very extension, its figuration in malleable clay. Either or both at once.

Extension of glory: "The whole Cosmos extended in space is only the expansion of God's heart" (Schelling). The Glory of extension: "Fire is found in the eyes; air in the tongue, forming speech; earth in the hands, whose proper function is touch; and water in the genital organs" (Bernard of Clairvaux).

In the human body that he gives himself—in this man, and woman, that he gives himself as a body—the creator doesn't reproduce his own image. The creator's strength comes from the original deconstruction of any recognizable image. The created world imitates only the inimitable. The body is an image—insofar as the body is the visibility of the invisible, the bright plasticity of spacing.

The very *idea* of "creation" is the idea, or thought, of an originary absence of Idea, form, model, or preliminary tracing. And if the *body* is par excellence the thing *created*, if "created body" is a tautology—or, rather, "created bodies," for *the* body *is* always in the plural—then *the body is the plastic material of spacing*, without form or Idea. It's the very plasticity of expansion, extension—where existences *take place*. The *image* (that it thus is) has no link to either the idea or, in general, to the visible (and/or intelligible) "presentation" *of* anything at all. The body's not an image-*of*. But it's the *coming to presence*, like an image coming on a movie or a TV screen—coming *from* nowhere behind the screen, *being* the spacing of this screen, existing as its extension—exposing, laying down this areality, not as an idea given *to* my own vision as a punctual subject (and still less as a mystery), but *right at* my eyes (my body), as their areality, themselves

un mystère), mais *à même* mes yeux (mon corps), comme leur aréalité, eux-mêmes venant à cette venue, espacés, espaçant, eux-mêmes écran, et moins «vision» que *video*. (Non «video» = «je vois», mais *la video* comme un nom générique pour la *techné* de la venue à la présence. La *techné:* la «technique», l'«art», la «modalisation», la «création».)

Ce corps aréal, ce corps-video, ce corps-clarté-d'écran est la matérialité glorieuse de la *venue*. La venue a lieu *à* une présence qui n'a pas eu lieu et qui n'aura pas lieu ailleurs, et qui n'est ni présente, ni représentable hors de la venue. Ainsi, la venue elle-même n'en finit pas, elle va en venant, elle est allée-et-venue, rythme des corps naissant, mourant, ouverts, fermés, jouissant, souffrant, se touchant, s'écartant. La gloire est le rythme, ou la plastique, de cette présence—locale, forcément locale.

Incarnation

Mais il y a, tout le long de la tradition, l'autre version de la venue en présence, et de sa *techné*. L'autre, la même, indiscernables et distinctes, accouplées comme dans l'amour. «Le» corps aura toujours été sur la limite de ces deux versions, là où elles se touchent et où elles se repoussent en même temps. Le corps—sa vérité—aura toujours été l'entre-deux de deux *sens*—dont l'entre-deux de la droite et de la gauche, du haut et du bas, de l'avant et de l'arrière, du phalle et du céphale, du mâle et du femelle, du dedans et du dehors, du sens sensible et du sens intelligible, ne font que s'entr'exprimer les uns les autres.

L'autre version de la *venue* se nomme l'incarnation. Si je dis *verbum caro factum est* (*logos sarx egeneto*), je dis en un sens que *caro* fait la gloire et la véritable venue de *verbum*. Mais je dis aussitôt, en un tout autre sens, que *verbum* (*logos*) fait la véritable présence et le sens de *caro* (*sarx*). Et si, *en un sens* (une fois encore), ces deux versions s'entr'appartiennent, et si «incarnation» les nomme toutes deux ensemble, cependant *en un autre sens* elles s'excluent.

Elles s'excluent *comme s'excluent déjà*, dans *la phrase de l'Évangile philosophique, les concepts de «logos» et de «sarx»*. Pour énoncer cette proposition, il faut avoir déjà disposé de ces concepts ou de ces Idées. L'Évangile philosophique fait fond sur cette disposition: il en est même tout d'abord l'annonce. *En archè èn o logos, in principio erat verbum*: il y a eu principe et commencement, il y a *déjà* eu cela, cet avant et cet après. Lorsqu'on commence, on est déjà sorti de l'entre-deux: l'entre-deux n'a pas lieu (comme si jamais nous ne pouvions commencer par l'entre-deux du lieu, jamais commencer par le corps, jamais avoir à faire au corps naissant: *alors même* que c'est ici, que cela veut être ici l'Évangile de la Naissance proprementdite; mais sans doute, en effet, le commencement en tant que *principium* n'est

coming into this coming, spaced, spacing, themselves a screen—less "vision" than *video*. (Not "video" = "I see," but *video* as a generic name for the *technē* of a coming into presence. *Technē*: "technique," "art," "modalization," "creation.")

This areal body, this video-body, this clear-screen-body, is the glorious materiality of *what is coming*. What is coming happens *to* a presence that hasn't taken place, and won't take place elsewhere, and is neither present, nor representable, outside of what is coming. Thus, the *coming* itself never ends, it *goes* as it comes, it's a coming-and-going, a rhythm of bodies being born, dying, open, closed, delighting, suffering, being touched, swerving. Glory is the rhythm, or the plasticity, of this presence—local, necessarily local.

Incarnation

But throughout the whole tradition, there's the other version of this *coming*, of the coming into presence and its *technē*. The other, the same, indiscernible and distinct, coupled as in love. "The" body will always have been at the limit of these two versions, where each at one and the same time touches and repels the other. The body—its truth—will always have been the intervallic space between two *senses*—amongst which the intervals between right and left, high and low, before and behind, phallus and cephale, male and female, inside and outside, sensory sense and intelligible sense, merely inter-express each other.

The other version of this *coming* is called incarnation. If I say *verbum caro factum est* (*logos sarx egeneto*), I say in one sense that *caro* gives rise to *verbum*'s glory and true *coming*. But I also instantly say, in an entirely different sense, that *verbum* (*logos*) gives rise to the true presence and sense of *caro* (*sarx*). And if, *in one sense* (once again), these two versions belong to each other, and if "incarnation" names them both together, they nevertheless, *in another sense*, exclude one another.

They exclude one another just as *the concepts of "logos" and "sarx" already exclude each other, in the sentence drawn from the philosophical Gospel.* For this proposition to be enunciated, one must have disposed of these concepts, or these Ideas. The philosophical Gospel is based on such a disposing: it is even first and foremost its declaration. *En archē en ho logos, in principio erat verbum*: there was a principle and a beginning, it was *already* there, this before and after. When one starts, one has already left the in between: the inter-space doesn't take place (as if we could never begin with the inter-space of a place, never start with the body, never be involved with a body being born: *even though* the Gospel of the Nativity itself is here, or wants to be here; but as

pas une naissance, et n'est donc pas un corps . . .). Lorsqu'on commence, il y a déjà une antécédence absolue.

(Lorsqu'*on* commence: qui donc commence ainsi, articulant «En archè èn o logos . . . »? C'est l'*ange*, le messager *sans corps*, qui porte la nouvelle de l'incarnation. Logique angélique de l'annonciation occidentale.)

Puisqu'une antécédence est donnée, le corps sera dans la descendance (*egeneto*). Il est saisi d'avance dans la filiation, et la filiation efface, ou du moins réduit l'espacement de la naissance. Parce qu'il est d'abord *fils*, le corps répond moins à l'espace qu'au temps, à la succession et à la progression. Il *descend* du père (de sa gloire), et il avance *sa lumière dans les ténèbres*. Le corps est la pénétration, la progression du principe dans les ténèbres de ce qui succède, de ce qui se tient en dessous.

Mais c'est dans la ténèbre, et comme ténèbre lui-même, que le corps a été *conçu*. Il a été conçu et conformé dans la caverne de Platon, et comme la caverne même: prison ou tombe de l'âme. L'incarnation fait pénétrer le principe dans cela qui l'obscurcit et qui l'offusque. Le corps est tout d'abord conçu dans l'angoisse de cet étouffement. Le corps-caverne est l'espace du corps *se voyant du dedans*, voyant du dedans (et sans naître) le ventre de la mère, ou se voyant lui-même sa propre matrice, sans père ni mère, pure ténèbre de l'autofiliation. Ainsi, l'œil nocturne de la caverne *se voit*, et il se voit nocturne, il se voit privation du jour. Le corps est le sujet de l'ombre—et son *voir* ténébreux est aussi bien, déjà, l'empreinte, le reste de lumière, le signe de la vision solaire. *Lux in tenebris*, le corps de l'incarnation est *le signe*, absolument.

Le signe, c'est-à-dire le signe *du sens*, c'est-à-dire, non la venue du sens, mais un *renvoi* au sens comme intériorité, comme «dedans». Le corps est le renvoi du «dehors» qu'il est à ce «dedans» qu'il n'est pas. Au lieu d'être en extension, le corps est en expulsion vers son propre «intérieur», jusqu'à la limite où le signe s'abolit dans la présence qu'il représentait.

De part en part, la logique angélique et le *corpus* entier des corps philosophiques sont soumis à la loi signifiante, de telle manière que c'est la signification (ou la représentation) qui donne sens au corps, en le faisant lui-même signe du sens. Tous les corps sont des signes, de même que tous les signes sont des corps (signifiants).

Corps signifiant

A proprement parler, nous ne connaissons et nous ne concevons, nous n'imaginons même que du corps signifiant. Du corps dont il n'importe guère qu'il soit *ici*, qu'il soit l'*ici* ou le *là* d'un lieu, mais dont il importe avant tout qu'il opère comme le lieu-tenant et le vicaire d'un sens. Nous ne nous

principium, the beginning, no doubt, is not in fact a birth, and is hence not a body . . .). As soon as one begins, there's already an absolute antecedence.

(As soon as *one* begins: who, then, begins like this, articulating "En archēn ho logos . . ."? It's an *angel*, a messenger *without a body*, who bears tidings of the incarnation. Angelic logic of Western annunciation.)

Since antecedence is given, the body will be in descendants (*egeneto*). It's caught beforehand in filiation, and filiation effaces, or at least reduces, the spacing of birth. Being a *filius* in the first place, the body responds less to space than to time, succession, and progression. It *descends* from the father (from his glory) and advances *his light in darkness*. The body is the penetration and progression of the principle into the darkness of what comes after, of what's kept beneath.

But the body was *conceived* in darkness, and as darkness itself. It was conceived and shaped in Plato's cave, as the cave itself: prison or tomb of the soul. Incarnation causes the principle to penetrate the thing that obscures and obfuscates it. From the outset, the body is conceived in the anxiety of this confinement. The cave-body is the space of the body *seeing itself from within*, seeing (without being born) from within the mother's womb, or seeing itself as its own matrix, with neither mother nor father, the pure darkness of autofiliation. Thus, the nocturnal eye of the cave sees *itself*, and sees itself as nocturnal, sees itself as the privation of day. The body is the subject of shadow—and its shadowy *seeing* is also, already, the imprint, the remainder of light, the sign of solar vision. *Lux in tenebris*, the body of the incarnation is *the sign*, absolutely.

The sign, meaning a sign *of sense*, meaning not the coming of sense but a *reference* to sense as interiority, as "inside." The body is the return of the "outside" that it is to this "inside" that it isn't. Instead of being in extension, the body is in expulsion toward its own "interior," right to the very limit where the sign is abolished in the presence it represented.

Through and through, angelic logic and the whole *corpus* of philosophical bodies are subjected to the signifying law, in such a way that signification (or representation) gives sense to the body, making it the sign of sense. All bodies are signs, just as all signs are (signifying) bodies.

Signifying Body

Properly speaking, we only know, conceive, and even imagine a signifying body. It doesn't matter that the body be *here*, be the *here* or *there* of a place, but that it should operate as the place-holder and vicar of sense. We only conceive of completely hysterical bodies, paralyzed by the representation of

représentons que des corps d'hystérie intégrale, tétanisés par la représentation d'un autre corps—d'un corps-de-sens—, et pour le reste, en tant que «corps» ci-gisants, simplement *perdus*. La convulsion de la signification arrache tout le corps au corps—et laisse le cadavre à la caverne.

Tantôt ce «corps» est lui-même le «dedans» où la représentation se forme ou se projette (sensation, perception, image, mémoire, idée, conscience)—et dans ce cas, le «dedans» apparaît (et *s'*apparaît) comme étranger au corps et comme «esprit». Tantôt, le corps est le «dehors» signifiant («point zéro» de l'orientation et de la visée, origine et récepteur des rapports, inconscient), et dans ce cas, le «dehors» apparaît comme une intériorité épaisse, une caverne comblée, bourrée d'intentionnalité. Ainsi, le corps signifiant ne cesse pas d'échanger dedans et dehors, d'abolir l'étendue dans un unique *organon* du signe: cela *où* se forme et *d'où* prend forme le sens. Les perspectives philosophiques particulières n'y changent pas grand-chose: dualisme de l'«âme» et du «corps», monisme de la «chair», symboliques culturelles ou psychanalytiques des corps, toujours le corps est structuré comme un *renvoi au sens*. L'incarnation est structurée comme une décorporation.

De cette manière, dans cette structure ou dans cette posture, le corps signifiant ne cesse pas de se construire. Il est par excellence instance de contradiction. Ou bien c'est par lui, et en lui, qu'il y a signification (par exemple, corporéité du langage), et la signification tombe dans ses limites, elle ne vaut que ce que vaut l'ombre dans la caverne, et pour finir, comme le signe en général, le corps signifiant fait *obstacle* au sens. Ou bien c'est *de* lui qu'il y a signification, c'est *lui en vérité* que le sens interprète, mais alors, son lieu propre de «corps» devient le lieu plus qu'intime d'une propriété incorporelle. De toute manière, le corps se tend le piège du signe et du sens—et s'y prend de part en part. S'il est le signe, il n'est donc pas le sens: il lui faut donc une *âme* ou un *esprit*, qui sera le *vrai* «corps du sens». S'il est le sens, il est alors le sens indéchiffrable de son propre signe (corps mystérique, et donc, et de nouveau, «âme» ou «esprit»).

Le corps signifiant—tout le corpus des corps philosophiques, théologiques, psychanalytiques et sémiologiques—n'*incarne* qu'une chose: l'absolue contradiction de ne pas pouvoir être *corps* sans l'être *d'un esprit*, qui le désincorpore.

La littérature ne le fait pas moins voir. On pourrait être tenté de dire que si, dans la philosophie, il n'y a jamais eu de corps (autre que *de l'esprit*), dans la littérature en revanche) il n'y aurait que des corps (ce qu'on affirmerait aussi de l'art en général). Cependant, la littérature—et du moins, cette interprétation de la littéraure (et de l'art) qui l'a déjà comprise comme *une incarnation de la philosophie* . . . —nous présente de trois choses l'une: ou bien la fiction, le jeu des représentations, qui *touche*, assurément (crainte et pitié,

an *other* body—a body of sense—and of the rest as "bodies" lying here, simply *lost*. The convulsion of signification completely tears the body from the body—leaving the cadaver in the cave.

Sometimes this "body" is itself an "inside" where representation is formed or projected (sensation, perception, image, memory, idea, consciousness)—in which case the "inside" appears (and appears *to itself*) as alien to the body, as "spirit." At other times, the body is the signifying "outside" (a "zero point" for orientation and aim, the sender and receiver of connections, the unconscious), and, in this case, the outside appears as a dense interiority, a cave overwhelmed, crammed with intentionality. Thus the signifying body never stops exchanging inside and outside, abolishing extension in the unique *organon* of a sign: exactly *where* and *whence* sense is formed and takes form. Particular philosophical perspectives don't greatly alter things: the dualism of "body" and "soul," the monism of "flesh," cultural or psychoanalytic symbolisms of bodies, the body always is structured as a *return to sense*. Incarnation is structured like a disembodiment.

In this way, in this structure, or posture, the signifying body never stops construing itself. It's an instance par excellence of contradiction. Either there's signification by means of it, and in it (the corporeality of language, for example), and signification falls within its limits, so that it's only as valuable as the cave's shadow, finally presenting, like the sign in general, an *obstacle* to sense. Or else signification is *of* it, it's *truly the body* that sense interprets—but then its own place as "body" becomes the more than intimate site of an incorporeal propriety. In whatever way, the body sets the trap of sign and sense—and is completely entrapped by it. If it's a sign, then it's not sense: therefore it has to have a *soul* or *spirit*, which will be the *true* "body of sense." If it's sense, then it's an indecipherable sense of its own sign (a mysterical body, and therefore, once again, "soul" or "spirit").

The signifying body—the whole corpus of philosophical, theological, psychoanalytic, and semiological bodies—*incarnates* one thing only: the absolute contradiction of not being able to be a *body* without being the body *of a spirit*, which disembodies it.

Literature doesn't make this any less evident. We might be tempted to say that, if there's never been a body in philosophy (other than *of the spirit*), there are, by contrast, only bodies in literature (something we'd also affirm about art in general). But literature—at least the interpretation of literature (and art) that has already understood it as *an incarnation of philosophy* . . .—presents us with three things at once: *either* a fiction or play of representations, which *touches*, certainly (fear and pity, laughter and mimicry), but with a

rire et mimique), mais d'un toucher lui-même réputé fictif, protégé, distancié et pour tout dire «spirituel» (la vraie question du *toucher* et en général de la *sensibilité* littéraire et artistique, la vraie question d'une *esthétique* reste entièrement à poser, ou peu s'en faut, tant que les corps sont d'abord signifiants); ou bien, d'inépuisables réserves de corps eux-mêmes saturés de signification, eux-mêmes engendrés pour signifier, et uniquement pour cela (comme par un excès de zèle philosophique . . .): sans même parler des corps de Don Quichotte ou de Quasimodo, ni de tous les corps de Balzac, de Zola ou de Proust, y a-t-il en littérature des corps qui ne fassent pas signe? (là où il y en a, j'y reviendrai, on sort de la «littérature»); ou bien encore, c'est la production même (la création?) de la littérature qui s'offre en personne et en corps (mémoires, fragments, autobiographie, théorie), abandonnée et bandée, hyper-signifiante comme le «*corps qui bat* (qui jouit) » de l'écrivain écrit de la main de l'écrivain même (ici, Roland Barthes), signifiant éperdument jusqu'au bord de la non-signifiante, mais signifiant, encore.

S'il y a autre chose, un autre corps de la littérature que ce corps signifié/signifiant, il ne fera ni signe, ni sens, et en cela il ne sera pas même écrit. Il sera l'écriture, si l'«écriture» indique *cela qui s'écarte de la signification*, et qui, pour cela, s'*excrit*. L'excription se produit dans le jeu d'un espacement in-signifiant: celui qui détache les mots de leur sens, toujours à nouveau, et qui les abandonne à leur étendue. Un mot, dès qu'il n'est pas absorbé sans reste dans un sens, *reste* essentiellement étendu *entre* les autres mots, tendu à les toucher, sans les rejoindre pourtant: et cela est le langage en tant que *corps*.

L'assomption dernière du corps signifiant est politique. «Corps politique» est une tautologie, ou du moins une évidence, pour toute la tradition, et quelles qu'en soient les figures variées. La fondation politique repose sur cette absolue circularité signifiante: que la communauté ait le corps pour sens, et que le corps ait la communauté pour sens. Par conséquent, que le corps ait la communauté—son institution—pour signe, et que la communauté ait le corps—du roi ou de l'assemblée—pour signe. La présupposition infinie est donc celle du corps-communauté, qui comporte une double implication. D'une part, le corps en général a pour sens sa propre intimité organique, son se-sentir et se-toucher de sujet (*res inextensa*): autrement dit, le corps a pour sens *le sens*, absolument et en totalité. D'autre part, et corrélativement, les corps individués s'entr'appartiennent dans un corps commun dont la substance (de nouveau, *res inextensa*) fait le fond de la révélation du mystère politique. (Autrement dit, sous le régime politique du sens, pas de *res extensa*, pas d'*espace* pour l'être-*entre*-nous ou pour l'être-*en*-commun—et pas d'espace pour les *corps*, leurs tracés, leurs

touch itself reputedly fictive, protected, and distanced, in a word, "spiritual" (the true question of *touching* and, in general, of literary and artistic *sensibility*, the true question of an *aesthetics*, is yet to be posed, or very nearly so, so long as bodies are signifiers above all); or else inexhaustible reserves of bodies, themselves saturated with signification, themselves engendered to signify, and for that one purpose alone (as with an excess of philosophical zeal . . .): leaving aside the bodies of Don Quixote, or Quasimodo, or all the bodies in Balzac, Zola, or Proust, are there any bodies in literature that do not constitute a sign? (Wherever there are, we take leave of "literature," I'll get back to this.) Or else, again, the very production (the creation?) of literature is offered in person and in body (memories, fragments, autobiography, theory), abandoned and bandaged, hyper-signifying as a writer's "*throbbing body* (that takes pleasure)," written in the hand of the writer himself (here, Roland Barthes), madly signifying to the very limit of nonsignificance, but signifying, nonetheless.

If there's anything else—a body of literature other than this signifying/signified body—it will furnish neither sign nor sense, and in this respect won't even be written. It will be writing, if "writing" indicates *the very thing that swerves from signification* and which, therefore, *is exscribed*. Exscription is produced in the loosening of unsignifying spacing: it detaches words from their senses, always again and again, abandoning them to their extension. A word, so long as it's not absorbed without remainder into a sense, *remains* essentially extended *between* other words, stretching to touch them, though not merging with them: and that's language as *body*.

The final assumption of the signifying body is political. "Body politic" is a tautology, or at least obvious, for the whole tradition, whatever its various figures may be. The political foundation rests on this absolute signifying circularity: that the community should have body as its sense, and that the body should have community as its sense. Consequently, that the body should have the community—its institution—as its sign, and that the community should have the body—of king or assembly—as its sign. Thus there's an infinite presupposition of a body-community, which bears a double implication. On the one hand, the body in general has its own organic intimacy for its sense, its feeling- and touching-itself as a subject (*res inextensa*); in other words, the body has *sense* as its sense, absolutely and totally so. On the other hand, and correlatively, individuated bodies belong with each other in a common body whose substance (once again, *res inextensa*) provides a foundation for the revelation of political mystery. (In other words, in the political order of sense there's no *res extensa*, no space for being-*between*-us or for being-*in*-common—and no space for *bodies*, their

rencontres, leurs accidents singuliers, leurs postes et postures dans le travail, l'échange et toute l'indéfinie déclinaison des «conditions communes». Parce que ce régime est à bout, le soupçon vient que la politique ne serait plus une affaire de *sens* incorporé: mais que la politique *commence et se termine aux corps*. Car ce n'est pas d'ailleurs qu'il y a, ou qu'il n'y a pas, du juste et de l'injuste, de l'égal et de l'inégal, du libre et du prisonnier: ces *choses*-là, il ne s'agit pas de les signifier, il s'agit de leur donner *lieu* [et lieux], et même de les *mesurer* [fussent-elles aussi incommensurables]. Les dimensions d'un logement, d'un atelier, d'un instrument, la durée d'un transport, le tracé d'une voie: *hoc est* l'étendue politique. S'il faut être plus clair, qu'on se représente ces réfugiés sous la pluie glaciale des montagnes, tenant à six une unique couverture au-dessus de leurs têtes.)

Trou noir

Signe de soi, et *être-soi du signe*: telle est la double formule du corps dans tous les états et dans toutes les possibilités que nous lui reconnaissons (dès lors que ce que nous «reconnaissons» relève *a priori* de l'ordre du sens). Le corps *se* signifie en tant que corps (de l')intériorité sensée: il n'est que de voir tout ce qu'on fait dire au corps humain, à sa station droite, à son pouce opposable, à ses «yeux où la chair se fait âme» (Proust). Ainsi, le corps présente l'être-soi du signe, c'est-à-dire la communauté accomplie du signifiant et du signifié, la fin de l'extériorité, le sens à même le sensible—*hoc est enim*.

Toutes nos sémiologies, toutes nos mimologies, toutes nos esthétiques tendent vers ce corps absolu, vers ce corps sur-signifiant, *corps du sens* dans le *sens du corps*. Toute fonction *symbolique* s'y accomplit: réunion sensible des parties de l'intelligible, réunion intelligible des parties du sensible. C'est bien pourquoi le corps de Dieu fait lui-même symbole pour toute notre tradition—c'est-à-dire, le corps de l'Homme, temple vivant de la divinité.

Mais le corps n'est ce Temple Vivant—la Vie comme Temple et le Temple comme Vie, le se-toucher comme mystère sacré—qu'à la condition d'achever sans reste la circularité qui le fonde. Il faut que le sens fasse corps, en soi et de toujours, pour que le corps fasse sens—et réciproquement. Ainsi, le sens du «sens» est «corps», et le sens du «corps» est «sens». Dans cette résorption circulaire, la signification accomplie s'évanouit aussi bien. Et c'est bien en ce point que le corps lui-même s'évanouit: c'est bien pour être ce comble de la signification que «le corps» n'a pas cessé d'être tendu, exaspéré, écartelé entre l'innommable et l'innommable: d'autant plus étranger que plus intime. *Le* corps est *l'organe du sens*: mais le sens du sens, c'est d'être *l'organe* (ou *l'organon*), absolument (on peut dire aussi bien: le système, la communauté, la communion, la subjectivité, la finalité, etc.). *Le*

tracings, their encounters, their singular accidents, their posts and postures in work, in trade, and in the whole indefinite series of "common conditions." Because this order is exhausted, the suspicion has arisen that politics is no longer an affair of incorporated *sense*: but that politics *begins and ends with bodies*. Because it's not really that there is, or isn't, something just or unjust, something equal or unequal, something free or something imprisoned: it's not a matter of signifying those *things*, but of giving them a *place* [and places] and even of *measuring* them [even if they're also incommensurable]. The dimensions of housing, of a studio or an instrument, the duration of a transport, the tracing of a way: *hoc est* the political extension. If this needs to be clearer, just recall those refugees in the mountains' glacial rain, six of them holding a single blanket over their heads.)

Black Hole

The sign of the self, and *the being-self of the sign*: such is the double formula of the body in all its states, with all the possibilities we grant it (since what we "grant" derives a priori from the order of sense). The body signifies *itself* as a body (of) sensed interiority: it's a matter merely of recognizing all the things that we make the human body say, along with its erect posture, its opposable thumb, its "eyes where flesh is made into a soul" (Proust). Thus the body presents the being-self of the sign, in other words, the accomplished community of signifier and signified, the end of exteriority, the sense right with the sensory—*hoc est enim.*

All our semiologies, all our mimologies, all our aesthetics tend toward this absolute body, toward this over-signifying body, a *body of sense* in the *sense of a body*. Every *symbolic* function is achieved in this body: a sensory joining of the elements of the intelligible, an intelligible joining of the elements of the sensory. This is certainly why the body of God itself serves as a symbol for our entire tradition—in other words, the body of Man, a living temple of divinity.

But the body is only a Living Temple—Life as a Temple and a Temple as Life—the being-touched as sacred mystery—if it achieves, without remainder, its founding circularity. In itself and always, sense has to make the body in order for the body to make sense—and conversely. Thus the sense of "sense" is "body," and the sense of "body" is "sense." In such circular reabsorption, achieved signification also promptly disappears. And it is precisely here that the body itself disappears: as the height of signification, "the body" hasn't stopped being stretched, exasperated, torn between the unnameable and the unnameable: all the stranger for being more intimate. *The body* is *the organ of sense*: but the sense of sense lies in being *the organ* (or

corps n'est donc rien d'autre que *l'auto-symbolisation de l'organe absolu*. Innommable comme Dieu, n'exposant rien dans le dehors d'une étendue, organe de l'organisation-de-soi, innommable comme la pourriture de sa digestion-de-soi (la Mort en Personne)—innommable aussi bien comme cette intime texture-de-soi vers laquelle s'évertue une philosophie du «corps propre» («ce que nous appelons chair, cette masse intérieurement travaillée, n'a de nom dans aucune philosophie»—Merleau-Ponty). Dieu, la Mort, la Chair: triple nom du corps de toute l'onto-théologie. Le corps est la combinatoire exhaustive, l'assomption commune de ces trois noms impossibles, où toute signification s'épuise.

Ce corps se retire au fond de lui-même—au fond du Sens—tout autant que le sens s'y retire jusqu'à son fond de mort. Ce corps forme très exactement ce que l'astrophysique nomme un *trou noir:* un astre d'une dimension telle que sa gravité y retient jusqu'à sa propre lumière, un astre qui s'éteint et s'effondre de lui-même en lui-même, ouvrant dans l'univers, au centre de l'astre et de sa densité inouïe, le *trou noir* d'une absence de matière (et une «fin des temps», l'inverse d'un «big bang», une dimension de cessation du monde dans le monde même). Que le corps métaphysique ou mystérique, que le corps de l'incarnation et du sens, soit pour finir un *trou* n'est guère surprenant: parce qu'il est le signifiant total d'un sens dont le sens est de faire-corps, le corps est aussi bien la fin du signifiant, la *crase* absolue du signe, le sens pur à même le sens pur, *hoc est enim corpus meum, hoc* désignant *ici* l'absence totale d'extériorité, la non-étendue en soi concentrée, non pas l'impénétrable, mais son excès, l'impénétrable *mêlé à* l'impénétrable, l' intussusception infinie, le *propre* s'avalant lui-même, jusqu'au vide de son centre—en vérité, plus loin que le centre, plus loin que toute trace d'espacement (que le «centre» retient encore), dans l'abîme où le trou absorbe jusqu'à ses bords.

Rien de surprenant si nos pensées, idées et images, au lieu de s'attarder dans l'étendue des bords, s'engouffrent dans les trous: cavernes, bouches hurlantes, cœurs transpercés, *inter feces et urinam*, crânes aux orbites béantes, vagins qui châtrent, non pas des ouvertures, mais des évidements, des énucléations, des effondrements—et le corps tout entier comme sa propre précipitation dans le non-lieu.

Une plaie

Ici, au lieu de non-lieu, et nulle part ailleurs qu'en ce « lieu » sans ailleurs, jaillit *l'esprit*, la concentration infinie en soi, le *souffle* ou le *vent* qui seul emplit les trous.

L'âme est la forme d'un corps, et donc, corps elle-même (*psyché étendue*). Mais *l'esprit* est la non-forme ou l'outre-forme du trou où le corps

the *organon*) absolutely (we could just as well say: the system, community, communion, subjectivity, finality, etc.). *The* body therefore is nothing other than the *self-symbolizing of the absolute organ.* Unnameable like God, exposing nothing in an extension's outside, an organ of self-organization, unnameable as the rot of its self-digestion (Death in Person)—unnameable also like this intimate self-texture, toward which a philosophy of the "body proper" struggles. ("What we call flesh, this inwardly worked mass, has no name in any philosophy"—Merleau-Ponty.) God, Death, Flesh: the threefold name of the entire body of onto-theology. The body is an exhaustive combining, a common assumption of these three impossible names, where all signification is exhausted.

This body retreats into its own depth—to the depth of Sense—just as sense withdraws all the way to its mortal depth. This body forms very precisely what astrophysicists call a *black hole*: a star whose dimension is such that its gravity withholds its own light, a star that extinguishes and collapses on its own into itself, opening, in the universe, at the center of the star and its extraordinary density, the *black hole* of an absence of matter (and an "end of time," the inverse of a "big bang," a dimension of the world's cessation within the world itself). That the metaphysical or mysterical body, the body of incarnation and sense, might finally be a *hole* is hardly surprising: as the all-signifying of a sense whose sense is body-building, the body is the end of the signifier as well, the absolute *crasis* of the sign, the pure sense of pure sense, *hoc est enim corpus meum*, with *hoc* designating *here* a total absence of exteriority, a nonextension concentrated in itself, not something impenetrable, but rather its excess, the impenetrable *mixed with* the impenetrable, infinite intussusception, the *proper* devouring itself, all the way to the void at its center—in truth deeper, even, than the center, deeper than any trace of spacing (which the "center" still retains), in an abyss where the hole absorbs even its own edges.

It's no surprise that our thoughts, ideas, and images are swallowed up in holes, instead of lingering within reach of their sides: caverns, crying mouths, hearts pierced through, *inter feces et urinam*, skulls with staring eyeholes, castrating vaginas, not openings, but evacuations, enucleations, collapses—and the whole body as its own precipitation into nonspace.

A Wound

Here, in the where of nowhere, and nowhere else than this "where" without elsewhere, *the spirit* emerges, infinite concentration in itself, the *breath* or *wind* that alone fills up holes.

The *soul* is the form of a body, and therefore a body itself (*psyche extended*). But the *spirit* is the nonform or the ultra-form of the hole into

se précipite. Dans l'âme, le corps *vient*, dans l'esprit, il *s'enlève*. L'esprit est la relève, la sublimation, la subtilisation de toute forme des corps—de leur étendue, de leur partage matériel, dans l'essence distillée et révélée du *sens* du corps: l'esprit *est* le corps du sens, ou le sens en corps. L'esprit est l'organe du sens, ou le *vrai corps*, le corps transfiguré. L'esprit du christianisme, c'est-à-dire, le christianisme en tant que théologie de l'Esprit saint, est ici tout entier: religion du souffle (judaïque, déjà), de la touche impalpable, religion du verbe, de la profération, de l'exhalaison—odeur délétère de la mort et parfums agréables à l'Éternel, odeur de sainteté (judaïques, déjà, islamiques, aussi)—, religion de l'expiration, et de l'inspiration, pneumatologie générale; religion de la filiation: l'Esprit va du Père au Fils (la mère, pour sa part, se suffit d'être un ventre intact, par où ce souffle aura passé); le fils est le corps, non pas l'expansion créatrice des corps, mais le corps de l'esprit, rassemblé, concentré sur son souffle, offert en sacrifice au père qu'il rejoint en expirant, corps du dernier cri, du dernier soupir où tout est consommé. *Pater, hoc est enim corpus meum: Spiritus enim sanctus tuus.*

Le Fils est le Corps de l'Esprit s'exhalant à la face du Père, se dissipant vers Lui dans les effluves et les flux du sacrifice qui le sanctifie: sueur, eau et sang, larmes, soupirs et cris. *Ici*, l'esprit qui s'exhale expose le plus proprement son propre corps: *Ecce homo.*

Mais ainsi se révèle ce qui le fait vraiment corps (de l') esprit: c'est une plaie, ce corps est passé dans ses plaies.

Ici, au même point du non-lieu de l'esprit, se présente le corps comme une plaie: l'autre façon d'épuiser le corps, d'en subtiliser le sens, de l'exhaler, de l'épancher, de le débrider, de l'abandonner, exposé à vif. L'esprit concentre ce que la plaie saigne: dans l'un et l'autre cas, le corps s'affaisse, plus et moins que mort, privé de sa juste mesure de mort, fouillé, souillé, supplicié.

C'est aussi de cette manière que s'annonce la mondialité des corps. Les corps meurtris, déchirés, brûlés, traînés, déportés, massacrés, torturés, écorchés, la chair mise en charniers, l'acharnement sur les plaies. Dans le charnier, les cadavres ne sont pas des morts, ils ne sont pas nos morts: ce sont des plaies amoncelées, collées, coulant l'une dans l'autre, et la terre jetée droit dessus, sans un linge pour définir l'espacement d'un mort, puis d'un autre mort. Il n'y a pas de cicatrice, la plaie reste à vif, les Forps ne retracent pas leurs aires. Comme au revers de l'esprit, ils se subliment en fumée, ils s'évaporent en brouillard. Ici aussi, le corps perd sa forme et son sens—et le sens a perdu tout corps. Par une autre concentration, les corps ne sont plus que des signes annulés: non, cette fois, dans le sens pur, mais dans son pur épuisement.

Il est difficile de dire à quel point la *concentration* (initiales: KZ) aura été la marque de naissance de *notre* monde: la concentration de l'esprit, le SOI

which the body throws itself. In the soul the body *comes*, in the spirit it is *taken away*. The spirit is the substitution, the sublimation, the subtilizing of all forms of bodies—of their extension, their material division, in the distilled and revealed essence of the *sense* of the body: the spirit *is* the body of sense, or sense in body. Spirit is the organ of sense, or the *true body*, the transfigured body. Here, then, the spirit of Christianity, meaning Christianity as a theology of the Holy Spirit, is entirely whole: a religion of breath (already Judaic), of impalpable touch, a religion of the word, of proferring, of exhaling—a deleterious odor of the dead, with perfumes pleasing to the One Eternal, an odor of sanctity (Judaic, already, and also Islamic)—a religion of expiration and inspiration, a general pneumatology, a religion of filiation: the Spirit passes from Father to Son (it's enough for the mother, for her part, to be an intact womb through which this breath will have passed); the son is the body, not the expansion that creates bodies, but the spirit's body, gathered up, concentrated in its breath, offered in sacrifice to the father it returns to by expiring, the body of the last cry, of the final sigh where everything is consumed. *Pater, hoc est enim corpus meum: spiritus enim sanctus tuus.*

The Son is the Body of the Spirit exhaling in the face of the Pater, dissipating toward Him in the effluvia and fluxes of a sacrifice that sanctifies him: sweat, water, and blood; tears, sighs, and cries. *Here*, the exhaling spirit most properly exposes its proper body: *Ecce homo.*

But what's revealed here is what makes it truly the spirit('s) body: it's a wound; this body has passed into its wounds.

Here, at the same point of the spirit's nonsite, the body is presented as a wound: the other way to exhaust the body, subtilize its sense, exhale it, pour it forth, unbridle it, abandon it, exposed in the raw. The spirit concentrates what the wound bleeds: in either case, the body subsides, more and less than dead, robbed of its fair share of death, dug up, soiled, sacrificed.

The world-wideness of bodies is also announced in this way. Bodies murdered, torn, burned, dragged, deported, massacred, tortured, flayed, flesh dumped into mass graves, an obsessing over wounds. The cadavers in a mass grave aren't the dead, they aren't our dead: they are wounds heaped up, stuck in, flowing into one another, the soil tossed right on top, no winding-cloth to define the spacing of one, and then another, death. There's no scar, the wound's still open, the bodies don't retrace their areas. As if on the reverse side of spirit, they're sublimated into smoke, vaporized in fog. Here, too, the body loses its form and sense—and sense has lost all body. Through another concentration, bodies are only signs annulled: this time not into pure sense, but into its pure exhaustion.

It's hard to say to what extent *concentration* (initials: KZ) will have been the birthmark of *our* world: a concentration of spirit, an incandescent SELF—

incandescent—et la concentration des corps, les masses, les rassemblements, les presses, les entassements, les accumulations, les bonds démographiques, les exterminations, les grands nombres, les flux, les statistiques, la présence obsédante, anonyme et exponentielle, pour la première fois, d'une *population du monde*. Mais ce que d'abord elle donne à voir et à toucher, c'est une plaie. Non pas d'abord la multiplication des corps, mais l'unicité, l'uniformité de la plaie: corps de misère, corps de famine, corps battus, corps prostitués, corps mutilés, corps infectés, corps bouffis, corps trop nourris, trop *body-builded*, trop bandants, trop orgasmiques. Ils n'offrent qu'une plaie: elle est leur signe, aussi bien que leur sens, autre et même figure de l'exténuation dans le signe-de-soi.

C'est ainsi que le monde des corps se produit, et qu'il est en somme l'unique et véritable production de notre monde. Tout revient à elle: il n'y pas de différence entre phénomènes «naturels» et «techniques» (un cyclone sur le Bengladesh, avec des centaines de milliers de morts, des dizaines de millions de victimes, est indissociable de la démographie, de l'économie, des rapports du Nord et du Sud, etc.); ou bien, sur un autre plan, une société qui fait proliférer les marges et les exclusions s'en affecte ou s'en infecte aussi par secousses jusque dans ses centres (drogue, SIDA), et ce sont encore des corps, et c'est encore leur plaie. Voilà ce qui tout d'abord est *mondial*: ce n'est pas nécessairement ce qui occupe toute la planète (encore que cela même devienne exact), mais c'est ce qui, en lieu et place d'un cosmos et de ses dieux, en lieu et place d'une nature et de ses hommes, distribue et assemble les corps, l'espace de leur étendue, l'exposition de leur dénudement.

Ce monde des corps—ou bien, *le monde = les corps = «nous»*—nous offre proprement notre chance et notre histoire. Ce qui veut dire aussi qu'il nous précède encore, et que nous avons à le découvrir. Jusqu'ici, pour le dire une fois de plus, c'est d'abord une plaie qui se présente. Depuis la Première Guerre *mondiale* (c'est-à-dire, depuis l'invention simultanée d'un nouvel espace juridique pour l'économie politique inter-nationale et d'un nouvel espace de combat pour un nombre inédit de victimes), ces corps partout pressés sont surtout des corps sacrifiés.

Ou plutôt, ils ne sont pas même sacrifiés. «Sacrifice» en dit trop ou trop peu, pour ce que nous faisons avec les corps. Cela dit (en principe) le passage d'un corps à une limite où il devient corps commun, esprit d'une communion dont il est l'effectif symbole matériel (*hoc est enim . . .*), rapport absolu à soi du sens dans le sang, du sang dans le sens. Mais nous n'avons plus de sacrifices, ce n'est plus notre monde. Le sang qui coule de nos plaies coule affreusement, et seulement affreusement, comme s'est écoulé et dissous goutte à goutte l'Esprit des plaies du Christ. Il n'y a pas de Graal pour

and a concentration of bodies, masses, gatherings, crowdings, crammings, accumulations, demographic spurts, exterminations, large numbers, fluxes, statistics, the haunting presence, for the first time, of a *world population*, anonymous and exponential. To begin with, however, concentration allows us to see and touch a wound. Not, first of all, a multiplication of bodies, but the unicity and uniformity of a wound: bodies of misery, bodies of famine, beaten bodies, prostituted bodies, mutilated bodies, infected bodies, swollen bodies, bodies over-nourished, too *body-built*, too erectile, too orgasmic. They offer only a wound: it's their sign, as well as their sense, another and the same figure of extenuation in the sign-of-self.

Thus the world of bodies is produced, and this is finally our world's unique and genuine production. Everything comes back to this production: there's no difference between "natural" and "technical" phenomena (a cyclone in Bangladesh, with its hundreds of thousands of deaths, its tens of millions of victims, being indissociable from demography, economy, the linkage of North and South, etc.); or else, on another level, a society causing margins and exclusions to proliferate is affected, and also infected, by shockwaves all the way into its centers (drugs, AIDS), and these are still bodies, and this is still their wound. This, then, is what *world-wide* means first and foremost; it's not necessarily something that occupies the whole planet (even though that too is becoming the case) but what, in place of a cosmos and its gods, in place of nature and its humans, distributes and gathers bodies, the space of their extension, the exposition of their denuding.

This world of bodies—or rather, *the world = bodies = "us"*—properly offers us our chance and our history. Which also means that it still precedes us, and that we have yet to discover it. Up until now, to state it once again, a wound, first of all, is what's presented. Since the First *World* War (in other words, the simultaneous invention of a new juridical space for an international political economy, *and* a new combat-space for a whole new number of victims), these bodies, crowded wherever they go, are bodies primarily sacrificed.

Or rather, not even sacrificed. As a word for what we do with our bodies, "sacrifice" says too much or too little. It states (in principle) the passage of a body to the limit at which it becomes a common body, the spirit of a communion for which it becomes the effective material symbol (*hoc est enim* . . .), an absolute self-bonding of sense in blood and of blood in sense. But we have no sacrifices today, this is no longer our world. The blood that flows from our wounds flows terribly, and only terribly, as the Spirit flowed from the wounds of Christ, dissolving drop by drop. No

recueillir ce sang. La plaie n'est désormais qu'une plaie—et tout le corps n'est qu'une plaie.

C'est donc aussi, et d'abord, cette plaie qui n'est que son propre signe, ne signifiant rien d'autre que la souffrance où le corps se rétracte, corps ramassé, concentré, privé de son espace de jeu. Ce n'est pas le malheur (qui fait un signe de tragédie, désormais indéchiffrable), et ce n'est pas la maladie (qui fait signe vers sa cause et vers la santé: il n'y a pas là de plaie sans pansement): mais c'est le mal, absolument le mal, une plaie ouverte sur soi, signe de soi résorbé en soi jusqu'à n'être plus ni signe, ni soi. «Œil sans paupière épuisé de voir et d'être vu»: c'est ce que dit Marcel Hénaff de notre corps occidental parvenant au bout d'un programme d'abord tracé par Sade. *Porno-graphie*: le nu gravé de stigmates de la plaie, blessures, fêlures, chancres du travail, du loisir, de la bêtise, des humiliations, des sales nourritures, des coups, des peurs, sans pansements, sans cicatrices, plaie qui ne se referme pas.

Corpus, anatomie

Par la plaie s'échappe le sens, goutte à goutte, affreusement, dérisoirement,— peut-être même sereinement, sinon joyeusement?

Cette question, c'est la question que propose l'aube exsangue en train de se lever sur un monde des corps. Saurons-nous faire avec cette perte de sens, aurons-nous le sens de cette perte—mais un sens sans concession, sans tricherie sur cette perte même? Saurons-nous aller jusqu'à ce qui, déjà, *s'é- tend* et *s'ouvre* à partir d'elle? A savoir, le monde des corps tel que le délivre ou le laisse venir la fin trouée de l'organon du sens?

Saurons-nous, par exemple et pour commencer, comprendre que cette perte du corps-du-sens—qui fait proprement notre temps, et qui lui donne son espace—, si elle nous donne de la douleur, pourtant elle ne plonge pas dans l'angoisse? Car l'angoisse s'angoisse précisément de l'absence du sens. Elle en est l'incorporation mélancolique ou l'incarnation hystérique (mys- térique?), mais elle lui donne son sens d'angoisse. L'angoisse *se donne comme sens*, et pour finir, elle est elle-même encore une forme de l'extrême concentration, cette forme-limite où il faut imaginer l'Esprit saint angoissé (sa sainteté perdue?). Mais la douleur ne se donne pas comme sens. Nous sommes dans la douleur, car nous sommes *organisés pour le sens*, et sa perte nous blesse, nous entaille. Mais pas plus que du sens perdu, la douleur ne fait sens de la perte. Elle en est seulement le tranchant, la brûlure, la peine.

Ici, au point de la douleur, il y a seulement un «sujet» ouvert, coupé, *anatomisé*, déconstruit, désassemblé, déconcentré. L'aube d'un espacement, la clarté même, le risque et la chance de l'*aréalité* en tant que *cela* à quoi

Graal gathers this blood. From now on, a wound is only a wound—and the whole body's only a wound.

This is also how, in the first place, this wound is only its own sign, signifying only the suffering of a body when it shrinks, gathered up, concentrated, deprived of its living space. This isn't sorrow (serving as a sign of tragedy, henceforth undecipherable), and it isn't sickness (sending a signal toward its cause and toward health, where no wound goes undressed): but evil is what it is, absolute evil, a wound opened up on itself, the sign of a self so far reabsorbed into itself that it's no longer a sign, no longer a self. "A lidless eye exhausted with seeing and being seen": so says Marcel Hénaff about our Western body, reaching the end of a project initially traced by Sade. *Pornography*: the nude engraved in the wound's stigmata, injuries, fractures, sores from labor, leisure, stupidity, humiliations, filthy foods, blows, fears, with no bandages or scars, a wound that doesn't heal.

Corpus, Anatomy

Sense escapes from the wound, drop by drop, frightfully, derisively—perhaps even serenely, if not joyfully?

This question is prompted by a bloodless dawn rising on a world of bodies. Can we deal with a loss of sense, and have a sense of that loss—but without concession or deceit concerning the loss itself? Can we reach what has already *been extended and opened* by this loss? Namely, the world of bodies, as the gaping end of the organon of sense delivers it, or lets it come?

To begin with, for example, can we understand that losing this body-of-sense—which properly makes our time, and gives it its space—won't bury us in anguish even while causing us pain? Because anguish is precisely anguish over an absence of sense. It's its melancholic incorporation, or hysterical (mysterical?) incarnation, but gives it its sense of anguish. Anguish *is given as sense*, and is itself, moreover, finally a form of extreme concentration, that limit-form at which we have to imagine the Holy Spirit as anguished (its sanctity lost?). But suffering isn't given as sense. We suffer because *organized for sense*, and the loss of it wounds us, cuts us. But of loss, suffering makes as little sense as it does of sense lost. It's only its edge, its burn, its pain.

Here, at the point of suffering, is only an open "subject," cut, *anatomized*, deconstructed, disassembled, deconcentrated. The dawn of a spacing, clarity itself, the risk and chance for *areality* as what we're exposed to, and what exposes us, as *we*—as a *we-world*.

nous sommes exposés, et qui nous expose, en tant que *nous*—en tant que *nous-monde*.

Plus de cinq milliards de corps humains. Bientôt huit milliards. Pour ne rien dire des. autres corps. L'humanité devient *tangible*: mais ce qu'on peut toucher n'est pas «l'homme», ce n'est justement pas cet être générique. Nous parlons de sa non-généricité, de sa non-généralité. Nous entamons l'ontologie modale et locale de son être-*ici*, de son être-l'ici-et-le-là, de son *ci-gît* et de son *allée-venue*. Quel est l'espace ouvert entre huit milliards de corps, et en chacun, entre phalle et céphale, entre les mille plis, postures, chutes, jets, coupes de chacun? Quel est l'espace où ils se touchent et s'écartent, sans qu'aucun d'eux, ni leur totalité, se résorbe en pur et nul signe de soi, en corps-de-sens? Seize milliards d'yeux, quatre-vingts milliards de doigts: pour voir quoi? pour toucher quoi? Et si c'est uniquement pour exister et pour être *ces corps*, et pour voir, toucher et sentir les corps de *ce monde*, que saurons-nous inventer pour célébrer leur nombre? Pouvons-nous même y penser, nous que la plaie fatigue, et seulement fatigue?

Tout est possible. Les corps résistent, dures *partes extra partes*. La communauté des corps résiste. La grâce d'un corps qui s'offre est toujours possible, comme est disponible l'anatomie de la douleur—qui n'exclut pas une joie singulière. Les corps exigent encore, à nouveau, leur création. Non pas l'incarnation qui insuffle la vie spirituelle du signe, mais la mise au monde et le partage des corps.

Non plus des corps employés à faire du sens, mais du sens qui donne et qui partage des corps. Non plus le pillage sémiologique, symptomatologique, mythologique et phénoménologique des corps, mais de la pensée, de l'écriture livrées, adonnées aux corps. L'écriture d'un corpus en tant que partage des corps, partageant leur être-corps, mais ne le *signifiant* pas, partagée par lui, divisée donc d'elle-même et de son sens, excrite tout le long de son inscription. Cela même, enfin, que dit dans le monde des corps ce mot d' «écriture»: corps anatomisé d'un sens qui ne présente pas la signification des corps, et qui réduit encore moins le corps à son propre signe. Mais un sens *ouvert* comme les sens «sensibles»—ou plutôt, ouvert *de* leur ouverture, exposant leur être-étendu—, une signifiance de l'espacement elle-même espaçante.

(Elle signifiera, quand même, inévitablement. Je le redis: nous sommes *organisés* pour ça. Mais *l'être* en nous, *l'existence* que nous mettons en jeu, est l'infini suspens fini de cette organisation, l'exposition fragile, fractale, de son anatomie. L'écriture ne vaut pas comme une débandade ou comme un chaos de la signification: elle ne vaut que dans la tension *à même* le système signifiant. C'est-à-dire, dans cette tension [que nous sommes] de l'être avec ce que nous sommes. Dans cette anatomisation de l'organisation, sans laquelle nous

More than five billion human bodies. Soon to be eight billion. Not to mention other bodies. Humanity becomes *tangible*: but what we can touch isn't "mankind," it's precisely not this generic being. We talk about its nongeneric nature, its nongenerality. We're starting the local and modal ontology of its being-*here*, its being-the-here-and-the-there, its *here-lies* and its *coming-going*. What is the space opened between eight billion bodies, and, within each one, between phallus and cephale, among the thousand folds, postures, falls, leaps and bounds of each? In what space do they touch each other and stray from each other, with none of them, or their totality, being absorbed into a pure and empty sign of the self, into a body-of-sense? Sixteen billion eyes, eighty billion fingers: seeing what? Touching what? And if it's only to exist and be *these bodies*, and to see, touch and sense the bodies of *this world*, what might we invent to celebrate their number? Can we even think about it, we whom the wound fatigues, and only fatigues?

Anything's possible. Bodies resist, hard *partes extra partes*. The community of bodies resists. The grace of a body offered is always possible, just as an anatomy of suffering is available—not excluding a singular joy. Bodies demand, yet again, their creation. Not an incarnation inflating the spiritual life of the sign, but a birthing and a sharing of bodies.

But also not bodies employed to make sense, but a sense that gives and divides bodies. No longer the semiological, symptomatological, mythological, and phenomenological pillaging of bodies, but thought and writing delivered, devoted to bodies. The writing of a corpus as a dividing of bodies, sharing their being-bodies, but not *signifying* it, shared by it, hence divided by, and from, itself and its sense, exscribed all along its inscription. The very thing, finally, that this word *writing* says in the world of bodies: the anatomized body of a sense that doesn't present the signification of bodies and, still less, reduce the body to its proper sign. But a sense *open* as "sensory" senses are—or rather, opened *by* their opening, exposing their being-extended—a significance, itself spacing, of spacing.

(It will still, inevitably, signify. And I say it once again: we're *organized* for this. But *the being* within us, *the existence* that *we* are putting into play, is an infinitely finite suspending of this organization, a fragile, fractal, exposition of its anatomy. Writing doesn't work as a stampede or chaos of signification: it only works with the tension *that is a part of* the signifying system *itself*. In other words, in the tension [that we are] of being with what we are. In this anatomizing of organization, without which we wouldn't be mortals, but we wouldn't be anything more than Death

ne serions pas mortels, mais nous ne serions rien de plus que la Mort en Personne. Cette tension est l'extension dénotée «corps» dans notre tradition).

Ce qui, d'une écriture, n'est pas â lire

Écrire le signe *anatomique* de «soi», qui ne se signifie pas, mais coupe, écarte, expose. Laisser courir l'animal du discours. Entailler le discours—ce qui, notez-le cependant, n'est pas non plus autre chose que d'en laisser aller le cours, sa répétition, ses aléas, son improvisation (négligeant le *dia* du dialogue et la médiation du contrat du sens, ou plutôt s'en détournant doucement, discrètement, et même avec pudeur). Glisser vers l'anatomie d'un corpus. Ce n'est pas l'anatomie philosophico-médicale de la dissection, le démembrement dialecticien des organes et des fonctions. Plutôt l'anatomie du dénombrement que celle du démembrement. L'anatomie des configurations, des plastiques, il faudrait dire des états-de-corps, façons d'être, allures, respirations, démarches, sidérations, douleurs, plaisirs, pelages, enroulements, frôlements, masses. Les corps, d'abord (c'est-à-dire: à les aborder) sont masses, masses offertes sans rien à en articuler, sans rien à y enchaîner, ni discours, ni récit: paumes, joues, ventres, fesses. L'œil même est une masse, comme la langue et comme le lobe de l'oreille.

Ce concept de la masse n'en est pas le concept physique, mais il est encore moins celui des «phénomènes de masse», celui de Tardes ou de Freud, qui relève de la concentration (et qui permettrait de montrer comment, dans la «masse populaire», il n'y a pas d'espace pour les corps). Les masses qui se distribuent, qui zonent l'étendue des corps, de manière toujours modifiable, sont des lieux de densité, non de concentration. Elles n'ont pas de centre, pas de trou noir. Elles sont à même la peau—et à même la paume qui peut les prendre. C'est de l'espace massé, de la masse spacieuse, l'étendue exposée comme un grain, comme un poids, comme un gonflement, comme un agencement limité, une couleur locale où les *partes extra partes* densifient leur aréalité, sans pourtant se précipiter *partes intra partes*.

Le paradigme en est sans doute le sein de la femme, masse qui localise de si nombreuses ectopies. Nourriture, objet séparé, visibilité du sexe, mouvement indépendant, érection, débordement, doublement, inversion du poitrail vigoureux, naissance de la courbe, naissance du fruit: la *naissance des seins* exemplifie toute naissance comme modalisation essentielle de l'aréalité—et fait aussi comprendre que cette modalisation peut se dire, en tous sens, *émotion*. Ce privilège d'are-alité dense et zonée se nomme et s'espace en tant qu'*aréole*.

Dans cette anatomie des masses, c'est à dire, donc, dans l'espace des émotions, le corpus n'a plus rien d'une surface d'inscription—en tant qu'un enregistrement de signification. Pas de «corps écrit», pas d'écriture à même le

in Person. This tension, in our tradition, is the extension denoted as "body.")

What in Writing Is Not to Be Read

Writing the *anatomical* sign of "self," which doesn't signify, but cuts, separates, exposes. Unleashing the discourse-animal. Cutting the discourse: which, however—and we should take note of this—is also only letting it run its course, its repetition, its chances, its improvisation (neglecting the *dia* of dialogue and the mediation of the contract of sense, or, rather, turning away from it quietly, discreetly, even modestly). Gliding toward the anatomy of a corpus. This isn't the philosophico-medical anatomy of dissection, a dialectician's dismembering of organs and functions. An anatomy more of numbering than dismembering. An anatomy of configurations, of the plasticity of what we'd have to call states of body, ways of being, bearing, breathings, paces, staggerings, sufferings, pleasures, coats, windings, brushings, masses. Bodies, to begin with, are masses, masses offered with nothing to be articulated about them, nothing to link them to, whether a discourse or a story: palms, cheeks, wombs, buttocks. Even an eye is a mass, as are tongue and ear-lobe.

While not drawn from physics, this concept of mass is even less the concept of "mass phenomena" as conceived by Tardes or Freud, deriving from concentration (which would allow us to show, in the "popular mass," that there's no space for bodies). Distributed masses, zoning the extension of bodies in always modifiable ways, are sites of density, not concentration. They have no center, no black hole. They are right at the surface of the skin—right at the surface of the hand that can grasp them. It's a massed space, a spacious mass, extension exposed like a grain, like a weight, like a swelling, like a limited arrangement, a local color where the *partes extra partes* make their areality more dense, but without falling into *partes intra partes*.

Its paradigm is probably the woman's breast, a mass that localizes many an ectopia. Nourishment, separate object, visibility of sex, independent movement, erection, overflowing, doubling, the obverse of a vigorous breastplate, the bearing of a curve, bearing fruit: the *b(e)aring of breasts* exemplifies every birth as an essential modalizing of areality—and also lets us see how this modalizing can, in every sense, be called *an emotion*. This privilege of dense and zoned areality is named, and spaced, as *areola*.

In this anatomy of masses, which is the same thing as saying a space of emotions, the corpus is no longer anything like an inscriptive surface—as a recording of signification. No "written body," no writing at the body, and

corps, ni rien de cette somatographologie dans laquelle on a parfois converti «à la moderne» le mystère de l'Incarnation, et de nouveau le corps en tant que pur signe de soi, et que pur soi du signe. Justement, voici: le corps n'est pas un lieu d'écriture (on voit bien, par exemple, que c'est par là qu'il faut commencer, si l'on veut parler avec justesse du tatouage). Le corps, sans doute, c'est *qu'on écrit*, mais ce n'est absolument pas où on écrit, et le corps n'est pas non plus ce qu'on écrit—mais toujours ce que l'écriture *excrit*.

Il n'y a d'excription que par écriture, mais l'excrit *reste* cet autre *bord* que l'inscription, tout en signifiant sur un bord, ne cesse obstinément d'indiquer comme son autre-propre bord. Ainsi, de toute écriture, un corps est l'autre-propre bord: un corps (ou plus d'un corps, ou une masse, ou plus d'une masse) est donc aussi le tracé, le tracement et la trace (*ici*, voyez, lisez, prenez, *hoc est enim corpus meum . . .*). De toute écriture, un corps est la lettre, et pourtant, jamais la lettre, ou bien, plus reculée, plus déconstruite que toute littéralité, une «lettricité» qui n'est plus à lire. Ce qui, d'une écriture et proprement d'elle, n'est pas à lire, voilà ce qu'est un corps.

(Ou bien, c'est clair, il faut comprendre la lecture comme ce qui n'est pas le déchiffrement: mais le toucher et l'être touché, avoir à faire aux masses du corps. Écrire, lire, affaire de tact. Mais encore—et cela aussi doit être clair— à la condition que le tact ne se concentre pas, ne prétende pas—comme fait le toucher cartésien—au privilège d'une immédiateté qui mettrait en fusion tous les sens et «le» sens. Le toucher aussi, le toucher d'abord est local, modal, fractal.)

Je répète: on demande, ce monde demande *le corps d'un sens* qui ne donne pas la signification du corps, encore moins qui le réduise à être son propre signe et l'essence accomplie de toutes les onto-théologies du signe. L'inverse ou l'exact revers—l'autre bord—de l'incarnation qui monopolisait dans l'ancien monde toutes les modélisations, tous les espacements du corps. Dans l'incarnation, l'esprit *se fait* chair. C'est du reste pourquoi ce Mystère par excellence *se révèle lui-même. Cet* esprit prononce de sa chair: *hoc est enim corpus meum*, il *s'articule* lui-même de toute présence sensible. Ce que le Mystère révèle, c'est donc *le corps comme mystère révélé*, le signe absolu de soi et l'essence du sens, le Dieu dans la chair retiré, la chair à soi-même subjectivée, ce qui se nomme enfin, dans le plein éclat du Mystère, la «résurrection».

Mais il s'agit ici de ce corps, ou plutôt de cette multitude de corps que nul esprit ne s'est faits ou engendrés.

Techné des corps

Pas des corps produits par l'autoproduction de l'esprit et sa reproduction— qui du reste ne peut produire qu'un seul corps, une seule image visible de

nothing whatsoever of a somatographology into which the mystery of the Incarnation was sometimes converted *à la moderne*, and the body, also, into a pure sign of the self, the pure self of the sign. Just so, therefore: the body's no place for writing (it's certainly clear, for example, that we have to start here, if we hope to do justice to tattooing). *That we write*, no doubt, is the body, but absolutely not *where* we write, nor is a body *what* we write—but a body is always what writing *exscribes.*

There is only exscription through writing, but what's exscribed *remains* this other *edge* that inscription, though signifying on an edge, obstinately continues to indicate as its own-other edge. Thus, for every writing, a body is the own-other edge: a body (or more than one body, or a mass, or more than one mass), is therefore also the traced, the tracing, and the trace (*here,* see, read, take, *hoc est enim corpus meum* . . .). In all writing a body is the letter, yet never the letter, or else, more remotely, more deconstructed than any literality, it's a "letricity" no longer meant to be read. What in a writing, and properly so, is not to be read—that's what a body is.

(Or else, clearly, we have to see reading as something that's not deciphering: touching, rather, and being touched, involved with the body's masses. Writing, reading, a matter of tact. But still—and this, too, has to be clear—under the condition that tact isn't concentrated, doesn't claim—as does Cartesian touch—the privilege of an immediacy that would fuse all senses and "sense." Touching, to begin with, is also local, modal, fractal.)

I repeat: we seek, this world seeks, *a body of sense*, providing not the signification of the body, still less reducing it to its own sign and to the achieved essence of every onto-theology of the sign. The inverse, or exact reverse—the other edge—of incarnation that monopolized all modalizings, all bodily spacings, in the ancient world. In the incarnation, the spirit *is made* flesh. Which is, furthermore, why, par excellence, this Mystery *reveals itself. This* spirit says of its flesh: *hoc est enim corpus meum*; it *articulates itself* from every sensory presence. What the Mystery reveals, therefore, is *the body as revealed mystery*, the absolute sign of self and the essence of sense, God withdrawn into flesh, flesh subjectivized to itself, which, finally, is called "the resurrection," in the full radiance of the Mystery.

But here we're concerned with this body, or rather, with this multitude of bodies, which no spirit has made or engendered.

Technē of Bodies

Not bodies produced by the autoproduction of the spirit and its reproduction—which, at any rate, can produce only a single body, a single visible

l'invisible (de là que le corps de la femme soit suspect d'être mal engendré, défectueux pour Aristote, marqué d'une plaie impure pour les Chrétiens). Mais un corps donné multiplié, multisexué, multifiguré, multizoné, plane et aphalle, céphale et acéphale, organisé, inorganique. Des corps ainsi *créés*, c'est-à-dire *venant*, et dont la venue espace chaque fois l' *ici*, le *là*. (Comme l'écrit Elaine Scarry dans *The Body in Pain*, lorsque «le monde, le soi, la voix sont perdus dans l'intensité de souffrance de la torture», c'est la «dissolution du monde, la décréation du monde créé».) La «création» est la *techné* des corps. Notre monde crée le grand nombre des corps, il se crée en tant que monde des corps (mettant au jour ce qui toujours fut *aussi* sa vérité de monde). Notre monde est le monde de la «technique», le monde dont le cosmos, la nature, les dieux, le système complet dans sa jointure intime s'expose comme «technique»: monde d'une *écotechnie*. L'écotechnie fonctionne avec des appareils techniques, sur lesquels elle nous branche de toutes parts. Mais ce qu'elle *fait*, ce sont nos corps, qu'elle met au monde et branche à ce système, nos corps qu'elle crée ainsi plus visibles, plus proliférants, plus polymorphes, plus pressés, plus en «masses» et «zones» que jamais ils ne furent. C'est dans la création des corps que l'écotechnie a ce *sens* qu'on lui cherche en vain dans des restes de ciel ou d'esprit.

Aussi longtemps qu'on ne pensera pas sans réserves la création écotechnique des corps comme la vérité de *notre* monde, et comme une vérité *qui ne le cède en rien* à celles que les mythes, les religions, les humanismes, avaient pu représenter, on n'aura pas commencé à penser ce monde-ci. L'écotechnie crée le monde des corps sur deux modes corrélatifs: aux projections d'histoires linéaires et de *fins* dernières, elle substitue des espacements de temps, avec différences locales, bifurcations nombreuses. L'écotechnie déconstruit le système des fins, rend celles-ci nonsystématisables, non-organiques, stochastiques même (*sauf* sous l'imposition de la fin de l'économie politique ou du capital, qui s'impose en effet aujourd'hui à toute l'écotechnie, re-linéarisant le temps, homogénéisant les fins: pourtant, le capital lui aussi doit renoncer à présenter une fin dernière, Science ou Humanité, et la création des corps détient aussi une force révolutionnaire . . .). En même temps, branchant et connectant les corps de toutes les manières, les plaçant aux lieux d'intersections, d'interfaces, d'interactions de toutes les procédures techniciennes, bien loin d'en faire des «objets techniques» (comme on dit, croyant du reste savoir ce que c'est qu'un «objet technique») l'écotechnie les met au jour comme tels, dans cette connexion *aréale* qui fait aussi l'espace du retrait de toute signification transcendante ou immanente. Le monde des corps n'a de sens ni transcendant, ni immanent. Si l'on tenait à garder ces mots, il faudrait dire que l'une a lieu dans l'autre, mais sans dialectisation—que l'une a lieu *comme* l'autre, et que *les*

image of the invisible (hence the fact that the body of woman is regarded by Aristotle as poorly engendered and defective, or marked, according to Christians, with an impure wound). But a body given as multiplied, multi-sexed, multi-figured, multi-zoned, phallic and aphallic, cephalic and acephalic, organized, inorganic. Bodies thus created, which is to say, *coming*, and whose coming spaces the *here*, the *there*, every time. (As Elaine Scarry puts it in *The Body in Pain*, when "the world, the self, the voice are lost in the intensity of the suffering of torture," it's the "dissolution of the world, the uncreation of the created world.") "Creation" is the *technē* of bodies. Our world creates the great number of bodies, creates itself as the world of bodies (shedding light on what was always *also* its worldly truth). Our world is the world of the "technical," a world whose cosmos, nature, gods, entire system is, in its inner joints, exposed as "technical": the world of the *ecotechnical*. The ecotechnical functions with technical apparatuses, to which our every part is connected. But what it *makes* are our bodies, which it brings into the world and links to the system, thereby creating our bodies as more visible, more proliferating, more polymorphic, more compressed, more "amassed" and "zoned" than ever before. Through the creation of bodies the ecotechnical has the *sense* that we vainly seek in the remains of the sky or the spirit.

Unless we ponder without reservation the ecotechnical creation of bodies as the truth of *our* world, and a truth *just as valid as* those that myths, religions, and humanisms were able to represent, we won't have begun to think *this* very world. The ecotechnical creates the world of bodies in two correlative ways: for the projections of linear histories and final *ends*, it substitutes the spacings of time, local differences, and numerous bifurcations. The ecotechnical deconstructs the system of ends, renders them unsystemizable, nonorganic, even stochastic (*except* through an imposition of the ends of political economy or capital, effectively imposed nowadays on the whole of the ecotechnical, thus relinearizing time and homogenizing all ends, but capital also has to stop presenting a final end—Science or Humanity—and, moreover, the creating of bodies harbors revolutionary force . . .). At the same time, the ecotechnical, linking and connecting up bodies in every way, placing them at sites of the intersections, interfaces, and interactions of every technical procedure, far from turning bodies into "technical objects" (as is often said today, by those who think, furthermore, that they know what a "technical object" is) sheds light on them as such, through this *areal* connection, which also creates space for the withdrawal of any transcendental or immanent signification. The world of bodies has neither a transcendent nor an immanent sense. If we wanted to keep these words, we'd have to say that one takes place within the other, but without being dialecticized—that one takes place *as* the

lieux sont cet avoir-lieu. Les lieux, les lieux de l'existence de l'être, désormais, *sont* l'exposition des corps, c'est-à-dire leur dénudement, leur population nombreuse, leurs écarts multipliés, leurs réseaux enchevêtrés, leurs métissages (techniques bien plus qu'ethniques). Pour finir, l'*aréalité* donne la loi et le milieu, en place d'une dialectique transcendante/immanente, d'une *proximité*, mondiale et locale à la fois, et l'une dans l'autre. Pour finir, nous sommes dans la *techné* du *prochain*.

Le «prochain» judéo-chrétien-islamique résidait dans le *particulier* et dans l'*universel*, dans la dialectisation des deux, qui ne manque pas de finir dans l'universel. Mais *ici*, le prochain serait ce qui vient, ce qui a lieu dans une approche, ce qui touche et s'écarte aussi, localisant, déplaçant la touche. Ni naturel, ni artificiel (comme il apparaissait tour à tour jusqu'ici), le «prochain» comme *techné* serait la «création» et l'«art» véritable de *notre* monde. Au surplus, soumettant à révision ces mots de «création» et d'«art», tout comme au premier chef le terme de «prochain». Je préfère donc dire que la *techné* est celle du partage des corps, ou de leur comparution: les divers modes de donner lieu aux tracés d'aréalité le long desquels *nous sommes exposés ensemble*, c'est-à-dire, *ni présupposés dans quelque autre Sujet, ni postposés dans quelque fin particulière et/ou universelle*. Mais exposés, corps à corps, bords à bords, touchés et espacés, *proches de n'avoir plus d'assomption commune, mais seulement l'entre-nous de nos tracés partes extra partes.*

Sans doute, le capital produit aussi bien une généralisation banalisante du corps, et du prochain. En témoignent les obsessions photographiques des foules, de leurs misères, de leurs paniques, du nombre en tant que tel, ou des hantises érotiques partout infiltrées. La proximité s'y fait tout pauvrement banalité de la reproduction du corps—réputé «singulier»—par millions d'exemplaires. (C'est aussi pourquoi «le corps» est déjà devenu le plus insipide, le plus plat et en somme le plus «débranché» des thèmes et des termes—en coma dépassé.)

Mais il faut y regarder de près. L'horreur de la banalité, de la reproduction, la cérébration de l'unique, de l'exceptionnel, sont des données banales du monde qui se retire sous nos pieds, ici même. Nous sommes tous *banalement* rétifs à la «banalité»—et à cette sorte de surcroît de banalité que nous attachons, précisément, au corps . . . Mais savons-nous ce que c'est que «banal»?

Il y a deux registres de banalité des corps: celle du *modèle* (registre des magazines, canonique des corps fuselés, veloutés)—et celle du *tout-venant* (n'importe quel corps, difforme, abîmé, usé). Dans l'écart ou dans la dialectique des deux—que l'écotechnie produit simultanément—, il n'y a pas beaucoup de proximité possible. Mais la banalité *tout à fait banale* est peut-être encore

other, and that such a taking-place is what *places* are. Places, places for the existence of being, henceforth, *are* the exposition of bodies, in other words, their being laid bare, their manifold population, their multiplied swerves, their interlinked networks, their cross-breedings (far more technical than ethnic). In sum, *areality* provides the rule and the milieu of a *proximity*, at once worldwide and local, one within the other, instead of a dialectic of transcendental/immanent. In sum, we're in the *technē* of the *neighbor.*

The Judeo-Christian-Islamic "neighbor" resided in the *particular* and the *universal,* in the dialecticization of the two, which doesn't fail to end up in the universal. But *here* the neighbor would be what comes, what takes place in an approach, and what also touches and diverges, thus localizing, displacing, the touch. Neither natural nor artificial (as by turns it has hitherto seemed), the "neighbor" as *technē* would be the "creation" and true "art" of *our* world. Submitting, moreover, these words *creation* and *art* to revision, as in, above all, the term *neighbor*. I therefore prefer to say that the *technē* is one of a sharing of bodies, or of their compearance: the various ways to make room for the tracings of areality along which *we are exposed together,* in other words, *neither presupposed in some other Subject,* nor *post-posed in some particular and/or universal end.* But exposed, body to body, edge to edge, touched and spaced, *near in no longer having a common assumption, but having only the between-us of our tracings partes extra partes.*

Capital, no doubt, also produces a banalizing generalization of the body and of the neighbor. Photographic obsessions with crowds attest to this fact, with their miseries, their panics, with number as such, or with erotic obsessions filtering in throughout. Most miserably, proximity becomes the banal reproduction of the body—supposedly "singular"—through millions of copies. (This, too, is why "the body" has also become the most insipid, the flattest, finally the most "disconnected" of themes and terms—in an irreversible coma.)

But we have to take a careful look. The horror of banality, of reproduction, the celebration of the unique, the exceptional, are the banal givens of a world that is crumbling under our feet, right now. We are all *banally* hesitant about "banality"—and about this overload of banality that we attach, precisely, to the body . . . But do we know what "banal" is?

The banality of bodies has two registers: that of the *model* (the magazine register, a canon of streamlined, velvety bodies)—and that of the *indiscriminate* (no matter what body, ruined, wrecked, deformed). In the gap or dialectic between the two—which the ecotechnical produces simultaneously—little proximity is possible. But *entirely banal* banality is perhaps elsewhere, in a space still hardly open, a space for the absence of a

ailleurs, dans un espace encore à peine ouvert, l'espace d'une absence d'assomption commune ou de *modèle du corps humain* (ni le mannequin, ni la foule). Alors, l'expérience des corps serait que ce qui est le plus commun (banal) est *commun à chacun* comme tel. L'exceptionnel d'*un* corps est commun en tant que tel: substituable à tout autre *en tant qu'insubstituable*.

C'est ainsi qu'il est sans doute largement faux, ou idéologique, de dire que «les images banalisent». Des milliers de corps souffrants, réduits, rongés, que peut montrer la télévision, il est aussi bien montré que c'est chacun, chaque fois à nouveau un «chacun» qui souffre.

Mais cela n'est visible que dans l'espace des corps, à un regard porté sur les corps—non à un discours de l'humanité générique et générale.

Un tel regard discerne que chacun n'est qu'un exemplaire substituable dans la foule ininterrompue *et* que le même chacun est exemplaire de la création qu'est un corps, chaque fois. Et que chacun est le «prochain» de l'autre *des deux manières à la fois*. Il y aurait ainsi une autre «banalité»: un espace commun où chaque corps serait modèle pour tous *et* substituable à tous et par tous. En vérité, un espace sans «modèle» ni «reproduction»: mais savons-nous penser le *sens* hors de ces repères? Un sens ni exemplaire, ni reproductible, cela peut-il faire «sens»? . . .

Pesée

Corpus du tact: effleurer, frôler, presser, enfoncer, serrer, lisser, gratter, frotter, caresser, palper, tâter, pétrir, masser, enlacer, étreindre, frapper, pincer, mordre, sucer, mouiller, tenir, lâcher, lécher, branler, regarder, écouter, flairer, goûter, éviter, baiser, bercer, balancer, porter, peser . . .

Même sans synthèse, tout finit par communiquer avec la pesée. Un corps toujours pèse, ou se laisse peser, soupeser. Aréalité dense, zones en masses. Un corps n'a pas un poids: même pour la médecine, il *est* un poids. Il pèse, il presse contre d'autres corps, à même d'autres corps. Entre lui et lui-même, c'est encore pesées, contrepoids, arc-boutants. Notre monde hérite du monde de la gravité: tous les corps pèsent les uns *sur* les autres et les uns *contre* les autres, les corps célestes et les corps calleux, les corps vitrés et les corpuscules. Mais la mécanique gravitationnelle est ici seulement corrigée de ce point: les corps pèsent légèrement. Ce n'est pas à dire qu'ils pèsent peu: au contraire—et on peut dire qu'un corps à soutenir, dans l'abandon d'amour ou de détresse, dans la syncope ou dans la mort, pèse chaque fois *le* poids absolu.

Mais les corps pèsent légèrement. Leurs poids est l'élévation de leurs masses à la surface. Sans cesse, la masse s'élève à la surface, elle s'enlève en surface. La masse est l'épaisseur, une consistance locale dense. Mais elle ne

common assumption or *model of the human body* (neither the fashion model nor the crowd). The experience of bodies, then, would be one where the most common (banal) is *common for each* as such. The exceptionality of *a* body is common as such: substitutable for every other *as unsubstitutable.*

This is what makes the idea that "images banalize" more or less false or ideological. Of the thousands of corroded, suffering, reduced bodies that television can show, it also shows that each one, each and every time again an "each one," is suffering.

But this is visible only in the space of bodies, to an eye attentive to bodies—not to a discourse about generic and general humanity.

This kind of attentive eye recognizes that each one is only a substitutable example in an uninterrupted crowd, *and* that the very same each one exemplifies the creation that the body each time is. And that each is the other's "neighbor" *in both ways at once.* Thus there would be yet another "banality": a common space in which every body would be a model for all, *and* substitutable for and by all. In truth, a space without "model" or "reproduction": but can we think of "sense" outside these parameters? Does sense, when it is neither exemplary nor reproducible, make "sense"? . . .

Weighing

A corpus of tact: skimming, grazing, squeezing, thrusting, pressing, smoothing, scraping, rubbing, caressing, palpating, fingering, kneading, massaging, entwining, hugging, striking, pinching, biting, sucking, moistening, taking, releasing, licking, jerking off, looking, listening, smelling, tasting, ducking, fucking, rocking, balancing, carrying, weighing . . .

Even without a synthesis, everything ends up communicating with weighing. A body always weighs or lets itself be weighed, poised. A dense areality, zones en masse. A body doesn't have a weight: even in medicine, it *is* a weight. It weighs on, it presses against other bodies, right up against other bodies. Between it and itself, it's still weighing, counterweight, buttressing. Our world has inherited the world of gravity: all bodies weigh *on* one another, and *against* one another, heavenly bodies and callous bodies, vitreous bodies and corpuscles. But gravitational mechanics is corrected here on just one point: bodies weigh lightly. This isn't to say that they don't weigh very much: to the contrary—and we can say that a body needing sustenance, abandoned in love or in distress, fainting or dying, weighs *the* absolute weight every time.

But bodies weigh lightly. Their weight is the raising of their masses to the surface. Unceasingly, mass is raised to the surface; it bubbles up to the surface; mass is thickness, a dense, local consistency. But it isn't concentrated

se concentre pas, «au-dedans», en «soi», son «soi» est l'«au-dehors» *comme quoi* son dedans s'expose. L'aréalité massive se soutient d'extension, non de concentration, d'étendue, non de fondement; à vrai dire, son principe et son attente ne sont pas de peser, mais *d'être pesée.* Peser se fait sur le seul support, et suppose le montage d'un univers; être pesé demande le concours d'un autre corps, et l'étendue d'un monde. Ce n'est plus l'ordre de la présupposition, c'est celui de la *venue.* Les corps viennent peser les uns contre les autres, voilà le *monde.* L'immonde, c'est le pré-supposé où tout serait pesé d'avance.

C'est bien ainsi que *Psyché est étendue* et qu'elle *n'en sait rien.* Psyché est ici le nom du corps en tant qu'il n'est présupposé *ni* selon la sous-couche basse, enfoncée d'une «matière», ni selon la sur-couche déjà donnée d'un savoirde-soi. L'un et l'autre mode de présupposition restent dans la puissance, où du reste ils ne cessent de se déliter et de se débiliter, à travers toute la tradition, matérialismes grossièrement idéalistes, idéalismes se prenant eux-mêmes à un piège toujours plus resserré de l'origine du sens (intentionnalité, temporalité originaire)—*alors que les corps viennent, alors que la déclinaison de leurs atomes a déjà lieu, ouvre déjà des lieux, exerce ses pesées de part et d'autre, de part en part dans tout l'écartement du monde.* Mais cela, il est vrai, n'est pas affaire de «savoir»: c'est affaire de corps, qui vient dans la pesée, qui prend et qui donne à peser. Ce n'est pas «origine du sens» ni «sens de l'origine»: c'est que *sens* est sans origine, c'est que c'est *cela même, le «sens», l'être-sans-origine et le venirêtre-étendu, l'être-créé, ou la pesée.*

C'est bien *à* cela que Psyché est présente en tant qu'étendue, c'est à cela qu'elle est intéressée, infiniment ectopisée, c'est de cela qu'elle est en charge, en souci, en affect, et c'est ainsi qu'elle est «la forme d'un corps en acte». Il n'y a que des corps en acte, et chaque corps est Psyché, ou l'agencement de psychés singulièrement modalisées à travers l'étendue des atomes et/ou du *ça.* (Notez la double propriété, la double communauté des «atomes» *et* du «ça»: l'extension, la pesée. En vérité, la pesée est l'intention de l'extension. Tout revient donc à l'extension, sur son double bord intensif/extensif. Mais «revenir à l'extension», ce n'est justement pas se rapporter à du pré-supposé. C'est au contraire suspendre sans appel toute présupposition: ce que fait en effet au mieux, aux deux bouts de la tradition, la double figure des atomes et du ça, ici dénommée *corpus*).

Le non-savoir par Psyché de sa propre étendue—de l'extension-pesée que l'*être* est dès lors qu'il *existe psychique* (et pour finir, que veut dire «psychique»? sinon, «existant» = «forme d'un corps en acte»—et il n'y a pas de corps en puissance, ni d'existence en essence, c'est même *ça,* «le corps», «l'existence», ce n'est rien d'autre, rien de plus, rien de moins que ça—et c'est bien pourquoi toute la «psychanalyse» a son véritable programme toujours

"inside," within "itself": its "self" is the "outside" *as that which* its inside is exposed. Massive areality is sustained by extension, not concentration, by extent, not foundation; truth be told, its principle and expectation are not to weigh but *being weighed*. Weighing is done on a single support, and presupposes the construction of a universe; being weighed requires the assistance of another body and the extent of a world. It belongs to the order no longer of presupposition but of *coming*. Bodies come to weigh against one another, such is the *world*. The non-world (*im-mundus*), and intolerable, is the presupposition that everything is weighed in advance.

This is certainly the way that *Psyche is extended*, as well as why *she knows nothing about it*. Psyche, here, is the name of the body, as presupposed *neither* according to a substratum sunk into matter *nor* according to an already-given superstratum of self-knowledge. Both kinds of presupposition remain in effect, and they also don't stop, throughout the whole tradition, breaking up and breaking down grossly idealistic materialisms, idealisms caught in the ever-constricting trap of an origin of sense (intentionality, originary temporality)—*even though bodies come, even though the declination of their atoms is already taking place, is already opening places up, exerting its weight from one place to another, through and through, throughout the swerve of the world.* But still, it's true, this isn't a question of "knowing": it's a matter of the body, which comes through weighing, which takes and gives something to weigh. This is neither an "origin of sense" nor a "sense of origin." Because *sense* has no origin, because *being-without-origin and coming-to-be-extended, being-created, or weighing—such, indeed, is "sense."*

This is what Psyche is present-*to*, as extension, it's what she's interested in, infinitely ectopized, it's what she's in charge of, in care of, feels for, and it's why she's "the form of a body in action." There are only bodies in action, and each body is Psyche, or the arrangement of psyches singularly modalized across the extention of atoms and/or of the *id*. (Observe the twofold propriety, the double community of "atoms" *and* the "id": extension, weighing. In truth, weighing is the intention of extension. So everything comes back to extension, to its double intensive/extensive boundary. But "coming back to extension" is precisely not to be bound to something presupposed. On the contrary, it's a matter of suspending, without appeal, any presupposition: at its best this results, at both ends of the tradition, in the two-fold figure of atoms and the id, here called *corpus*.)

Psyche's nonknowledge of her proper extent—of the extension-weighing that *being* is, once the *psychic exists* (and what, finally, does "psychic" mean? if not that "existant" = "the form of a body in action"—and there's neither a potential body nor an essential existence, it's *this*, even, "the body," "existence," it's nothing else, nothing more, nothing less than this—which

à venir dans cette seule note de Freud)—ce non-savoir, donc, *est le corps même* de Psyché, ou plutôt, il est ce corps que Psyché est elle-même. Ce non-savoir n'est pas un savoir négatif, ni le négatif d'un savoir, c'est simplement l'absence du savoir, l'absence de ce rapport dit «savoir». En un certain lexique, on pourrait dire: le savoir veut de l'objet, mais avec le corps il n'y a que du sujet. Mais on pourra dire aussi bien qu'en l'absence d'objet il n'y a pas non plus de sujet: Psyché n'est pas Sujet. Ce qui reste est précisément corps, les corps. Ou bien: *«corps» est le sujet de n'avoir pas d'objet*: sujet de n'être pas sujet, sujet *à* n'être pas sujet, comme on dit «sujet *à* des accès de fièvre». La substance dont toute la substantialité, non présupposée, est de toucher à d'autres substances: déclinaison d'atomes, pesées mutuelles, et/ou réseaux, contagions, communications du «ça», autres modes de pesée.

Pesée: création. Ce par quoi commence une création, sans pré-supposition de créateur. Sujet d'avant tout sujet, pesée, poussée exercée, reçue, communauté toute archi-primitive des forces, des corps en tant que forces, des formes des corps—psychés—en tant que forces qui se poussent, s'appuient, se repoussent, s'équilibrent, se déstabilisent, s'interposent, se transfèrent, se modifient, se combinent, s'épousent. Les pesées distribuent l'étendue, extensions et intensions. L'étendue est le jeu des pesées: *partes extra partes* (le tort de Descartes est de concevoir l'extra comme du vide et comme de l'indifférencié, alors que c'est très exactement le lieu de la différenciation, le lieu de la «corporation», l'avoir-lieu de la pesée et par conséquent de la communauté du monde). C'est le toucher, le tact d'avant tout sujet, ce «soupeser» qui n'a lieu dans aucun «dessous»—ni, par conséquent, dans aucun «avant».

Un corps n'a ni avant, ni après, ni soubassement, ni superstructure. Toute la «puissance» de deux gamètes n'est encore rien par rapport à l'*acte*, non pas l'action de leur union, mais l'acte propre, *le corps psychique et la psyché étendue* qui font, ici ou là, la venue, l'avoir-lieu et l'écartement singulier d'une pesée, d'une nouvelle pesée locale au sein du monde des corps. De manière symétrique, aucune Mort/Résurrection ne succède au *ci-gît* de *ce* corps: mais il reste *ce* mort, espace re-venant à notre communauté, et partageant son étendue.

Infime dépense de quelques grammes

Les corps ne «savent» pas, ne sont pas non plus dans l'«ignorance». Ils sont ailleurs, ils sont d'ailleurs, d'autre part (des lieux, des parages, des frontières, des limites, mais aussi de coins casaniers, ou de boulevards à promenades, ou de voyages par les pays dépaysants: en fait, ils peuvent *venir* de partout, et de sur place, *ici* même, mais jamais du non-lieu du savoir). Il ne faut donc

is why, in this one note by Freud, all of "psychoanalysis" really has its true program always yet to come)—this nonknowledge, then, *is* Psyche's *very body*, or rather, it is this body that Psyche herself is. This nonknowledge is not a negative knowledge or the negative of knowledge, it's only an absence of knowledge, an absence of this bond called "knowing." In a certain vocabulary we could say: knowledge wants an object, but with the body there's only a subject. But we could also say that in the absence of an object there's also no longer a subject: Psyche isn't a Subject. What's left is precisely body, bodies. Or else: *"body" is the subject of having no object*: the subject of not being a subject, subject *to* not being a subject, as we say "subject *to* fits of fever." A substance all of whose substantiality, not presupposed, is to touch other substances: the declination of atoms, mutual weighings, and/or networks, contagions, communications of the "id," other modes of weighing.

Weighing: creation. What creation starts with, creation without the presupposition of a creator. A subject before any subject: weighing, pressure exerted and received, an entirely archi-primitive community of forces, of bodies as forces, of forms of bodies—psyches—as forces pushing each other, supporting, repelling, balancing, destabilizing, interposing, transferring, modifying, combining, and marrying each other. Weighings distribute extent, extensions, and intensions. Extent is the play of weighings: *partes extra partes*. (Descartes' error consists in conceiving the *extra* as a void, undifferentiated, when it's very precisely the place of differentiation, of "corporation," a taking-place of weighing, and consequently of the community of the world.) It's the touch, the tactile as preceding any subject, this "weighing down" that doesn't take place in an "under"—nor, therefore, in a "before."

The body has neither a before, an after, a sub-basement, nor a superstructure. The total "power" of two gametes is still nothing when compared to the *act* of their union, not to the action, but to the *act* proper, *the psychical body and the extended psyche* creating, here or there, the coming, the taking-place, and the singular swerve of a weighing, of a new local weighing at the heart of the world of bodies. Symmetrically, no Death/Resurrection follows upon the *here-lies* of *this* body: but *this* dead one remains, a ghostly space coming back to our community, and sharing its extent.

A Tiny Expenditure of a Few Grams

Bodies don't "know," nor are they in "ignorance." They're elsewhere, they're from elsewhere, from another side (of places, regions, frontiers, limits, but also of household plots, boulevards with promenades, trips through estranging lands: in fact, they can *come* from anywhere, from the spot, even *here*, but never from the nonplace of knowledge). In them especially, then, we

surtout pas leur chercher l'assise d'un savoir «obscur», «pré-conceptuel», «pré-ontologique», ou «immanent» et «immédiat». Je l'ai dit: ils sont d'emblée dans la clarté de l'aube, et tout est net. Il ne s'agit pas un instant de tous ces sous-produits des «théories de la connaissance», «sensation», «perception», «cœnesthésie», tous avatars laborieux de la «représentation» et de la «signification». Mais il ne s'agit même pas des médiations immédiates et des intrications en soi des «chairs» et des «corps propres». Le corps créé est là, c'est-à-dire *entre* ici et là, abandonné, toujours improprement abandonné, créé: sans raison d'être *là*, car *là* ne donne aucune raison, et sans raison d'être ce corps ni cette masse de ce corps (car *ce* ne rend raison de rien, ou rend «raison» du *rien* dans le créé: *res*, réel aréal—*hoc est enim corpus, rei ratio*). Corps seulement posés, pesés d'être seulement posés, et pesants, ouvrant, s'ouvrant leurs lieux.

Corps serait l'expérience de cette pesée, qui tout d'abord n'est pas propre, mais qui fait événement, série d'événements qui rendent possible l'appropriation de l'avoir-lieu. Et cette appropriation, pas plus que l'avoir-lieu, n'est le fait d'une circonstance unique et organique disposée dans un destin, dans un dessein, dans le mûrissement d'un progrès, dans la décision d'une occasion. Cela n'enlève rien, au demeurant, à la possibilité de nommer encore, soit *kairos* (ou chance), soit «révolution» (ou colère, et défi jeté sur l'inappropriable), les événements d'appropriation (ou d'inappropriation). Un corps n'est pas «propre», il est appropriant/inappropriant.

Mais l'expérience de pesée s'offre d'abord comme *corpus*, non comme corps-de-sens-et-d'histoire. Elle ouvre au sens possible d'un corps par le corpus proliférant, par le corpus *créateur* de ce corps. (La création comme corpus: sans créateur, logos empirique, variété aléatoire, ordonnance extensible, modalisation permanente, absence de plan et de fin—*seule la création serait la fin, ce qui veut dire aussi, seuls les corps, chaque corps, chaque masse et chaque intersection, interface de corps, chacun, chacune et toute leur communauté désœuvrée ferait les fins infinies de la techné du monde des corps.*)

Corpus des pesées d'une matière, de sa masse, de sa pulpe, de son grain, de sa béance, de son môle, de sa molécule, de sa tourbe, de son trouble, de sa turgescence, de sa fibre, de son jus, de son invagination, de son volume, de sa pointe, de sa tombée, de sa viande, de sa concrétion, de sa pâte, de sa cristallinité, de sa crispation, de son spasme, de sa fumée, de son nœud, de son dénouement, de son tissu, de sa demeure, de son désordre, de sa blessure, de sa douleur, de sa promiscuité, de son odeur, de son jouir, de son goût, de son timbre, de sa résolution, de son haut et bas, droite et gauche, de son acidité, de son essoufflement, de son balancement, de sa dissociation, de sa résolution, de sa raison . . .

should never seek the foundation of an "obscure," "preconceptual," "pre-ontological," or "immanent" and "immediate" knowledge. As I've already said: from the outset they're in the clarity of the dawn, and everything is clear. Not for a moment is it a question of "sensation," "perception," "cenesthesia"—derivatives, all, of "theories of knowledge," all laborious avatars of "representation" and "signification." But it's not even a matter of immediate mediations or intrications in and of themselves of "flesh" and "bodies proper." The created body is there, meaning *between* here and there, abandoned, always improperly abandoned, created: with no reason for being *there*, since *there* doesn't offer any reason, and with no reason for being *this* body or *this* mass of this body (because *this* doesn't justify anything, or "justifies" the *nothing* in the thing created: *res*, the real areal—*hoc est enim corpus, rei ratio*). Bodies merely posed, weighed just by being posed, and weighing, opening, opening up their places.

Body would be the experience of this weighing, which, to begin with, isn't proper but gives rise to an event, a series of events making possible the appropriation of the taking-place. Nor is this appropriation, any more than is a taking-place, the outcome of some unique and organic circumstance laid out in a destiny, in a design, in the ripening of a progress, in the seizing of an opportunity. Nevertheless, this in no way removes the possibility of still naming the events of appropriation (or nonappropriation) either as *kairos* (or luck) or as "revolution" (or as rage, and a challenge thrown against the inappropriable). A body isn't "proper," it's appropriating/inappropriating.

But the experience of weighing presents itself first of all as *corpus*, not as a body-with-sense-and-history. It opens onto the possible sense of a body through this body's proliferating corpus, its *creator* corpus. (Creation as *corpus*: without a creator, empirical logos, random variety, extendable grouping, permanent modalization, an absence of plan and end—*creation alone would be the end, meaning also that only bodies, every body, every mass, and every intersection or interface of the body, every male, every female, and their whole inoperative community, would provide the infinite ends of the technē of a world of bodies.*)

A corpus of the weighings of a material, of its mass, its pulp, its grain, its gulf, its mole, its molecule, its turf, its trouble, its turgidity, its fiber, its juice, its invagination, its volume, its peak, its fall, its meat, its coagulation, its paste, its crystallinity, its tightness, its spasm, its steam, its knot, its unknotting, its tissue, its home, its disorder, its wound, its pain, its promiscuity, its odor, its pleasure, its taste, its timbre, its resolution, its high and low, right and left, its acidity, its windedness, its balancing, its dissociation, its resolution, its reason . . .

Mais *expérience* n'est autre chose, ici, que le corpus de ces pesées, de ces pesées qui pèsent sans être pesées ni mesurées par rien, qui ne déposent nulle part leurs poids, ne s'apaisent d'aucune mesure. *Experitur*: un corps, une *psyché*, tente, est tentée, touchée, elle fait l'essai, elle se risque, elle est risquée, elle est poussée à venir à ce qu'elle est «déjà», mais «déjà» dans sa venue, non présupposée, *existant par essence imprésupposé*. Elle vient, elle va tout de suite—déjà, à l'instant, et cela prend toute une existence—jusqu'aux bords: rien de moins que naître et mourir, circonscrire, inscrire et excrire *à la fois* le lieu multiple d'un corps. *Experitur*: ça va, ça vient le long de ces bords, confins et fins sans fin bordés à d'autres fins, recommencements de soi autant qu'abords des autres, touches données et reçues, pesées, soupesées, tombées, levées, lèvres, plèvres, voix, visions, manières d'être aux bouts de soi et des autres bien avant d'être à soi ou à quiconque.

Expérience de la liberté: corps délivrés (de rien, de nulle caverne), livrés donc, mis au monde qu'ils *sont* eux-mêmes, naissant à ces pesées, n'étant que ces pesées, leurs caprices pris *dans* leurs nécessités, cette infime dépense de quelques grammes (poids, déclinaisons de fléaux, balances atomiques, glissements tectoniques, sismographes, engrammes, greffes, griffes)—quelques grammes, un corps, livré à tressaillir au tact de tant d'abords, de tant d'extrémités communes et distinctes de tous les corps, tous étrangers qu'ils sont, si prochains, si intimes, si absolument prochains et lointains dans la non-présupposition de la liberté. Car la liberté *est* la non-présupposition commune de cette intimité et de cet éloignement mutuels où les corps, leurs masses, leurs événements singuliers et toujours indéfiniment multipliables ont leur absence de fondement (et donc, identiquement, leur rigoureuse égalité).

C'est à l'absence de fondement, c'est-à-dire à la «création», que le monde des corps doit sa *techné* et son existence, ou mieux, *l'existence en tant que techné*. Elle engage l'infime dépense de quelques grammes qui ouvre un lieu, qui espace une exposition. *L'exposition* n'est pas le contraire du fondement, elle en est plutôt la vérité corporelle. L'«absence de fondement» ne doit pas s'entendre en termes de gouffre et d'abîme: mais en termes de bougé tectonique local, de quelques grammes de couleur plaçant *ici* l'éclat d'un corps (c'est-à-dire, chaque fois, *quelque* éclat: car un corps n'est jamais *tout entier*, et c'est aussi cela, l'être-exposé).

Parce qu'on ne fait pas le tour du tout d'un corps, comme le montrent l'amour, et la douleur, parce que les corps ne sont pas plus totalisables qu'ils ne sont fondés, il n'y a pas d'expérience *du* corps, pas plus qu'il n'y a d'expérience de la liberté. Mais la liberté elle-même est l'expérience, et le corps lui-même est l'expérience: l'exposition, l'avoir-lieu. Il faut donc qu'ils aient même structure, ou qu'une même structure les replie et les

But *experience*, here, is only the corpus of these weighings, of these weighings that weigh without being weighed or measured by anything, that do not set their weights down anywhere, are quieted by no measure. *Experitur*: a body, a *psyche*, tries, is tempted, touched, attempts, puts itself at risk, is risked, is driven to reach what it is "already," but "already" in its coming, not presupposed, *existing essentially unpresupposed*. It comes, it goes right away—already, right now, which takes an entire existence—right up to the edges: nothing less than being born and dying, circumscribing, inscribing, and exscribing, *at the same time*, a body's multiple place. *Experitur*: it goes, it comes all along the edges, the confines and the ends without end bordered by other purposes, fresh starts for the self as much as approaches to others, touches given and received, weighings, heftings, falls, rises, lips, lungs, voices, visions, ways of being at the ends of oneself and of others, long before being unto oneself or unto anyone.

The experience of freedom: bodies delivered (from nothing, from no cave), left therefore, borne into the world that they themselves *are*, awakening to these weighings, being nothing but these weighings, their caprices caught *in* their necessities, this tiny expenditure of a few grams (weights, the tiltings of beams, atomic scales, tectonic shifts, seismographs, engrams, graftings, claws)—a few grams, a body, left to jump at the touch of so many approaches, so many common and distinctive extremities of all bodies, all strangers as they are, so neighborly, so intimate, so absolutely near and far in the nonpresupposition of freedom. For freedom *is* the common nonpresupposition of this mutual intimacy and distancing where bodies, their masses, their singular and always indefinitely multipliable events have their absence of ground (and hence, identically, their rigorous equality).

The world of bodies owes its *technē* and its existence, or better, *its existence as technē*, to the absence of a foundation, that is, to "creation." It incurs the tiny expenditure of a few grams that open a place, spacing an exposition. An *exposition* isn't the opposite of a foundation, but rather its corporeal truth. An "absence of foundation" shouldn't be understood as a gulf or abyss but as a local tectonic stirring, a few grams of color placing the burst of a body *here* (in other words, every time, *some* burst, because a body is never *completely whole*, and being-exposed is also that fact).

Because we aren't ever done with a body's entirety, as love and suffering show, because bodies are no more totalizable than they are founded, there's no experience *of* the body, any more than there is an experience of freedom. But freedom itself is experience, and the body itself is experience: an exposition, a taking-place. They must therefore have the same structure, or the same structure must fold or deploy them into one another, the one

déploie l'un en l'autre et l'un par l'autre. Ce qui ressemblerait trait pour trait à la double structure du signe-de-soi et de l'être-soi-du-signe: à l'essence de l'incarnation.

De fait, le corps a la structure même de la liberté, et réciproquement: *mais aucun des deux ne se présuppose, ni en soi, ni en l'autre, comme la raison ni comme l'expression de la structure*. Le *sens* de la structure ne tient pas dans un renvoi de l'un à l'autre—renvoi de signe et/ou de fondement—mais le *sens* tient précisément à l'écart in-fini de la venue de l'un à l'autre. Il n'y a pas de «corps libre», il n'y a pas de «liberté incarnée». Mais de l'un à l'autre s'ouvre un *monde* dont la plus propre possibilité tient à ceci que «corps» et «liberté» *ne sont ni homogènes, ni hétérogènes l'un à l'autre*.

Il n'y a pas de *schème* qui prescrit la liberté comme le «sens» du monde des corps, et il n'y a pas non plus de *figure* qui (re)présente ce «sens» en ce monde. Ainsi, il n'y a pas de corps, pas d'*organon* du monde—pas plus qu'il n'y aurait deux «mondes» (pluriel contradictoire). En cela, il est vrai que le monde des corps est «im-monde», presse et plaie des corps qui sont aussi bien dans la clarté de l'espacement que dans l'implosion du trou noir.

L'infime dépense de quelques grammes, le tressaillement du monde créé, s'inscrit et s'excrit aussi bien comme un tremblement de terre: la *dislocation* est aussi le craquement de la gravité tectonique, et la ruine des lieux.

L'immondice

Le monde des corps se partage d'immonde. Identiquement. Ce n'est pas une simple respiration dialectique du «même» à l'«autre», finissant par relever l'ordure, et par la sublimer ou par la recycler. Il y a dans ce monde et dans sa création quelque chose qui excède et qui tord les cycles. (En général, les cercles, les sphères, leurs harmonies emboîtées: toutes les formes d'*annulation* de l'espace. Nos corps ni le monde ne sont circulaires, et c'est la loi la plus sérieuse de la création écotechnique que de ne pas *tourner rond*.)

«Partes *extra* partes», c'est identiquement, bord à bord de la délinéation des corps, l'extension et la distension, l'aréalité traçante et la crevaison purulente. Monde du corps pressé, fébrile, fibrillé, engorgé, s'engorgeant de sa propre proximité, tous les corps dans une promiscuité touffue de microbes, de pollutions, de sérums déficients, de graisses excessives, de nerfs crissants, obèses, décharnés, ballonnés, fouillés de vermines, barbouillés de crèmes, brûlants, luisants, bourrés de toxines, perdant leurs matières, leurs eaux, se perdant en gaz dans des nausées de guerre ou de famine, d'infection nucléaire ou d'irradiation virale. L'are-alité n'est pas l'épure de l'étendue sans l'impureté

through the other. Which would resemble, feature for feature, the double structure of the sign-of-self and the being-self-of-the-sign: the essence of incarnation.

In effect, the body has the structure of freedom, and conversely: *but neither of the two, either in itself or in the other, is presupposed as either the reason or the expression of the structure.* The structure's *sense* doesn't consist in one referring to the other—the sign referring and/or the foundation—but this *sense* depends precisely on the in-finite swerve of the coming of the one to the other. There's no "free body"; there's no "freedom incarnate." But a *world* opens up from the one to the other, a world whose ownmost possibility depends on the fact that "body" and "freedom" *are neither homogeneous nor heterogeneous to each other.*

There's no *schema* that would stipulate freedom as the "sense" of the world of bodies, nor is there any *figure* that would (re)present this "sense" in this world. Thus, there's no body, there's no *organon* of the world—any more than there might be two "worlds" (a contradictory plural). In this respect, it's true that the world of bodies is *im-mundus*, "non-world," a pressing and wounding of bodies, which *are* as much in the clarity of spacing as in the black hole's implosion.

The tiny expenditure of a few grams, the shiver of the created world, is inscribed and exscribed equally well as an earthquake: *dislocation* is also the splitting of tectonic gravity and the wrecking of places.

Immunditia

The world of bodies is shared with and divided by *immundus*. Identically. This isn't a simple dialectical respiration from the "same" to the "other," finally gathering up the trash and sublimating or recycling it. In this world and its creation, something exceeds and twists the cycles. (Circles, spheres, and their imbricated harmonies generally: forms, every one, of the *annulment* of space. Neither our bodies nor the world are circular, and ecotechnical creation's most serious law is *not to come full circle*.)

Side by side with the delineation of bodies, "partes *extra* partes" is at once extension and distension, a tracing areality and a suppurating burst. A world where the body is squeezed, febrile, fibrillated, engorged, engorging on its own proximity, all bodies in a promiscuity thick with microbes, pollutions, defective serums, excessive fat, and grinding nerves, obese, emaciated, ballooning, vermin-mined, cream-smeared, burning, gleaming, toxin-stuffed, losing their materials, their waters, turning to gas in the vomit of war or famine, nuclear infection or viral irradiation. Areality is not the reduction

de la propagation, de la dissémination sournoise ou brutale. Si le monde des corps, dans sa création, est bien la prise en masses et la dérive archi-tectonique de tous les macro/micro-cosmes, alors c'est aussi le monde d'une imprégnation de tous les corps, et d'une commune exposition spongieuse où tous les contacts sont contagieux, où chaque corps qui s'espace délite et débilite aussi tous les espaces. En vérité, l'«ouvert» n'est pas une béance, mais bien la masse, le massif de nos corps. Aussi n'est-il ouvert qu'à être recreusé, fouillé dans l'ouverture jusqu'à l' engorgement.

La bouche sèche à dire ce qu'il faut dire, mais il faut qu'elle sèche: le corps spacieux est identiquement zoné de jouissance et de cancer. Aréole du sein.

L'ouverture est aussi bien lâchage, les corps se lâchent, se relâchent, les traits se retirent, la couleur s'avale elle-même, ou se recrache. Les touchers sont infectés, les lieux sont autant de spasmes, de frottements, de vrillements de virus et de bactéries, de corps vibrillonnaires, de corps immunitaires, immuno-dépresseurs, dans une réticulation indéfinie de corps-séquences, de corps-messages dissolvants, coagulants, contaminants, réplicants, clonants, brisants, rayants, mordants, tout le corpus chimique, archichimique, la surpopulation de psychés acides, ioniques, hérissées des signaux aveugles d'un monde des corps où les corps, identiquement, décomposent le monde. Identiquement: dis-location, dis-localisation.

Un corps est à lui-même, aussi, sa dévoration, sa dégradation, et jusqu'à la sanie puante, ou jusqu'à la paralysie. L'existence ne comporte pas seulement l'excrément (comme tel, élément cyclique): mais un corps est aussi, et *se fait* sa propre excrétion. Un corps s'espace, un corps s'expulse, identiquement. *Il s'excrit comme corps*: espacé, il est corps mort, expulsé, il est corps immonde. Le corps mort dé-limite l'immonde et revient au monde. Mais le corps qui s'expulse enfonce l'immonde en plein monde Et notre monde fait les deux: double suspens du sens.

Les ouvertures du sang sont identiquement celles du sens. Hoc est enim: ici *a lieu* l'identité même du monde, l'identité absolue de ce qui ne fait pas corps-de-sens, de ce qui s'étale comme le corpus «sang»/«sens»/«sans»/«100» (= l'in-fini du *corpus*). Tensions, pressions, débits, caillots, thromboses, anévrismes, anémies, hémolyses, hémorragies, diarrhées, drogues, délires, invasions capillaires, infiltrations, transfusions, souillures, cloaques, puits, égoûts, écumes, bidonvilles, mégalopoles, tôles, dessèchements, déserts, croûtes, trachomes, usures des sols, massacres, guerres civiles, déportations, blessures, chiffons, seringues, souillures, croix rouges, croissants rouges, sangs rouges, sangs noirs, sangs caillés, sangs électrolysés, perfusés, infusés, refusés, giclés, imbibés, embourbés, plastifiés, bétonnés, vitrifiés, classifiés,

of extension without the impurity of propagation—of brutal or crafty dissemination. If, in its creation, the world of bodies is really an amassing and archi-tectonic drift of all macro/micro-cosms, then it's also a world where all bodies are impregnated, the world of a common, spongelike exposition, where all contacts are contagious, where each body, spacing itself, also splits and degrades all spaces. In truth, the "open" isn't a yawning gap but rather a mass, the massiveness of our bodies. Therefore it's only opened by being repeatedly excavated, dug up at its opening to the point of being clogged.

In saying what has to be said, the mouth goes dry, but it has to go dry: the spacious body is identically zoned by pleasure and by cancer. The areola of the breast.

The opening is also a letting go: bodies let go, they loosen up, features retreat, color swallows itself or else spits itself up. Touchings are infected, places are just so many spasms, rubbings, viral and bacterial swirls, gasolating bodies, immunitary bodies, immuno-depressors, in an indefinite reticulation of sequence-bodies, message-bodies, dissolving, coagulating, contaminating, replicating, cloning, breaking, streaking, biting, the whole chemical, archi-chemical corpus, an overpopulation of acidic, ionized psyches, bristling with the blind signals of a world of bodies in which bodies, identically, decompose the world. Identically: dis-location, dis-localization.

In and of itself, a body is also its consumption, its degradation, even as stinking pus or paralysis. Existence not only requires excrement (as such, a cyclic element): a body is also, and *makes itself*, its own excretion. A body spaces itself, a body expels itself, identically. *It exscribes itself as body*: being spaced, it's a dead body; being expelled, it's a filthy body. A dead body delimits the nonworld and returns to the world. But a body expulsing itself sinks the nonworld right into the world. And our world does both: a double suspension of sense.

Openings for blood are identical to those of sense. *Hoc est enim*: here the very identity of the world *takes place*, the absolute identity of what doesn't make a body-of-sense, of what's spread out as the corpus "sang(uine)"/ "sense"/"sans"/"cent"/"100" (= the in-finity of the *corpus*). Tensions, squeezings, pressures, calluses, thromboses, aneurisms, anemias, hemolyses, hemorrhages, diarrheas, drugs, deliriums, capillary invasions, infiltrations, transfusions, soilings, cloacae, wells, sewers, froth, slums, megalopolises, sheet-roofs, dessications, deserts, crusts, trachomas, soil erosions, massacres, civil wars, deportations, wounds, rags, syringes, soilings, red crosses, red

énumérés, comptes sanguins, banques de sang, banques de sens, banques de sans, trafics, réseaux, écoulements, coulures, flaques.

Les corps de notre monde ne sont ni sains, ni malades. Les corps écotechniques sont un autre genre de créatures, pressées de toutes parts, de toutes masses en elles-mêmes, à travers elles et entre elles, branchées, échographiées, radiographiées, les unes à travers les autres, communiquant leurs résonnances nucléaires, contrôlant leurs déficits, s'ajustant sur leurs défaillances, appareillant leurs handicaps, leurs trisomies, leurs muscles fondus, leurs synapses effondrées, de toutes parts accolées, collées, mêlées, infiltrées par milliards de corps dont pas un seul ne tient en équilibre sur *un* corps, tous glissants, ouverts, répandus, greffés, échangés. Plus d'*état* sain, ni de *stase* malade: une allée-venue, une palpitation saccadée ou filante de bords à bords de peaux, de plaies, d'enzymes de synthèse, d'images de synthèse. Pas une seule psyché intègre, close sur un plein ou sur un vide.

L'*étendue* de Psyché, c'est cette exsudation et cette agitation intimes du corpus du monde. Peut-on ne pas les comprendre ou les ressentir comme immondes? Pour peu que notre monde comprenne qu'il n'est plus temps de se vouloir Cosmos, pas plus qu'Esprit surdimensionnant la Nature, il semble qu'il ne peut rien que toucher en soi l'abjection de l'immonde. Ce n'est pas seulement l'effet ambivalent de tous les narcissismes. *De fait*, dès que le monde *est monde* il *se* produit (s'expulse) aussi comme immondice. Le monde *doit* se rejeter im-monde, *parce que sa création sans créateur ne peut pas se contenir elle-même*. Un créateur contient, retient sa création, et se la rapporte. Mais la création du monde des corps ne revient à rien, ni à personne. *Monde* veut dire sans principe et sans fin: et c'est ce que veut dire *espacement des corps*, ce qui, à son tour, ne veut rien dire d'autre que l'in-finie impossibilité d'homogénéiser le monde avec lui-même, et le sens avec le sang. Les ouvertures du sang sont identiquement celles du sens—*hoc est enim . . .* —, et *cette* identité n'est faite que de l'absolu rejet-de-soi qu'est le monde des corps. Le sujet de sa création est ce rejet. La figure de l'écotechnie, propageant dans tous les sens le foisonnement mondial et la contagion immonde, est bien la figure de cette identité—et sans doute est-elle pour finir cette identité elle-même.

Un corps s'expulse: comme corpus, espace spasmé, distendu, rejet-de-sujet, «immonde» s'il faut garder le mot. Mais c'est ainsi que ce monde a lieu.

En un sens, la création du monde des corps est l'impossible même. Et en un sens, en un coup répété de sens et de sang, c'est l'impossible qui a lieu. Que le sens et le sang n'aient pas de schème commun—sinon le «sans» et l'infini du «100»—, que la création soit un incontenable écartement, une catastrophe fractale architectonique, que la venue au monde soit

crescents, red bloods, black bloods, clotted bloods, bloods electrolyzed, per-fused, infused, refused, spurted, imbibed, mired, plastified, cemented, vit-rified, classified, enumerated, blood counts, blood banks, sense banks, cents banks, traffics, networks, flowings, flash-floods, splashes.

Our world's bodies are neither healthy nor ill. Ecotechnical bodies are an-other kind of creature, pressed in on all sides, by all the masses themselves, across and between themselves, plugged in, echographed, radiographed, one crossing another, communicating their nuclear resonances, controlling their deficits, adapted to their defects, outfitting their handicaps, their trisomies, their collapsed muscles, their broken synapses, coupled, glued, mixed, infil-trated all over by billions of bodies, not one of which stays balanced on *a* body, all of them sliding, opened, spread out, grafted, exchanged. Neither a healthy *state* nor a sick *stasis*: a coming-and-going, a jumpy or smooth palpitation of skins side to side, wounds, synthetic enzymes, synthetic im-ages. Not a single integrated psyche, closed in upon a solid or hollow space.

This intimate exsudation and agitation of the world's corpus are Psyche's *extension*. Are we able not to see and feel them as filthy, as nonworld? If the world understands only that the time has passed for wanting to be a Cosmos, as it has passed for wanting to be a Nature-enlarging Spirit, then, apparently, it can only touch the abjection of its own filth. This isn't merely the ambiva-lent effect of every narcissism. De facto, as soon as the world *is world* it also produces (expels) *itself* as *im-munditia*. The world *must* reject itself as *non-world, because its creation without a creator can't contain itself.* A creator con-tains, retains his creation, and relates it to himself. But the creation of the world of bodies doesn't return to anything or anyone. *World* means no prin-ciple and no end: and this is the sense of the *spacing of bodies*, which, in turn, only means the in-finite impossibility of homogenizing the world with itself, sense with blood. The openings of blood are identical to those of sense—*hoc est enim . . .*—and *this* identity is made up of no more than the absolute re-jection of the self that *is* the world of bodies. The subject of its creation is this rejection. The figure of the ecotechnical, propagating in every sense a world-wide proliferation and filthy contagion, is indeed the figure of this iden-tity—and no doubt ends up, finally, as this identity itself.

A body expels itself: as corpus, as spasmic space, distended, subject-reject, "*im-mundus*," if we have to keep the word. But that's how this world takes place.

In one sense, the creation of the world of bodies is the impossible itself. And in one sense—in the repeated blow of sense and sang(uinary)—it's the impos-sible that happens. That sense and the sang(uinary) should have no common schema—except for the "sans" and the infinity of the "cent" (*100*)—that cre-ation should be an uncontainable swerve, an architectonic fractal catastrophe,

un irrépressible rejet, voilà ce que veut dire corps, et voilà ce que désormais *sens* veut dire. Le sens du monde des corps est le sans-limites, le sans-réserves, l'extrême assuré de l'*extra* partes. En un sens, c'est cela le sens, en *un* sens toujours renouvelé, toujours espacé, en *un* sens et en *un* autre, en *un* corpus de sens et donc en tous les sens—mais sans totalisation possible. Le sens absolu du monde des corps, sa mondialité et sa corporéité *mêmes*: l'excrétion du sens, le sens excrit.

Cette pensée rend fou. Cette pensée, si c'est une pensée, ou bien la pensée qu'il s'agit de penser *ça*—et rien d'autre. Cette pensée: hoc est *enim*, voici, le monde est son propre rejet, le rejet du monde est le monde. Tel est le monde des corps: il a en lui cette désarticulation, cette inarticulation du *corpus*. L'énonciation de toute *l'étendue du sens*. Une énonciation in-articulante: *non plus la signification, mais un corps-* «*parlant*» *qui ne fait pas* «*sens*», *un* «*parler*» *-corps qui ne s'organise pas*. Enfin, le sens matériel—c'est-à-dire en effet une folie, l'imminence d'une intolérable convulsion dans la pensée. On ne peut pas penser à moins: c'est ça ou rien. Mais penser ça, c'est encore rien.

(Ce qui peut être: *rire*. Surtout pas ironiser, ni moquer, mais rire, le corps secoué de pensée pas possible.)

Travail, capital

Où sont les corps, d'abord? Les corps sont d'abord au travail. Les corps sont d'abord à la peine du travail. Les corps sont d'abord en transport vers le travail, au retour du travail, à attendre du repos, à le prendre et vite à s'en déprendre, et à travailler, à s'incorporer dans de la marchandise, marchandise soi-même, force de travail, capital non accumulable, vendable, épuisable sur le marché du capital accumulé, accumulateur. La *techné* créatrice crée les corps d'usine, d'atelier, de chantier, de bureau, partes extra partes composant par figures et mouvements avec tout le système, pièces, leviers, embrayages, emboîtages, décolletages, encapsulages, fraisages, découplages, emboutissages, systèmes asservis, asservissements systémiques, stockages, manutentions, décharges, casses, contrôles, transports, pneumatiques, huiles, diodes, cardans, fourches, bielles, circuits, disquettes, télécopies, marqueurs, hautes températures, pulvérisations, perforations, câblages, canalisations, corps canalisés vers rien d'autre que leur force monnayée, rien d'autre que la plus-value de capital qui se ramasse et se concentre *là*.

N'essayez surtout pas de prétendre que ce discours est archaïque.

Capital veut dire: corps marchandé, transporté, déplacé, replacé, remplacé, mis en poste et en posture, jusqu'à usure, jusqu'à chômage, jusqu'à famine,

that coming to the world should be an irrepressible rejection, such is the sense of body, and henceforth the sense of *sense*. The sense of the world of bodies is the unlimited, unreserved, extreme certainty of the *extra* partes. This, in a sense, is sense, in *one* always renewed sense, always spaced, in *one* sense and in *an* other, in *one* corpus of sense and thus in every sense—but without any possible totalization. The absolute sense of the world of bodies, its *self-same* worldliness and corporeality: sense's excretion, sense exscribed.

This thought drives us crazy. This thought, if it is a thought, or else the thought that we have to think *this*—and nothing else. This thought: hoc est *enim*, here, the world is its own rejection, the world's rejection is the world. Such is the world of bodies: it has in itself this disarticulation, this unarticulating of the *corpus*. A statement of *the whole extension of sense*. An unarticulating statement: *no longer signification, but a "speaking" body that doesn't make "sense," a "speech"-body that isn't organized*. Finally, the material sense—meaning, in effect, a madness, the onset of an intolerable convulsion of thought. We can think of nothing less: it's either this, or it's nothing. But thinking this, it's still nothing.

(Which might be: *laughing*. Above all, not to ironize, not to mock, but to laugh, the body shaken with no way thought.)

Work, Capital

Where are the bodies, anyway? Bodies are first of all at work. First of all, bodies are hard at work. First of all, bodies are going to work, coming home from work, waiting for rest, taking it and promptly leaving it, and working, incorporating themselves into merchandise, themselves merchandise, a work force, nonaccumulable capital, sellable, exhaustible in the market of accumulated, accumulative capital. Creative *technē* creates bodies for the factory, shop-floor, construction site, office, *partes extra partes* combining with the entire system through figures and movements, pieces, levers, clutches, boxes, cutouts, encapsulations, milling, uncoupling, stamping, enslaved systems, systemic enslaving, stocking, handling, dumping, wrecks, controls, transports, tires, oils, diodes, universal joints, forks, crankshafts, circuits, diskettes, telecopies, markers, high temperatures, pulverizings, perforations, cablings, wirings, bodies wired to nothing but their minted force, to the surplus-value of capital collected and concentrated *there*.

Above all, don't try to pretend that this discourse is archaic.

Capital means: a body marketed, transported, displaced, replaced, superseded, assigned to a post and a posture, to the point of ruin, unemployment, famine, a Bengali body bent over a car in Tokyo, a Turkish body in a Berlin

corps bengali plié sur un moteur à Tokyo, corps turc dans une tranchée de Berlin, corps noir chargé de colis blancs à Suresnes ou à San Francisco. Ainsi, capital veut dire aussi: système de sur-signification des corps. Rien n'est plus signifiant/signifié que la classe, et la peine, et la lutte des classes. Rien n'échappe moins à la sémiologie que les efforts subis par les forces, la torsion des muscles, des os, des nerfs. Regardez les mains, les cals, les crasses, regardez les poumons, les colonnes vertébrales. Corps salis salariés, saleté et salaire comme un anneau bouclé de signification. Tout le reste est littérature.

Fin de la philosophie, et surtout de toute philosophie du corps, comme de toute philosophie du travail. Mais libération des corps, réouverture de l'espace que le capital concentre et surinvestit en temps toujours plus resserré, plus aigu, plus strident. Corps *made in time*. La création, elle, est éternelle: l'éternité, c'est l'étendue, la mer mêlée au soleil, l'espacement comme la résistance et la révolte des corps créés.

Autre citation

«Au crépuscule d'un jour où la pluie d'automne fait rage (présage de typhon sans doute), comme envoûté par un appel du fond de la montagne, dans le train sur la ligne Chuô, l'autre moi, rythmant de la jambe, appuyant sur le frein, secouant le wagon.

Petites ombres noirâtres ! Il y a dix heures et quelques, le tract "Pour que vive la mine d'Yûbari" distribué à la sortie du métro, oscillations des corps de deux mineurs (messieurs mineurs), des deux côtés de la sortie, (c'est ça!), leurs deux corps restèrent au fond des yeux, (le temps) se mettant à couler.

Envoûté par l'appel du fond de la montagne, violente pluie d'automne.

Depuis la ligne de partage des eaux du fond, le col Daibosatsu (Grand Bodhisattva) appela. Dans la pluie, tout en marchant et imaginant la forme de la montagne qui n'existe pas en ce monde, *la pluie* frappa comme des cailloux la capuche, je devenais la forme de la montagne qui n' existe pas.

La *forme* de cette montagne, la pluie qui frappe la capuche (mince blouson). Deux cailloux mis dans le sac. Tout cela à la fois, je descendis à la gare Ishigamimae (la gare Devant-le-dieu-des-pierres), marchai (attiré par le bruit de l'eau), atteignis le milieu, pont lumineux?» (Gôzô Yoshimasu).

Un corps est l'in-fini d'une pensée

Un corps ne cesse pas de se penser, de se peser—sous cette condition précise que se qui est à penser—ce «se», *hoc* «ipse», hoc *meum*—n'est pas à «sa» disposition, n'est disponible que dis-posé à travers toute une aréalité qui ne *se*

trench, a black body loaded down with white packages in Suresnes or San Francisco. Capital therefore also means: a system of over-signified bodies. There's nothing more signifying/signified than class, and suffering, and class-struggle. Nothing less escapes semiology than the stress suffered by work-forces, the twisting of muscles, bones, nerves. Look at the hands, the calluses, the dirt, look at the lungs, the spinal columns. Salaried, soiled bodies, toiling and earning as a closed ring of signification. Everything else is literature.

The end of philosophy, and especially of any philosophy of the body, as of any philosophy of labor. But the liberation of bodies, the reopening of a space where capital concentrates and overinvests in time that's more and more constricted, more intense, more strident. A body *made in time*. As for creation, it is eternal: eternity is extension, a mingling of sea and sun, spacing as the resistance and revolt of created bodies.

Another Citation

"At the dawn of a day when the rains of autumn are raging (foretelling, no doubt, a typhoon), as if spellbound by a call from the mountain's depth, in a train on the Chūō line, an other me, beating time with his leg, pulling at the brake, shaking the wagon.

"Small darkened shadows! Ten or more hours ago, the tract 'Saving the Yūbati Mine,' distributed at a subway exit, the swaying bodies of two miners (mister miners), on both sides of the exit (there it is!), both their bodies resting in the depths of their eyes, (time) starting to flow.

"Spellbound by a call from the mountain's depth, a violent autumn rain.

"From the depth of the watershed, the hill Daibosatsu (Great Bodhisattva) called out. In the rain, while walking and imagining the form of the mountain that doesn't exist in this world, *the rain* hit the hood like pebbles, I was becoming the form of the mountain that doesn't exist.

"The *form* of this mountain, the rain that strikes the hood (a light jacket). Two pebbles placed in the sack. All this at one and the same time, I went down to the Ishigamimae station (the Before-the-god-of-stones station), was walking (drawn by the sound of the water), reached the middle, a luminous bridge?"[2]

A Body Is the In-finity of a Thought

A body doesn't stop thinking itself, weighing itself—specifying under this precise condition that the *self* to be thought—*hoc* "ipse," hoc *meum*—is not at "its" disposal, is available only as dis-posed across a whole areality that

revient jamais sans s'écarter (ne s'écartant pas «de soi», si ce «soi» n'est nulle part donné, mais il faudrait dire, «écartant-soi-à-même-soi»). Ainsi, un corps ne cesse pas de se: matière, masse, pulpe, grain, fente, môle, molécule, tourbe, turgescence, fibre, jus, invagination, volume, tombée, viande, ciment, pâte, cristal, crispation, dénouement, tissu, demeure, désordre, odeur, saveur, résonnance, résolution, raison.

Il n'en sait rien, il ne sait pas qu'il *se*, ni ce qu'il *se*. Mais il n'y a pas là le moindre manque, car les corps n'appartiennent pas au domaine où «savoir» fait l'enjeu (et pas non plus «non-savoir», ni sous une forme mystérique, ni sous la forme d'une immédiate immanente science infuse du corps, d'un de ces délicats «s'éprouver» tels qu'en exposent les «philosophies de la vie»). Expérience n'est pas savoir, ni non-savoir. Expérience est traversée, transport de bord à bord, transport incessant d'un bord à l'autre tout le long du tracé qui développe et qui limite une aréalité.

Penser n'appartient pas non plus à l'ordre du savoir. La pensée est *l'être* en tant qu'il pèse sur ses bords, *l'être* appuyé, ployé sur ses extrémités, pli et détente d'étendue. Chaque pensée est un corps. (C'est pourquoi, à la fin, tout système de pensée se désagrège en soi-même, et il n'y a que *corpus* des pensées.)

Chaque pensée *est* (ou bien: dans chaque pensée *l'être est*- c'est ici que Parménide énonce «*c'est même chose être et pensée*»; songez donc à présent que *cette* pensée même de Parménide *est* la même chose que l'*être*, absolument, et qu'elle ne «pense» donc rien d'autre que l'être-là de l'être, c'est-à-dire qu'elle est *le même* que ce *là*, qu'elle est la *pesée* de l'être en tant que ce *là*, c'est-à-dire encore qu'elle est *ce lieu* de l'être ou *ce lieu* d'être, et vous comprendrez qu'une pensée est un corps, une *location* d'être, c'est-à-dire encore une existence). Une pensée *ne dit pas* «hoc est», mais une pensée *est* «hoc est», position sans présupposition, exposition. *Hoc est* n'est pas, pour sa part, quelque chose: *c'est très exactement l'inarticulation ontologique pensée/corps.* «Ceci, tout ceci, chaque ceci, rien que ceci est—le sens.» Hoc est: hoquet.

Corps, la pensée est l'être se montrant, l'être-son-propredéictique et l'être-l'index-de-son-propre. «Hoc est» énoncé par l'être, voilà ce qu'est penser. Mais comment l'être énonce-t-il? L'être ne parle pas, l'être ne s'épanche pas dans l'incorporel de la signification. L'être est *là*, l'être-lieu d'un «là», un corps. Le problème de la pensée (si on veut le nommer un «problème»), c'est *comment le corps énonce.*

(Bien sûr, le corps énonce aussi dans le langage: il y a là bouche, langue, muscles, vibrations, fréquences, ou bien mains, claviers, graphes, traces, et tous les messages sont de longues chaînes de griffes et greffes matérielles. Mais il s'agit précisément de ce qui, du langage, n'intéresse plus le message, mais son excription.)

never returns to *itself* without moving *itself* aside (not moving itself aside "from itself," if this "self" is nowhere given, but, as we'd have to say, "moving itself aside inside itself"). Thus, a body never stops *selving*: matter, mass, pulp, grain, slit, mole, molecule, bog, turgescence, fiber, juice, invagination, volume, flaccidity, meat, cement, paste, crystal, tensing, untying, fabric, home, disorder, odor, flavor, resonance, resolve, reason.

It knows nothing about it, doesn't know that it *selves*, or what it *selves*. But not the slightest thing is lacking there, because bodies don't belong to an order where "knowing" is at stake (and not "not-knowing," either, not in mysterical form, not in the form of an immediate, immanent, innate science of the body, one of those delicate "self-testings" expounded by "philosophies of life"). Experience is neither knowledge nor nonknowledge. Experience is a passage, a transport from border to border, an endless transport from shore to shore, all along a tracing that develops and limits an areality.

Nor does thinking pertain to the order of knowing. Thought is *being* insofar as it weighs on its borders, *being* supported, bending onto its extremities, a fold and release of extension. Each thought is a body. (Which is why, finally, every system of thought is disgregated within, and thoughts form only a *corpus*.)

Each thought *is* (or else: in each thought *being is*—what Parmenides states as "*Being and thinking are the same thing*"; imagine for a moment, then, that *this* very thought of Parmenides *is* the same thing as *being*, absolutely, and that it therefore "thinks" nothing but the being-there of being, meaning that it's *the same* as this *there*, the *weighing* of the being as this *there*, meaning, moreover, that it's *this place* of being or *this reason* being, and then you'll understand that a thought is a body, a *location* of being, meaning an existence as well). A thought *doesn't say* "hoc est," but a thought *is* "hoc est," a position without presupposition, exposition. *Hoc est* is not, for its part, one thing: *it's very precisely the ontological nonarticulation thought/body.* "This, all this, each this, nothing but this is—sense." *Hoc est*: hiccup.

Body, thought, is being displaying itself, being-its-own-deictic and being-the-index-of-its-own. "Hoc est" declared by being, such is thought. But how does being declare? Being doesn't speak, doesn't pour forth in the incorporeality of signification. Being is *there*, the being-place of a "there," a body. The problem with thought (if you want to call it a "problem") is *how the body declares.*

(Of course the body also declares in language: there is mouth there, tongue, muscles, vibrations, frequencies, or else hands, keyboards, graphs, traces, and all the messages are long chains of material scratches and grafts. But it's precisely a question of what, in language, no longer involves the message, just its exscription.)

Le corps énonce—il n'est pas silencieux ni muet, qui sont des catégories langagières. Le corps énonce hors-langage (et c'est ce qui du langage s'excrit). Le corps énonce de telle manière que, étranger à tout intervalle et à tout détour du signe, il *annonce* absolument tout (il *s'*annonce absolument), *et* son annonce se fait à elle-même obstacle, absolument. *Le corps énonce, et il s'énonce, en s'empêchant comme énoncé* (et comme énonciation). Sens du rejet-de-sens.

Soupesez donc une parole encore non dite, non échappée d'une bouche, encore à même le larynx, la langue, les dents (qui la feraient, à l'instant, résonner, si elle venait à être dite—mais son «encore là» est sans avenir, elle sera toujours *encore* là).

Parole prononcée non dite, annoncée non prononcée, dénoncée, posée, glissante comme une salive, salive elle-même, infime écoulement, exsudation, entraille. Parole avalée non dite, non pas ravalée, non pas reprise, mais avalée dans l'instant dérobé d'être dite, avalée dans l'a-peine de goût d'une salive, à peine écumeuse, à peine visqueuse, dissolution distincte, imprégnation sans immanence d'une fadeur savoureuse avalée, lavée au bord d'être dite. Malgré l'étymologie, cette saveur n'est pas savoir, ni cette voix n'est langage, ni vocable, ni vocalise, ni voyelle. Pareille donc au silencieux dialogue de l'âme avec soi, mais ni dialogue, ni monologue, étendue seulement de l'âme, schème sans signification, aire, mesure, scansion, rythme. L'être, en tant que le rythme des corps—les corps, en tant que le rythme de l'être. La pensée-encorps est rythmique, espacement, battement, donnant le *temps* de la danse, le *pas* du monde.

Rock: sous cette cadence de *corps*, il se trouve que notre monde a déployé une mondialité rythmique, de jazz en rap et au-delà, une presse, un foisonnement, un encombrement, une popularité de postures, une peau électronique zonée, massée, qu'on peut bien dire, si l'on y tient, *du bruit*, car il s'agit d'abord en effet du bruit de fond qui monte lorsque les formes n'ont plus cours, ne font plus sens (social, commun, sentimental, métaphysique)—et lorsqu'au contraire les *esthétiques* sont à refaire à même des corps aux *sens* nus, privés de repères, désorientés, désoccidentés, et que les *arts* sont à refaire, de part en part, comme la *techné* de la création des corps. Oui, du bruit: c'est comme le revers d'une pensée, mais c'est aussi comme ce qui gronde dans les replis des corps.

Corpus: cortex

Pensée du corps: la pensée que le corps est lui-même, et la pensée que nous voulons penser au sujet du corps. Ce corps, ici, le mien, le vôtre, qui cherche à penser le corps, où le corps cherche à se penser, ne peut le faire avec rigueur

The body declares—it isn't silent or mute, categories that are language related. The body declares outside-language (and that's the part of language that's exscribed). The body declares in such a way that, foreign to any interval and any detour of the sign, it *announces* absolutely everything (it announces *itself* absolutely), *and* its annunciation poses an obstacle for itself, absolutely. *The body declares, and is declared, by stopping itself as what is declared* (and as declaration). The sense of rejection-of-sense.

Weigh, then, a word as yet unspoken, not escaping the mouth, not even the larynx, the tongue, the teeth (which would, if it came to be said, make it resound promptly—but its "still there" has no future, it will always *still* be there).

A word pronounced unsaid, announced not pronounced, denounced, posed, slippery like saliva, itself saliva, a tiny outflow, an exsudation, an entrail. A word swallowed unspoken, not taken back, but swallowed in the snatched moment of being said, swallowed in the hardly any taste of saliva, hardly foaming, hardly viscous, a distinct dissolution, impregnation without immanence of a swallowed savory insipidity, washed at the brink of being spoken. Etymology notwithstanding, this savor isn't savant, and this voice isn't language, vocable, vocalized, or vowel. Similar, then, to a silent dialogue between self and soul, but not a dialogue or a monologue, just an extension of the soul, a schema without signification, area, measure, scansion, rhythm. Being, as the rhythm of bodies—bodies, as the rhythm of being. The thought-in-body is rhythmic, spacing, pulsing, giving the *time* of the dance, the *step* of the world.

Rock: under this body cadence of *body*, it turns out that our world has deployed a rhythmical world-wideness, from jazz to rap and beyond, a crowd, a proliferation, a glut, a popularity of postures, a zoned, massed, electronic skin, which, if we insist, we can certainly call *noise*, because in fact it is, to begin with, background noise arising where forms no longer hold sway, no longer make sense (social, common, sentimental, metaphysical)— and where, to the contrary, *aesthetics* will have to be reworked at the level of bodies with *naked* senses, deprived of reference points, disoriented, disoccidented, and where *arts* have to be reworked, through and through, as the *technē* of the creation of bodies. Yes, noise: it's like the other side of thought, but also like rumblings in the coils of the body.

Corpus: Cortex

Thinking of the body: the thought that the body itself is, and the thought that we want to think about the body. This body, here, my own, yours, which tries to think the body, where the body tries to think itself, can do

(renonçant à signifier le corps) qu'en se laissant reconduire à *ce* corps qu'il *est pensant*, à sa propre matière pensante, à même là où ça se dépense, sur la *res extensa* du *cogito*.

Ici est le point dur de cette chose—cette dureté absolue qui blesse la pensée dès que sérieusement elle pense (et qu'elle y pense)—, de cette chose dite «la pensée», le nodule ou la synapse, l'acide ou l'enzyme, le gène ou le virus, un corpuscule du cortex, un rythme encore, un saut, une secousse—et sa pesée.

Un gramme de pensée: pesée minime, poids d'une petite pierre, appelée scrupule, poids de presque rien qui embarrasse et qui fait demander pourquoi il n'y a pas rien, mais quelques choses, quelques corps, pourquoi cette création, et tout ce qu'elle énonce et qui n'est pas énoncé. Un gramme de pensée: trace de ce caillou, de ce calcul, gravure, incision minuscule, entaille, entame, point dur d'une pointe, poinçon, corps même de l'entame, corps entamé, corps partagé *d'être ce corps* qu'il est, de l'*exister* (verbe transitif). Le cortex n'est pas un organe, c'est ce corpus de points, de pointes, de traces, gravures, rayures, lignes, plis, traits, incisions, scissions, décisions, lettres, chiffres, figures, écritures engrammées les unes dans les autres, déliées les unes des autres, lisses et striées, planes et granuleuses. Corpus des grains de la pensée en corps—ni «corps pensant», ni «corps parlant»—, granit du cortex, égrènement d'expérience.

Pensée en retrait de penser. Toucher ce gramme, cette série, cette étendue. La pensée se touche, sans être soi, sans se revenir à soi. *Ici* (mais où est ici? il n'est pas localisable, il est la localisation *ayant lieu*, l'être *venant* aux corps), ici donc il ne s'agit pas de rejoindre une «matière» intacte: on n'oppose pas d'immanence à la transcendance. De manière générale, on n'*oppose* pas, les corps n'opposent ni ne s'opposent. Ils sont posés, déposés, pesés. Il n'y a pas de matière intacte—ou bien il n'y aurait rien. Au contraire il y a le tact, la pose et la dépose, le rythme de l'allée-venue des corps au monde. Le tact délié, partagé de lui-même.

Corps joui

Le corps jouit d'être touché. Il jouit d'être pressé, pesé, pensé des autres corps, et d'être cela qui presse, et pèse, et pense les autres corps. Les corps jouissent et sont jouis des corps. *Corps*, c'est-à-dire aréoles retirées, *partes extra partes*, de la totalité indivise qui n'existe pas. Corps jouis-sable *parce que* retiré, étendu à l'écart et ainsi offert au toucher. Le toucher fait joie et douleur—mais il n'a rien à voir avec l'angoisse (l'angoisse n'accepte

so with rigor (refusing to signify the body) only by letting itself be redirected to *this* body that it *is thinking*, to its own thinking matter, to the very place where it is expended, on the *cogito's res extensa*.

Here's the hard point about this thing—this absolute hardness that wounds thought as soon as it thinks seriously (and thinks seriously *about this*)—about this thing called "thought," nodule or synapse, acid or enzyme, gene or virus, a corpuscle of cortex, a rhythm once again, a leap, a shudder—and its weighing.

A gram of thought: a minimal weighing, the weight of a small stone, called a scruple, the weight of an almost nothing that's embarrassing and makes us ask why there isn't nothing but some things, some bodies, why this creation, and all it declares, and that's not declared. A gram of thought: a trace of this pebble, this calculation, this engraving, a minuscule incision, a notch, a cut, the hard point of a point, an awl, the very body of the cut, the body cut, the body divided *by being this body* it is, by *existing* it (transitive verb). The cortex is not an organ, it's this corpus of points, of peaks, of traces, engravings, grooves, lines, folds, figures, incisions, scissions, decisions, letters, numbers, figures, writings engrammed in one another, untied from one another, smooth and striped, flat and granular. Corpus of the grains of thought in body—neither a "thinking body" nor a "speaking body"—the granite of the cortex, the shedding of experience.

Thought in retreat from thinking. Touching this gram, this series, this extension. Thought touches itself without being itself, without returning to itself. *Here* (but where's here? it's not localizable, it's localization *taking place*, the being that's *coming* to bodies), so here it's not a question of rejoining an intact "matter": immanence isn't being opposed to transcendence. In a general way, we don't *oppose*, bodies neither oppose nor are opposed. They are posed, deposed, weighed. There's no intact matter—or else there'd be nothing. On the contrary, there's tact, the pose and deposing, the rhythm of the coming-and-going of the bodies in the world. Tact untied, divided unto itself.

Body Enjoyed

The body delights in being touched. It delights in being squeezed, weighed, thought by other bodies, and being the one that squeezes, weighs, and thinks other bodies. Bodies delight in and are delighted by bodies. *Bodies*, meaning areolas withdrawn, *partes extra partes*, from an undivided totality that doesn't exist. A body delectable *because* withdrawn, extended to one side and thereby offered to touch. Touch creates joy and pain—but has nothing to

pas le *pas* du toucher, l'écart de l'autre bord: elle est toute mystérique, fantasmatique).

Joie et douleur sont les opposés qui ne s'opposent pas. Un corps est joui *aussi* dans la douleur (et cela reste absolument étranger à ce qu'on nomme masochisme). Il y reste étendu, exposé—oui, jusqu'à l'insupportable rejet. Cet impartageable partage du jouir vrille et rend folle la pensée. (La pensée folle crie ou rit: tout reste à dire d'un cri sans pathétique et d'un rire sans ironie.)

Le corps joui s'étend dans tous ses sens, faisant sens de tous à la fois et d'aucun. Le corps joui est comme le pur signe-de-soi, sauf à n'être ni signe, ni soi. Le jouir même est corpus de zones, de masses, épaisseurs étendues, aréoles offertes, toucher lui-même démultiplié dans tous ses sens qui ne communiquent pas entre eux (les sens *ne se touchent pas*, il n'y a pas de «sens commun», ni de sentir «en soi»: Aristote le sait, qui dit que chaque sens sent *et* se sent sentir, chacun à part et sans contrôle général, chacun retiré comme vue, comme ouïe, comme goût, odorat, toucher, chacun jouissant et se sachant jouir dans l'écart absolu de son jouir; toute la théorie des arts s'engendre à partir de là).

Le corps joui jouit de soi en tant que ce *soi* est joui (que jouir/être joui, toucher/être touché, espacer/être espacé *font ici l'essence de l'être*). *Soi* de part en part étendu dans la venue, dans l'allée-venue au monde.

Cela ne veut pas dire que le corps vienne avant le sens, comme sa préhistoire obscure ou comme son attestation préontologique. Non, il lui donne lieu, absolument. Ni antérieur, ni postérieur, le lieu du corps *est l'* avoir-lieu du sens, absolument. L'ab-solu est le détaché, le posé-à-part, l'étendu, le partagé. (On peut dire le sens *fini*, à la condition de penser que *finir c'est jouir*.)

Corpus

Il n'y a pas «le» corps, il n'y a pas «le» toucher, il n'y a pas «la» *res extensa*. Il y a qu'il y a: création du monde, *techné* des corps, pesée sans limites du sens, *corpus* topographique, géographie des ectopies multipliées—et pas d'u-topie.

Pas de lieu hors-lieu pour le sens. Si le sens est «absent», c'est sur le mode d'être ici—*hoc est enim*—, et non sur celui d'être ailleurs et nulle part. *L'absence-ici*, voilà le corps, l'étendue de psyché. Pas de lieu d'avant la naissance, ni d'après la mort. Pas d'avant/après: le temps *est* l'espacement. Le temps *est* le surgissement et l'absente-ment, l'allée-venue à la présence: il n'est pas l'engendrement, la transmission, la perpétuation. Les «pères» et les «mères» sont d'autres corps, ils ne sont pas le lieu d'un Autre (comme ils le sont dans

do with anguish (anguish doesn't accept the *not*, and the *step*, of touch, the swerve of the other edge: it's entirely mysterical, fantasmatic).

Joy and pain are opposites unopposed to one another. A body is *also* enjoyed in pain (and this remains absolutely alien to what gets called masochism). It remains extended, exposed there—yes, to the point of unbearable rejection. This unshareable division of delight twists thought and drives it insane. (Insane thought laughs or cries: everything has yet to be said about a cry that's not pathetic and a laugh that's not ironic.)

The delighted body is extended in all its senses, making sense of all at once and of none. The delighted body is like a pure sign-of-self, subject to being neither sign nor self. Delight itself is a corpus of zones, masses, thicknesses extended, areolas offered, touch itself dispersed in all its senses, which do not communicate with each other (senses *don't touch each other*, there's no "common sense," no sensing "in itself": Aristotle knows it, saying that each sense senses *and* senses itself sensing, each on its own with no overarching control, each one withdrawn, as sight, as hearing, as taste, smell, touch, each delighting and knowing that it delights in the absolute apartness of its delight; all theory of art issues from this starting point.)

The delighted body delights in itself insofar as this *self* is enjoyed (as delighting / being delighted, touching / being touched, spacing / being spaced *make, here, the essence of the being*). *Self* extended through and through in the coming, in the coming-and-going into the world.

This doesn't mean that the body comes before sense, as its obscure prehistory or preontological attestation. No, it gives it its place, absolutely. Neither before, nor after, the body's place *is* the taking-place of sense, absolutely. The ab-solute is the detached, the set-apart, the extended, the imparted. (We can say the *finite* sense, on the condition of thinking that *finishing is delighting*.)

Corpus

There is not "the" body, there is not "the" touch, there is not "the" *res extensa*. There is that there is: creation of the world, *technē* of bodies, weighing without limits of sense, topographical *corpus*, geography of multiplied ectopias— and no u-topia.

No place beyond place for sense. If sense is "absent," it's by way of being here—*hoc est enim*—and not by way of being elsewhere and nowhere. *Absence-here*, that's the body, the extent of psyche. No place before birth or after death. No before/after: time *is* spacing. Time *is* the rising up and absenting, the coming-and-going into presence: it's not engendering, transmission, perpetuation. "Fathers" and "mothers" are other bodies; they aren't

la névrose, qui n'est qu'un accident très provisoire, même si nécessaire, de notre histoire, une difficulté à entrer dans ce temps du monde des corps). Pas de lieu pour un Autre des lieux, pas de trou, d'origine, pas de mystère phallomédusant.

Pas de lieu pour la Mort. Mais les lieux sont des corps morts: leurs espaces, leurs tombes, leurs masses étendues, et nos corps allant et venant entre eux, entre nous.

L'entre-les-corps ne réserve rien, rien que l'extension qu'*est* la *res* elle-même, la réalité aréale selon laquelle il arrive que les corps sont entre eux exposés. L'entre-les-corps est leur avoir-lieu d'images. Les images ne sont pas des semblants, encore moins des fantômes ou des fantasmes. C'est comment les corps sont offerts entre eux, c'est la mise au monde, la mise au bord, la mise en gloire de la limite et de l'éclat. Un corps est une image offerte à d'autres corps, tout un corpus d'images tendues de corps en corps, couleurs, ombres locales, fragments, grains, aréoles, lunules, ongles, poils, tendons, crânes, côtes, pelvis, ventres, méats, écumes, larmes, dents, baves, fentes, blocs, langues, sueurs, liqueurs, veines, peines et joies, et moi, et toi.

the place of an Other (as they are in neurosis, which is only a very provisional, even if necessary, accident in our history, a hardship of entering into this era of the world of bodies). No place for an Other of places, no hole, no origin, no phallomedusing mystery.

No place for Death. But places are dead bodies: their spaces, their tombs, their extended masses, and our bodies coming and going among them, among ourselves.

The between-bodies reserves nothing, nothing but the extension that *is* the *res* itself, the areal reality through which it happens that bodies are exposed to each other. The between-bodies is their images' taking-place. The images are not likenesses, still less phantoms or fantasms. It's how bodies are offered to one another, it's being born unto the world, the setting on edge, the setting into glory of limit and radiance. A body is an image offered to other bodies, a whole corpus of images stretched from body to body, local colors and shadows, fragments, grains, areolas, lunules, nails, hairs, tendons, skulls, ribs, pelvises, bellies, meatuses, foams, tears, teeth, droolings, slits, blocks, tongues, sweat, liquors, veins, pains, and joys, and me, and you.

On the Soul

Before starting, I'd like to say that, while I was on the way here yesterday, I was extremely troubled by the fact that I am taking part in a colloquium about the body just as the headlines of *Le Monde* are announcing the tortures and cruelties currently being committed in Bosnia. It's just that, I don't know how to put this, I'd like to give some thought to them before starting, to all those tortured, violated, wounded, humiliated bodies in Bosnia, at this very moment. And I'd add, for those bodies being denied their being as bodies.

I decided not to give a lecture in the form of a written and continuous text to be read, since the organizers offered us the possibility of an intervention to be recorded and subsequently transcribed. I prefer to leave room for a bit of improvising in my intervention, so as not to produce a *body effect*, precisely in Plato's sense when he says that a discourse is like a big animal, well organized, with a head, a tail, and a heart in the middle. I don't want to produce the effect of a closed or finite thing, because when we talk about the body we talk about something entirely opposed to the closed and the finite. With the body, we speak about something open and infinite, about the opening of closure itself, the infinite of the finite itself. That's what I want to try to develop: the body is the open. And in order for there to be an opening, something has to be closed, we have to touch upon closure. To touch on what's closed is already to open it. Perhaps there's only ever an opening by way of a touching or a touch. And to open—to touch—is not to tear, dismember, destroy.

We could start with this point: a closed, shut, full, total, immanent world, a world or a thing, whichever, so on its own and within itself that it wouldn't even touch itself, and we wouldn't either, a world alone to itself and in itself, wouldn't be a body. For me, this observation seems to suffice. Most of the time when we say "body," in opposition to "soul" or "mind" (or "spirit"), we have in mind something closed, full, on its own and in itself. If a closed-up body exists, if we can provide ourselves a kind of equivalent in the image of the inorganic, physical body—of a stone, for example (but perhaps even this is only an image; it isn't clear that a stone wouldn't be a body as *we* are a body)—if we suppose that there could be something of the sort, completely closed up in itself, to itself, I'd say that this isn't a body, it's a mass, however spiritual this mass might be: it can be purely spiritual (it's a certain image of God, for example). A mass is what is massed, gathered up in itself, penetrated with self and penetrated within itself such that, precisely, it's impenetrable. So there is nothing that articulates a mass to itself.

The mass is the impenetrable, in the sense of something penetrated without remainder or limit, thoroughly self-penetrating. The mass is also the absolute ground, which is at the ground and only there, grounded on its ground, completely. It's what's grounded [*se fonde*] in itself and *melts* [*fond*] into itself. In certain respects, it's something with a very long tradition in our philosophical thought, with a very simple name that everyone knows: the name is *substance*, that which is *under* something and no longer belongs to anything else. This is the definition of *substantia*, itself a term that translates Aristotle's *hypokeimenon*: what's under something and what, underneath a certain number of attributes or accidents, no longer belongs to anything other than itself. Substance, taken in this sense (because it's definitely more complicated in Aristotle, and undoubtedly in the whole philosophical tradition, as we shall shortly see), the substance of what we think of when we speak of "a substance," is what we think the body is. We often tend to think that the body is a substance, that something bodily is substantial. And opposed to this, or elsewhere, under another rubric, there would be something else—for example, something like the subject—that would not be substantial. I'd like to show that the body, if there is a bodily something, is not substantial but a subject. Let's keep this word for the moment and keep it simple. Substance—what for the moment I'm calling mass—has no *extension*. The true idea of substance is not even the stone, but the *point*, which has no dimension, in exactly the sense that Saint Augustine, who didn't much like extension and bodies—perhaps for having loved them too much in his early years—said that the body in general is a *tumor*, a tumor, an excrescence (he wasn't thinking of

tumor in its modern sense), a protuberance, which, "as such," is not "good." Only the point is "good," the self that is unto itself, without extension, which also means that it is without *exposition*.

That's the whole point: the body's a thing of extension. The body is a thing of exposition. It's not just that the body is exposed but that the body *consists* in being exposed. A body is being exposed. And to be exposed, it has to be extended, not perhaps in the sense of Descartes' *res extensa*, which we think of right away, a thing that's flat, mechanical, and absolutely deprived of soul or spirit (although we'll see that it's more complicated even for Descartes).

Let's start there: what isn't body is mass, or substance in the sense of mass, without extension, without exposition, a point. We can just as well call this spirit itself, spirit taken as concentration in itself, which we can call, in a still more terrible way, precisely, *concentration* as such. I need say no more. What concentration in itself means for us today is effectively the annihilation of bodies, the annihilation of the body as extension, of the body of which there are always several. Of the body, there's always *a lot*. There's always a *crowd* of bodies, there's never a *mass* of bodies. Where there's a mass of bodies, there's no more body, and where there's a mass of bodies, there's a mass grave. And this is concentration. It's one of those aspects of the corpse that we discussed this morning; it's the cadaver forming a mass. That's also why, when we want to discuss the body, we confront a major problem (which is why I didn't want to offer a seamless, polished text). In order to speak about the body, or, to put it in the Latin and professorial mode, to speak *de corpore* ("on the subject of the body"), we always have to speak about the body *ex corpore*: we should speak from the body, speaking should be projected out of the body—*ex corpore*, as in *ex cathedra*. A discourse of the body should always be a discourse *ex corpore*, coming out of the body, but also exposing the body, in such a way that the body would come out of itself. But I'd say this isn't the affair of discourse, as something that is *held*. On the contrary, the great temptation of thinking that we can hold a discourse adequate to the body, a discourse that would come "ex-corporate," project, cry, howl, sigh, and laugh the body, is naïve. It's an unavoidable temptation that at the same time is a thing that *ought to be*. I learned that at the opening of this colloquium you listened to Artaud's lecture "To be done with God's Judgment," one that I have heard elsewhere. And that's what's going on with Artaud: his lecture is truly a discourse "ex-corporated" and without naïveté, but we also see the limits of that discourse. It's not the business of discourse as such, as a discourse, merely to mime "ex-corporation." The issue is rather that discourse, which is necessarily in and of itself incorporeal, is also the

incorporeal. (This word comes from our tradition: for the stoics, everything is body except discourse, or what's said, the *lekton*, which is the "incorporeal.") The whole point about a discourse on the body is that the incorporeal of the discourse should nonetheless *touch* on the body.

But what's the touching of the incorporeal and the body? Necessarily, this has to do with a certain interruption of the one by the other. The incorporeal is necessarily interrupted when it touches on the body, and the body is necessarily interrupted, or open, when it touches upon, or as soon as it's touched by, the incorporeal. This is what is at stake. I mean that what is at stake is that a discourse on the body, of the body, is not simply "dis-corporated" like an object, like the object of an anatomy lesson; as Annie Le Brun showed us this morning, a discourse of the body or on the body is both touched by and touches upon something that isn't discourse at all. Which means quite simply that the body's discourse cannot produce a *sense* of the body, can't give sense to the body. Rather, it has to touch on what, from the body, interrupts the sense of discourse. That's the whole point. If this colloquium exists, and we're interested in the body today, it's because we sense, more or less obscurely, that the body of the body—the affair of the body, the affair of what we call body—has to do with a certain suspension or interruption of sense, which is where we are and is our current, modern, contemporary condition. Every day we put our finger on the fact that, concerning sense, there's no longer any available, in a certain mode of sense—some sense said, pronounced, enunciated, some incorporeal sense that would come to make sense of everything else. We are touching on a certain interruption of sense, and this interruption of sense has to do with the body, it is body. And it's no accident that the body has to do with sense, in the other sense of sense, sense in the sense of sensing, in the sense of touching. Touching on the interruption of sense is what, for my part, interests me in the matter of the body.

This is why I've called this lecture "On the Soul." Why this title? To begin with, certainly, it's a provocation. I've been asked to talk about the body, so I'm going to talk about the soul. But of course it isn't that simple, I ask you to credit me that. *On the soul*: because such a title causes an interruption, a rupture. But, to say it up front, *On the Soul* (*De anima*) is also the title of a very famous treatise by Aristotle. Now, in this treatise Aristotle talks only about the body. I'm now going to make use of this paradox. But first of all, to reassure you, in relation both to that silly provocation (or what could have been merely silly) and to the fear of hearing a Christian sermon, I'd say that, with the soul, there is, in effect, an effect of rupture, a rupture that is the body itself, in that the body can only

break with sense. In saying "of the soul," I simply wanted to indicate this: "of the soul" or "of the body outside the self." If the body isn't mass, if it isn't closed in on itself and penetrated by itself, it's outside itself. It is being outside itself. And this is what is at stake in the word *soul*. It in no way involves an understanding of the ineffable interiority behind this word, a sublime or vaporous identity escaping from the prison of the body. To put it in an extremely simplified way, it therefore has nothing whatsoever to do with the soul as it appears in the Platonic or Christian tradition, though this tradition itself is surely far more complex than it seems.

The premise of this proposition is therefore this: with the soul, it's not a matter of another spiritual body. In the whole of traditional iconography, we see the soul as a little person, a little angel with wings, exiting the mouth of a dying person and taking off. This states very clearly a certain representation of the soul. But it means that the soul is another body, simply a more subtle body, more aerian, a spiritual body, but another body—*something else*, if you will. What it ought to involve, on the contrary, is the fact that here, as with Aristotle, as with Saint Thomas, and, as we'll also see, with Spinoza and Descartes, surprising as this may seem, the soul, in all these "figures" of our tradition, doesn't represent *anything other* than the body, but rather the body outside itself, or this other that the body is, structurally, for itself and in itself. We have to talk about the soul, even if this gives rise to all sorts of ambiguities (it's true that beyond today's intervention, I won't necessarily remain attached to this word *soul*), if "on the soul" means: "on the body's relation with itself," insofar as it is a relation to the outside—being out.

The soul is the body's difference from itself, the relation to the outside that the body is for itself. In other words, and this allows me to return to Aristotle, the soul is the difference from itself that makes the body, what Aristotle declares by defining the soul as the *form* of a living body. The soul is not specifically human, even if the human soul has its proper characteristics. Here it therefore has to do with the soul of every organized living body. The soul is the form of a body. We have to understand that the form is not an exterior in relation to an interior. What would a body without form be? I hinted at this just now: it would be a mass, a pure substance. The form of a body is above all the body itself. If there is a body, it has a form—but even this is poorly stated, given that this verb *to have* makes us think of a certain exteriority of form in connection with the body. The body is the form. If there's indeed a thing that our whole climate of modern thought makes us think about directly, it's that the

form of a body—my body—is nothing other than the body; it's not an exterior aspect in relation to which there'd be an interior.

The form of a body is the body itself, insofar as it is not mass, or formless mass, or pure punctuality. Without wishing to be provocative, I'd say that a body, insofar as it is a form, is what is neither shit nor spirit. Shit and spirit are the excretions of the body, what the body rejects, even if rejecting and expelling are essential to the functioning of a body. But in expelling, the body gives itself form. Thus the form of the body is not the opposite of matter. There isn't, to begin with, the body's matter and something that would then come and give it its exterior appearance, because then the material would itself be the formless and we could ask: But what's the meaning of the form of the formless? We're accustomed to manipulating the couple form-matter, but if we notice that it signifies the form of the formless, we understand, strictly speaking, that it's meaningless. The form of the body doesn't mean the form of a material that would be a body, of a material that would be exterior to the form—this is nothing but excrement—but signifies, on the contrary, the body insofar as it is form, essentially form, in other words, *body*. Form means that body is articulated, not in the sense of the articulation of members but as the relation to something other than itself. The body is a relation to another body—or a relation to itself. This Aristotelian form has another name, which is at the midpoint between the three big instances of the organic body, the merely living (vegetal), the sensory (animal), and the human (which, in addition to being alive and sensory, is also thinking). The term common to these three instances is *sensing*, and this is the term for the body as form in Aristotle. The soul as form of the body—which is not the beautiful form according to the aesthetics of the moderns—signifies that the body is what is *sensing*. The body senses and is sensed. At this very moment, the body's matter, for Aristotle, is nothing other than its form. He literally says that we can't distinguish matter and form. The matter of the body is sensing matter. And the form of the body is the sensing of this matter. At most, we can say that matter designates the impenetrability of form. If I penetrate the form of a body, I destroy it, I dissolve it as form and then make it into a mass, a rotting or a mass grave. If we wish to keep the word *matter*, then we should say that it's the impenetrability of what is form—in other words, relation, articulation, and therefore, yet again, the relation between sensing, sensing oneself, being sensed, and sensing something as from the outside.

The last definition of the soul that Aristotle gives, further along in his development, is the following: the soul is the primal *entelechy* of a natural organized body. "Entelechy" means being accomplished with regard to

its end (*telos*). Entelechy is a thing's being completely achieved. Which means two things. First, the soul is the ensemble of form-matter (but we shouldn't put it that way: there isn't matter on one side and form on the other—the one takes place only through the other, and as the other), the soul as the entelechy of a body is this body as a complex, as a whole—as a body, finally! The entelechy of a body is thus the fact that the body is matter as form, and form as matter—a sensing. Second, the true entelechy for Aristotle in general, and this is very important for us, is always the *individual*, a word heavy today with many moral and political ambiguities. Entelechy doesn't aim at the *notion* of the body, but *a* body. The soul as entelechy of a body means this body, and this body is *this one here*. There is no body other than that of a "this one," and we should immediately add that "this one" is often feminine. Singular determination is essential to the body. We can't define a body as sensing and as relation if we don't define it at the same time by this indefinable fact of its being each time a singular body—this body here and not another. It is only on the condition of having this body here and not another that this body here can *sense itself* as a body and sense others. The soul as the *first entelechy of a natural organized body* (*Of the Soul*, 412b) is not some thing but the fact that there is a body, its *existence*. We can accentuate this word, as Heidegger has done, by saying *ex*-istence. The soul is the presence of the body, its position, its "stance," its "sistence" as being *out-side* (ex). The soul is the fact that a body exists, in other words, that there is extension and exposition. It is therefore offered, presented open to the outside. A body touches on the outside, but at the same time (and this is more than a correlation, it's a co-appurtenance), it touches itself as outside. A body accedes to itself as outside.

Have you already encountered yourself as pure spirit? No. This means that you are like me, that we only gain access to ourselves from outside. I am an outside for myself. This isn't simply through the fact, long recognized and repeated, that the eye doesn't see itself, that the face is something *turned* to the exterior and that we never see it, that we never appropriate not only the face but also the whole body. This is what skin is. It's through my skin that I touch myself. And I touch myself from outside, I don't touch myself from inside. There are some celebrated analyses by Husserl and Merleau-Ponty on this question of "self-touching," of my own hands' "self-touching." But curiously—and this comes up over and over again in the whole tradition—everything always returns in interiority. The phenomenological analyses of "self-touching" always return to a primary interiority. Which is impossible. To begin with, I have to be in exteriority in order to touch myself. And what I touch remains

on the outside. I am exposed to myself touching myself. And therefore—but this is the difficult point—the body is always outside, on the outside. It is from the outside. The body is always outside the intimacy of the body itself. Why do we always speak of the intimacy of the body? The only veritable intimacy of the body is in silence. This is Bichat's definition of health: health is life in the silence of the organs, when I don't sense my stomach, my heart, or my viscera. There's an intimacy there, but an intimacy that is merely not there, not sensible, it's of the order of the mass. But when I sense my stomach or my heart, or my lung, I sense it, and if I sense it, it's from the outside. That's what I'd want to have understood by "soul": by this name that, for us, symbolizes the other of the body, through this couple, which generally expresses a couple of exteriority, of contrariety, of opposition and negation, I'd like something else to be understood, which departs from this Platonic and Christian tradition but which would not simply and purely be something else. I don't want to speak of a body without a soul, any more than of a soul without a body. It's not a matter of reconstituting a pure immanence, because that would be, as I've said, the mass, or excrement. No, instead it has to do with trying to make use of the word *soul* as a lever to help us understand this outside of the body, this outside that the body is *for itself*. The soul is the being outside of a body, and it is in this being outside that it has its inside.

Without wishing to bore you with philosophical technicalities, I'll confirm this idea by appealing to Spinoza, when he says that the soul is the idea of the body. (Here we should remember that, when Aristotle says that the soul is the form of the body, he uses the word *eidos*, which gives us the word "idea.") We might get the impression of ending up back in a simple dualism: the soul is the idea of the body, something of which we have an idea, a representation, an image. But in fact, not at all. See how this works in Spinoza: to say that the soul is the idea of the body means, more precisely, that it's the idea that God has of the body, of my body or of every body. What's God for Spinoza? God is the unique substance. There's nothing else. The unique substance for Spinoza is not a mass, it is in itself double: it is thought and extension—the two being co-extensive and parallel to one another. And this very duality is God. Which is why, from that point on, we can forget God—Spinoza has been more than abundantly treated as an atheist, and, I think, rightly so. Let's forget God, then. The idea of the body is the idea, the vision and form of something that is both an expanse and an extension—insofar as this expanse or this extension is not merely exterior to the idea but visible or sensible in itself and as a form of itself. The body is linked to the soul, which is its idea. So the idea of the body is the soul's idea of itself, the form of self as it can

be seen or sensed in general by itself and as itself. In other words, I'd say, very quickly, and using Spinoza's terms: God sees himself as *this* body, mine, yours. And, for Spinoza, God doesn't see himself as anything else. If God is the thought of extension, it's because he's the extension of thought. Which enables Spinoza to utter this famous sentence: "I feel I'm eternal." What does this mean? "I feel I'm eternal" in no way signifies that I feel that I last forever—how could I feel such a thing? "Eternal" doesn't mean sempiternal—Spinoza is very precise on this point. It doesn't mean that I last indefinitely. To sense that I last all the time, I'd have to last *the whole time*, waiting for time. No. Eternity is of the order of necessity. If I feel I'm eternal, this means that I feel I'm necessary. This means that in my body, or rather, as my body, as my body itself, along the extension and exposition of my body, God (or substance) feels itself necessary. In consequence, we understand that God feels and knows himself to be necessary in his contingency. To say that my body is eternal doesn't mean that it's sempiternal or immortal.

That's the complete schema of what I'd like to say: for Aristotle or Spinoza, the soul—or at least the fact that we have had recourse to a word other than the word *body* and that the word *soul* was chosen—signifies that *the body is what knows or senses it is necessary in its contingency*. The body is only this singular body, but this singularity is felt and sensed as necessary, as irreplaceable, as irreplaceable exposition. That's what the body is. And we can complete this with Descartes, as surprising as that may seem. We're used to thinking that the body, for Descartes, is geometrical extension, the thing extended—there's only figure and movement—and then there's the thinking thing, the famous *cogito* which is completely and entirely of itself and in itself. In the *Second Meditation*, when Descartes sets out the celebrated imaginary experiment of a piece of wax, he writes that a piece of wax has a figure, a color, that tapping it yields a sound. Then, when we heat it up, it melts, it loses all its qualities, and, to the mind's view, to the *inspectio mentis*, there's nothing left but extension. In this reading, we seem to have, quite clearly, on the one hand, pure extension and, on the other, pure cogitation, an outside-the-self completely pure and an inside-the-self completely pure. We could already very simply ask: how are they related to one another? How does one touch the other? And that's just it: *they touch one another*. It's in Descartes' text. The wax that melts loses its color, its smell, it no longer yields a sound, and then the author hesitates: "we touch it *just barely* if at all," *just barely* because he can't say that we don't touch it any more. Of course, we always touch the wax. Since it's been melted, we might be under the impression

that we can't touch it because it's burning hot—but we can get burned, we always have to get burned in order to touch.

For Descartes, thought is sensing, and as sensing, it touches upon the extended thing, it's touching extension. We can say, to refine the analysis, that this barely but still touching, this sensing that still remains as touching, is the asymptote of seeing. Descartes seems to suppress the sight of the piece of wax: there's no more figure, no more color, but we certainly see something. This seeing is a touching. For Descartes himself, the famous *ego* (which I'm now using in place of the soul) is only *ego* by virtue of being outside itself, by touching the wax. And therefore, to put it in an arrogant way, I'm claiming to show that, for Descartes, the *res cogitans* is a body. Descartes knows this very well. At this point, we should develop everything he says about the union of the soul and the body, which is evidence as strong as that of the *ego sum* itself. *Ego* is being outside with reference to the *ego*. *Ego* is also being a body. A body is sensing, but sensing such that there's no sensing that wouldn't be a "sensing one's self." To sense, we have to sense ourselves sensing—this is also a proposition of Aristotle that we find in the *On the Soul*. Body means very precisely the soul that feels it's a body. Or: the soul is the name of the sensing of the body. We could say it with other pairs of terms: the body is the ego that senses itself to be other than ego. We could say it by using all the figures of the self's interiority facing exteriority: time, which is sensed as space; necessity, which is felt as contingency; sex, which is felt as another sex. The formula that sums up this thought would be: the inside, which senses it is outside.

That's what the body is. This means we shouldn't say, or we should try to stop saying, that being body, the body self, the being to itself of a body, the relation to self as a sensing oneself outside, as an inside that feels it is outside—we should say not that this is the property of a subject or of an ego, but that it *is* the "Subject." And even "subject" is extremely fragile, since we should say, not that "I," body, am touched and touch in turn—that I'm sensed—but rather try to say (and this is the whole difficulty) that "I" is a touch.

"I" is nothing other than the singularity of a touch, of a touch that is always at once active and passive, and that, as a touch, evokes something punctual—a touch in the sense of a touch of color, in the sense of a pianist's touch, and, why not?, in the sense of the old argot, when we would say that we put the touch on someone (scoring . . .). The unity of a body, its singularity, is the unity of a touch, of all the touches (of all the touchings) of this body. And it's this unity that can make a self, an identity. But it's not a matter of a self, an identity or a subject as the interior of an

exterior. It's not, in accordance with the old image that we've dragged along since the beginning of philosophy, about a very ugly Socrates who's very beautiful inside: interiority, the inside; subjectivity as incommensurable with exteriority, extension, and exposition. No, it's a matter of a "one," and a "some*one*," of the unity or singularity of what I in effect really want us to keep calling an identity, an ego, a self, a subject, provided that the subjectivity of this subject is clearly understood as a being outside the self, as a "self-sensing," but as a "self-sensing" that is exactly not a being posed by oneself and an appropriating of oneself to oneself in a pure interiority, but a being in exteriority in relation to itself. We sense ourselves as an outside. This is not just a question of the hands, but basically concerns the sense of existence. Kant wrote, in a note to the *Prolegomena* (a note to paragraph 46), that the "self" is without substance and without concept, that it is "only sentiment of an existence" (*Gefühl eines Daseins*). Furthermore, Kant doesn't put the article with *Gefühl*, he doesn't say a sentiment, or the sentiment, but "self" is sentiment of an existence. "Self" is sensing an existence. If we develop Kant's formula rigorously, sensing an existence doesn't mean that a self senses an existence outside itself, as of a table, say. Existence is what's sensed as existence. This doesn't mean that there's a little subject back behind, sensing itself as existence. There's no longer a subject "back behind." There's only a "self-sensing," as a relation to self as outside. And that's what being one's self is. Self being is necessarily being outside, on the outside, being exposed or extended. This is what Heidegger tries to make the word *Dasein* ("existence") say: *Dasein* is being the there (*da*).

With the body, it's only a question of this: how is it that *I* am the there. When we say "I'm here," we presuppose that there's an exterior place that the "I," an unassignable interiority, would come to occupy—as soon as we say this, we involve ourselves in enormous difficulties, because how can "I," which has no place, come into a place? It's the mystery of the incarnation. But that's just it, we can in no way think the body in terms of incarnation. I am speaking not only of the Christian dogma of incarnation, where that which is without place, without exteriority, without form, without matter (God) comes into flesh, but of the incarnation that is the model (itself Christian, in effect) of all our thought on the subject. This idea of incarnation is impossible: what does it mean that something without place would come to occupy a place? It isn't a question, then, of being there. Rather, it has to do, following a perhaps impenetrable formula in Heidegger, with "being the there"—exactly in the sense that when a subject appears, when a baby is born, there's a new "there." Space, extension in general, is extended and opened. The baby is nowhere else

but *there*. It isn't in a sky, out of which it has descended to be incarnated. It's spacing; this body is the spacing of a "there." Thereafter, things do indeed become more complex: the "there" itself is not simply there; it isn't there as a geometrical point, an intersection or a marker on a geographical map. The "there" itself is made only of opening and exposition.

When we want to talk about the body, we need to break with a certain reflex. We spontaneously think of body *against* soul. The body is considered as physical, material, carnal reality. I'm disturbed by certain discourses of the body that either adopt "bodybuilding" and reduce it to Schwarzenegger or else, very subtly, very underhandedly, turn the body into a soul in the traditional sense: the signifying body, the expressive body, the orgasmic body, the suffering body, etc. In saying this, we put the body in the place of the soul or the spirit. Very curiously, I believe that a provisional reflex is necessary. We have to do justice to the ugly Cartesian dualism, Platonic and Christian in origin, that opposes the soul to the body, because we won't respond to the injunction that comes to us in the form of a body if, as contraband and in the name of a "unity" of soul and body, we put the soul back in the place of the body. At any rate, when we speak about the body, we are soon all too ready to reject, to "excrete" something (bad, "material" . . .), by denouncing, for example, the "objectified body." Machines are reputed to be inhuman, soulless, and bad for the body, even though at the same time we're quite content to use them. In wanting to keep a "good," "signifying" body, we reproduce the same schema of the exclusion of the body by the soul. Through the appeal or injunction of what falls under the name of *body*, we must first of all— and I say this as something of a provocation, but not merely so—restore something of the dualism, in the precise sense that we have to think that the body is not a monist unity (as opposed to the dualist vision), having the immediacy and self-immanence with which we earlier endowed the soul.

The body is the unity of a being outside itself. Here, I abandon the word *dualism*, and I also don't say that this is the unity of a duality. The provocative recourse to the word *dualism* lasts only for a second. After that, it becomes instead a question of thinking the unity of being outside the self, the unity of the coming to self as a "self-sensing," a "self-touching" that necessarily passes through the outside—which is why I can't sense myself without sensing otherness and without being sensed by the other. It involves thinking the unity of what a little earlier I called articulation, unity as a form, which is inevitably an articulation. Then what we were calling "soul" (and we can perhaps try to dispense with this word, which is all very heavy anyway) is exactly what makes this *being*

outside, not this being on the outside, but this *being outside without inside that completely forms the inside*—or all *being to self*. The soul is the extension or the expanse of the body. Therefore one has to give it back its rights to extension, even Cartesian extension, even *partes extra partes*, not necessarily as a way to reduce it to the simple position of geometrical points one outside the other, but to give every right to the *extra*, the being outside of, and to ex-tension. And after having insisted on the "ex" of extension, we should think *tension* as such. What makes for an extension? Tension does. But an extension is also an in-tension, in the sense of an intensity. And it's perhaps precisely here that the subject of an intention disappears, in the phenomenological sense of that word, in the sense of an intentional aiming at an object—an aiming that, charged with sense, will endow my perception of an object with sense. For that kind of intentionality, we should substitute intensity, extension in the sense of a tension of the outside as such.

A body is therefore a tension. And the Greek origin of the word is *tonos*, "tone." A body is a tone. I don't say anything here that an anatomist couldn't agree with: a body is a tonus. When the body is no longer alive, has no more tonus, it either passes into *rigor mortis* (cadaverous rigidity), or into the inconsistency of rotting. Being a body is being a certain *tone*, a certain tension. I'd also even say that a tension is also a *tending*. Consequently, there are possibilities for ethical developments that we might perhaps not expect to find here.

I'm going to conclude with a few words that will try to pull together the results of this very minimal analysis. If we've talked about the soul, if our entire tradition has spoken, and in various ways, about the soul, it's because, for good or ill, and partly in spite of itself, it has thought, not in the soul alone but in the *difference* between body and soul, the difference that the body *is* in itself, for itself—this difference in tension, in extension, in a certain tone of the outside. And what's been thought under the name of *soul* is nothing other than the experience of the body. It's simple, and it's on the textual surface of the whole tradition. What's the soul, if not the experience of the body, not as an experience among others, but as the sole experience? The whole of experience is there, *in nuce*, in the experience of the body—in the experience that the body is. The soul is a name for the experience that the body *is*. *Experiri*, in Latin, is precisely going outside, leaving without a destination, crossing through something without knowing whether we will return from it. A body is what pushes to the limit, blindly, while groping, hence while touching. Experience of what? Experience of "self-sensing," of touching upon the self. But touching upon the self is the experience of touching on what is untouchable in a

certain way, since "self-touching" is not, as such, something that can be touched. The body is the experience of indefinitely touching on the untouchable, but in the sense that the untouchable is not anything that would be back behind, anything interior or inside, or a mass, or a God. The untouchable is the fact that it touches. We can also use another word to say this: what touches, what we're touched by, is on the order of *emotion*. Emotion is a very weak word for us, but emotion means: set in movement, in motion, shaken, affected, breached. We can add another word as well, which is perhaps too spectacular: *commotion*. This word has the advantage of introducing "with" (*cum*). Commotion is being set in motion with. What we have thought under the name *soul* for some time is not the emotion or commotion of the body, the body as emotion or commotion. In a sense, this implies such an exposition to the outside, such a being outside, such an *experiri* of the outside or as the outside, that it inevitably introduces something that always induces the word *soul*, a kind of placing in inferiority, a placing of the body as waste or refuse. This is precisely what should be, not gathered up (which would imply a valorization of the waste or refuse of the body), but understood.

We have to understand that outside all the gestures of valorization, hierarchization, and evaluation that have been attached, by a whole huge tradition, to the subordination of the body, to its submission, and even to its abjection, beyond all these indices of *de*valorization, there is, in effect, in the body as such, as "self-sensing," a structure of being set outside, such that we cannot speak of the body without speaking about it as an *other*, an other indefinitely other, indefinitely outside. Which means that without refusing it or disposing of it as waste, we must also not reanimate and reincorporate it as if *it* were the soul. Which is what I find very well articulated in the title of this colloquium: *The Weight of the Body*. We don't think the body if we don't think of it as weighing. And if the body is weighing, it must weigh with all its weight and impart its full measure (a weight is a measure), and this measure is always the measure of an outside, a measure that is not allowed to revert to the unitary measure of the inside or the interior. The weight of the body has to weigh to the point that it becomes impossible to sublimate this weight, to animate it, to spiritualize it—in a word, to withdraw it from its outside. I wanted to make us a little more sensitive to this weight of the body by speaking, as if for one last time, about the soul as the experience of the body.

The Extension of the Soul

Let's begin by reading a long passage from the letter that Descartes wrote to Elizabeth on June 28, 1643, which undoubtedly constitutes his major text on the knowledge of the union of soul and body.

> Metaphysical thoughts that exercise the pure understanding make the notion of the soul familiar to us; and the study of mathematics, which exercises primarily the imagination in thinking about shapes and movements, gets us accustomed to forming very distinct notions of body. Finally, it is only by using our lived experience and ordinary interactions, and by abstaining both from meditation and from studying things that use the imagination, that one learns to conceive the union of the soul and the body.
>
> I am almost afraid that Your Highness may think that I am not speaking seriously here; but that would be contrary to the respect I owe you, which I would never fail to show. I can also say truthfully that the main rule that I followed in my study—and the rule that I believe has helped me most to acquire some knowledge—is that I never gave more than very few hours a day to thoughts that occupy the imagination, and very few hours a year to thoughts that occupy the understanding on its own; I spent all the rest of my time in relaxing the senses and reposing my mind. I even include, among the uses of the imagination, all serious conversations and everything that requires attention. This is what made me retire to the country;

for although, in the busiest city of the world, I could have had as many hours' study as I currently enjoy, I could not spend them as usefully if my mind was distracted by the attention required by the ordinary business of daily life. I take the liberty of writing to Your Highness here that I genuinely admire the fact that, among the cares and business which are never absent in the case of people who, simultaneously, are of noble birth and have great minds, you have been able to find time for the meditations that are required to know the distinction between mind and body.

But I thought that, more than thoughts that require less attention, these meditations were responsible for making you find obscure the notion we have of the union of mind and body, because it seemed to me that the human mind is incapable of conceiving very distinctly, and simultaneously, both the distinction and union of body and soul. The reason is that, in order to do so, it would be necessary to conceive of them as two things—which is self-contradictory. Assuming that Your Highness still retains a vivid memory of the reasons that prove the distinction of the soul and body, and not wishing to ask you to get rid of them in order to conceive of the union that everyone constantly experiences in themselves without philosophizing—viz. of being a single person who has a body and thought together, and being of such a nature that thought can move the body and can sense the changes that occur in it—I therefore used an analogy above with heaviness and with the other qualities that we commonly imagine are united with certain bodies, for the way in which thought is united with our body. I was not worried that this analogy might be defective on account of the fact that these qualities are not real, as they are imagined to be, because Your Highness was already completely convinced that the soul is a substance which is distinct from the body.

However, since Your Highness suggested that it is easier to attribute matter and extension to the soul than to attribute to the soul the ability to move, and to be moved by, a body without having any matter itself, I beseech you to take the liberty to attribute this matter and extension to the soul, for that is nothing more than conceiving of its union with the body. Having conceived of that union properly and having experienced it in yourself, you will find it easy to think that the matter that you have attributed to this thought is not the thought itself and that the extension of this matter has a different nature from the extension of thought, in this sense: the former is determined to a certain place from which it excludes every other

bodily extension, whereas this does not apply in the latter case. In this way Your Highness will easily recover your knowledge of the distinction between the soul and the body, despite the fact that you conceive of their union.

Finally, although I think that it is very necessary to have understood well, once in a lifetime, the principles of metaphysics because they provide us with knowledge of God and our soul, I also think that it would be very harmful to occupy one's understanding frequently in thinking about them because the understanding would find it difficult to leave itself free for using the imagination and the senses. It is best to be satisfied with retaining in one's memory and one's belief the conclusions that have once been drawn from the principles of metaphysics, and to devote one's remaining study time to those thoughts in which the understanding acts together with the imagination and the senses.[1]

꒰꒱

The union of body and soul is thus conceived through the activity of ordinary life, and not through thought and imagination as isolated faculties. It's conceived "without philosophizing," and anyone can so conceive it. The evidence for this union works just like the evidence for "*ego sum*," which also had to be accessible to anyone's mind. The union is an object of evidence, analogous to the evidence of each of the substances it unites. The modality of this evidence differs by virtue of the fact that it's "experienced" rather than thought or figured. Not only is there a union but it has its own mode of evidence and certitude, its own mode of distinction, which is the distinction of the indistinct. But the structure of the evidence remains identical in this evidence: the known and the knowing are intermixed or separated from one another through a link of the same to the same. Thought thinks itself thinking, imagination pictures extended figures for itself, and union is experienced in the inattention of an activity that feels itself acting, and acted upon, without thinking about it. Moreover, thoughts of metaphysics and imaginings of mathematics should, once acquired and committed to memory, merely open the way to study, where the three registers of knowing are employed together and are therefore able to contribute to a knowledge that will itself be an active knowledge of ordinary life and of the mastery and possession of nature. The evidence of the union is the moment when the mind, endowed as it is with truth's certain foundations, and able to turn itself toward action, stops turning back on itself. Truth, here, is not an end but a means for this more ample, ever-moving truth, which is the usage of life and the world.

In acting this way, the evidence of union is offered in some fashion on two sides or in two moments—a fact that is congruent with the nature of its content, at once single and double. In one of its aspects, in effect, this evidence belongs to the order of obscurity, to the indistinction and internal contrariety of an antinomic conception; but under another of its aspects it is very certain and very clear by virtue of being what one "experiences in oneself," as Descartes puts it twice in a few lines. What we experience in ourselves is the self united with the self just as the body is united with the soul, since this union is the only place where "a single person who has a body and soul together" is present, in such a way that this ensemble makes it possible for the body to make itself felt in thought and for thought to make itself the driver of the body.

What, then, is this clear-obscure, passive-active ensemble, which is the ensemble of a *self* completely present to itself, present in itself and for itself, and of a *self* at once another and the same, extended out of the self, sensing the world and also sensing itself there, with this evidence whose certainty is proportional to its inattention to the self?

When the union is conceived, what's inconceivably conceived? Is it an object or a subject of knowledge? First of all, who knows? Assuredly not thought, which knows only itself or objects. Might it be the body? Certainly not, because the body doesn't know; it only senses. Sensing, however, is one mode of thought, at least insofar as an ego relates to itself in the body, as much as it does in conception, imagination, or will. The body knows itself as a soul, or as intimately united with soul. But the soul thus knows itself as what is extended, not across the body but along the body's extension. So the soul should be recognized as having an extension that is linked to the whole extension of the body, though without sharing the character of the impenetrability and exclusion of extended places. The soul is extended right along what is extended, not as a content in a container (nor as a pilot in a ship) but as the extension of the unextended, through which the thing extended (or the body) is known in its union with the unextended.

This is precisely not a form of knowledge: it's an obscure evidence whose obscurity makes for certitude. It's not a matter here of thinking a "body proper," which would, in fact, be only a figure of the soul, alone knowing itself properly through an extended figure. It's the opposite: the unextended soul is given over to an extension that is improper to it, and its union with this impropriety is what it conceives without conceiving and what it conceives as inconceivable.

When I struggle or breathe, when I digest or suffer, fall or jump, sleep or sing, I know myself only as being what struggles or sings, grimaces or

scratches itself; that, and not that person, or at any rate not as an ego distinct from every other thing. That, then, instead of this one, or this one who is only that.

That which knows, therefore, is nothing other than that which is known, but what's known in this way is the fact that these are two distinct things in a single indistinction. The more effective this identity is, the more indistinct it is, and the less there is to know, properly speaking. The less, therefore, is there also knowledge of a "body proper," since the instance of propriety has evaporated. I can't introduce this instance—a "self" able to say "my body" or "I am my body"—without keeping the body at a distance, distinct and disunited. And so I weaken the evident knowledge of the union.

This doesn't mean that this evidence would be an immediate immersion in the supposedly intimate density of the union, represented as a presence to self comparable to the impenetrable in itself, which defines matter, as well as to the absolute penetration in itself and in everything pertaining to the mind. For the union would then be only the improbable penetration of the impenetrable, conceived as a being in itself. But what it isn't, and what it makes, is indeed the penetration of the impenetrable. Evidence, here, is the very penetration of this penetration, but it therefore is not the conception of a presence in itself.

Whatever its nature, a substantial presence can be only a negation of presence as of the self, of presence in itself as to itself. For a presence is nothing if it's not somehow a setting before—*prae-sentia*—an ex-position, and a self is nothing if not, at its heart (the heart of a self is its very self), apart from and touching on itself, a pulsing of self to self, by which the "same" decomposes the "self" that we would have thought to be posed and supposed.

From this it follows that the evidence of the union, far from being a reply and a retort to the evidence of the mind and extension—as certain apologies for the "body" or certain approaches to "flesh" would have us understand—is evidence of a different order. It's neither "evident" nor "clear and distinct," and it cannot relate to itself as the self-grounded certitude of an *inspectio mentis*. And, in the fact, it's a fact subject not to "inspection" but to an "exercise," or a "test."

Its proper modality pertains to its content. This is the substantial union. This signifies, first of all, that it is not a third substance: if that were so, given that a substance relates only to itself, it would be impossible for this one to have the slightest relation to the other two. Yet the union is precisely the relation between the two substances.

But the union does not unite the two substances accidentally: it is, precisely, substantial.[2] Or we could say that it enacts the substantiality of an accident.[3]

The union unites substances: it is neither substance nor accident; it is neither a thing nor the quality or property of a thing (unless it's the property of the union as a property shared by the two substances). It depends on another order: not that of *res* but that of relation. But this relation is very specific: it is neither inclusion nor inherence, neither dependence nor causality, neither disjunction nor exclusion, without, however, being reduced to contiguity or proximity, which are no longer relations (except as relations "of proximity"). It is as if distinct from all these modes, which it nonetheless also includes.

It forms a pertaining of each substance to the other, such that it is not a matter of the assumption or subsumption of one by the other but rather of the susceptibility of one to the other. The soul can be touched by the body, and the body by the soul.

From the one to the other, there is touch: a contact that communicates while leaving both the two *res* intact. Touch, for Descartes, always touches the impenetrable: but the mind, "mixed, so to speak, with the body," "is touched by the vestiges imprinted in it." Wherever they touch each other, the mind and the body are impenetrable to one another and, by virtue of that fact, are united. Touch makes contact between two intacts.

What touch communicates is not *res* (or *réal*) but of the order of touch, which itself is real without being *réal*: it's an impulsion or a drive, a pressure, an impression or expression, an unhinging. The union is made in the order of the movement: it is that in which, or as which, one of the soul's movements is transmitted to the body, or one of the body's movements to the soul.

Movements of the soul are of the order of thought, in other words, of the relation to self: an ego is related to itself in this movement, in the mode of sensing or conceiving, imagining or wishing. In a broad sense, and staying with the terminology of the *motum*, we could say that these movements are e-motions. Emotion is the percussion of an ego that is altered or affected by itself. At the same time, all e–motion presupposes an egological auto-affection or cogitatio, which is the co-agitation of the ego, announced in the doubling, indeed in the e-moted stuttering, of *ego sum, ego existo*.

Movements of the body are of the order of local transport: they go from one place to another. In itself, extension is outside itself: distance between places, *partes extra partes*, figures and movements (the figures

themselves being the effect of a movement that traces them). Let's say, broadly, that all movements of the body are extensions: settings outside itself of the pure coincidence of self, which is here the definition of the point and which is the negative of extension. Extension is the negation of this punctual negativity (but the latter denies a previous movement, the tracing of the two perpendicular lines that divide at the point).

ॐ

From the preceding, two inferences follow.

1. The analysis of the union as a union of movements (motor or mobilizing union) confirms the reciprocal independence of the substances. Every *cogitatio* presupposes itself *cogito*, and every *extensio* presupposes itself *extenditur*. I think on one side, and it's extended on the other, and I always think "I," in one way or another, as extension itself is extended. Each substance is first and last for itself.

2. The union is therefore one of emotion and extension, which are two heterogeneous presuppositions. It's the touching of two mobilities, or rather, it's the mobility or motility proper to touching: a contact of intacts.

At a point (it's the pineal gland, seat of incessant agitation), the two movements touch each other in the same movement. There, the incorporeal is corporeal, and reciprocally so. This is not a transubstantiation but a communication (though we could, undoubtedly, seek to identify the two). This communication extends emotion and moves ex-tension. Now this double movement is nothing but the duality comprised in the identity of a same *e* or *ex*, which is the prefix for both emotion and extension. The union is the unique and double operation of an ex-position that is like the same motoric property of the two substances. The union, if one may say so, is a re-union, which would have to be understood as an ex-union or as a union exogenous in and of itself . . .

This provides a better approach to the evidence we ex-perience. It's a knowledge that is not distinguished from its object and, for that very reason, is not at all distinguished, but in-distinguishes itself to the extent of its ex-perience. It is simultaneously and indistinctly emotive and extensive. Whenever I know myself in this way, I am moved by my knowledge, just as I extend this knowledge to the things in which it is invested, like the beating of my heart, the attachment of a nail, or the gray tint and granulated surface of a table on which my hand is resting. I know myself as a beating, nail, tint, and surface. Which is to say that I know all these extensions of ego, which is moved by this, and that I reciprocally know the egoity of these extensions: the latter is called a world, in the contemporary if not the Cartesian sense of the word. A world is a totality of

extended emotion and moving extension: in other words, a totality of ex-position, which we can also name "sense," in the sense that "sense" is here precisely the sharing of the ex: that which is in itself refers to the self as outside the self—but this outside is precisely the inside of the world, which consists only in this exposition, which we understand (without dis-tinguishing it) as the indistinctly corporeal and incorporeal movement of that which is extended in an indissociable double sense: which is endlessly divided into impenetrable *partes extra partes* and which endlessly pene-trates and is penetrated as *extra*-position in itself. The *extra* of the impene-trable parts is here confounded with the *existo*: ex-ist, being *ex*, is to be exposed according to corporeal exteriority, it is to be in the world, and, in a more radical fashion, is being world.

Being world does not mean being immanent to oneself: to the con-trary, it means being outside oneself. It means being an extended sense: we should say that the sense of the world gets confused with the extension of the world, with no possible appeal to another world or to an outer world, but we should also say, indistinctly, that the sense of the world is outside the world.[4] This indistinct identity, which is also that of the evi-dence in which its knowledge is exposed and im-posed, is ex-perienced in its confused proof and is therefore the identity of the inside and the outside.

But the identity of the outside and the inside does not effectuate the resorption of one substance into another: it effectuates, on the contrary, very precisely, the exposition of the one to the other as the exposition of the world to itself and therefore as the necessity of comprehending sense (or truth) as this exposition itself—and consequently, too, insofar as it cannot simply be called "itself." For it is, in itself, different from itself: it is distinct from itself in its indistinction.

What we so often designate Cartesian "dualism" can therefore be un-derstood as entirely different from an ontological cut between body and soul. It is just as much, and may be even more, an ontology of the "be-tween," of the swerve or exposition by which alone something like a "sub-ject" can emerge. A subject that would henceforth have two fundamental characteristics: that of not being substance and that of being exposed to other subjects. These two characteristics are in turn the internal division of the *ex*—which makes for the motoricity and mobility of the union. A world of subjects can only be a world in internal expansion along this double line of ex-position, and thus a common and insubstantial world, common by virtue of its insubstantiality—in other words, common by the ontological impossibility of a common substance (no more common

to all subjects than common to the subject and to itself). This impossibility alone opens the possibility, the chance, and the risk of being in the world.

ॐ

When I look at extension—the spilled wax spread without quality—and when the extension is extended to my eyes, then an emotion and an extension touch one other. Without this contact, my *inspectio mentis* would see nothing, and the extension wouldn't extend to my *mens*. The mind is then moved, in its very *inspectio*, even into extension, and the latter is extended all the way to the mind, through all the channels and all the fibers of the body, where the mind exposes itself by inspecting.

The soul is then touched: meaning at once that it is disturbed and that it is impressed by the "imprinted vestiges" in the body, in other words, by the extended traces of the world's extension. The soul is exposed there in a proper modality of extension and marries the impulse of the body: if I walk, it's a walking soul; if I sleep, a sleeping soul; if I eat, an eating soul. If a blade or a shard cuts through my skin, my soul is cut to the exact depth, force, and form of the wound. And if I die, the soul becomes death itself.

In other words, the soul doesn't experience the body, any more than the body does the soul. But someone experiences, and the "one" of this someone is altogether justly the indistinct motion of this "experiencing." It senses itself, which doesn't mean that it distinguishes itself as "self," or at least not as a substance—but that it in-distinguishes itself insofar as it is exposed to itself. By experiencing in this way, it is distinguished as distinct from the distinct in general, and thus as in-distinct. But this in-distinction is not a weak and mixed-up character of the object: it is the very force and movement of what we can name the ex-piration of the subject: how it arrives by falling outside the self.[5]

Psyche is extended, knows nothing about it, writes Freud in a posthumous note. As extended, Psyche doesn't know itself as extended. Extension in general is not to be known; it is to move, to be moved. But in the being moved or being exposed of the union, in an inextricably single and double mode, two in one and one in two, the nonknowledge of the self is known, which makes the self, moves sense, and makes sense—even the sense of knowledge itself—an emotion exposed, from the soul, to the whole body, and to the end of the world.

The body is the extension of the soul to the ends of the world and to the confines of the self, the one tied to the other and indistinctly distinct, extension tensed to the breaking point.

To Exist Is to Exit the Point

ANTONIA BIRNBAUM

Outside is the world, and we're all outside. Jean-Luc Nancy's thought worries about the outside. Worried, it doesn't settle for, or settle on, any of the classical figures for the relation to exteriority that philosophy crosses, retrieves, and displaces. Outside: exteriority doesn't derive from an alterity that would divide the self on the inside, even if such a division were primary and constitutive. Because it's not a question of keeping one's own negation inside but of thinking each self as some "one" existing with others: one of us all. Outside: exteriority isn't the sublime or transgressive experience of the failure of every limit, in which the self, swept up in the vacillation of something exceeding the presentable, fails to recover itself. Access to the world doesn't happen when confronting something beyond the self, the immensity of a starry sky, the boundless chasms of the sea, the chaos of mountains. . . . The world's boundlessness, far more discretely, lies in as many worlds as are needed to make a world: in as many things and existences as are peopling our own. Outside: exteriority isn't anxiety, where *Dasein* is brought back to its own disappearance, finding itself, in the process, referred to the finitude of its being-in-the-world. Because the possibility of death is always already someone else's as well, and finitude so considered is felt as much in the simple everyday presence of "anyone" (each and every one) as in the anxiety-producing imminence of our own death.

If we're all outside, present to the world in the first place—someone among other "someone's"—then there is no dialectical split to produce a

scene for enacting the division of interiority, no "inner" consciousness opposing nature's opaque exteriority, no improper existence redoubled by the more proper possibility of being authentically oneself in solitude. There's none of this, since interiority continues to weigh on all such grounds for exteriority, even when that interiority is constitutively alienated from the other, or bound by a moral law transcending the sensuous realm, or promoted in solitude's privilege as the most proper mode of being.

Or rather, all this is certainly in Nancy, but as the material for a thinking that is always eager to cross borders, to suffer no restriction, to leave nothing self-enclosed: not even to leave the soul cloistered and confined in a prison intended as the envelope for its corporeal existence. Here, in a text whose brevity is equaled only by its density ["The Extension of the Soul"], Nancy applies himself to restoring extension to this thing that, by definition, lacks extension, namely, the soul itself . . .

Why seek "the extension of the soul" in Descartes? Nancy notes that "what we so often designate Cartesian 'dualism' can therefore be understood as entirely different from an ontological cut between body and soul." This dualism has in fact many other characteristics, primarily that of cutting Descartes' philosophy off from the Christian ontology of incarnation. Such an ontology rests on a twofold concept of the image. God draws the world's image after himself, in keeping with the principle of resemblance, and out of himself, in keeping with the principle of generation. Thus the image is at once effigy and child. The sensuous, as exteriorization of the Word, resembles the intelligible, which created it. This spiritual transitivity underlies all material proximity, all recognition. Granted this fact, everything in this world, first of all humanity itself, depends in its heart of hearts on an intelligible essence, to which its sensuous existence owes its reality, giving that essence only an exterior form. The relation of the sensuous to the intelligible is therefore one of subsumption. Spirituality constitutes the interior essence of all the sensible world's exterior manifestations. Or, to put it more precisely: materiality is only the expression of the mind's relation to itself.

Descartes' rationalism certainly remains deeply anchored in Christianity by taking divine perfection to be the origin of reason. Nevertheless, his persistence in posing the autonomy of the two substances—*res cogitans*, res extensa—prevents him from resorting to a transitive relationship between flesh and word when trying to determine the link that constitutes the lived union of body and soul. In fact, as Nancy emphasizes, Descartes never ignored the fundamental importance of the problem of this union. As a philosopher having posed the obligation to think for oneself, he

knows that in life we're never involved with distinct substances, but always with someone. But he's in the quasi-aporetic position of wanting to account for this union without at the same time retreating from the gains of his system, in which each of the related substances nonetheless remains first and last for itself. How, then, are we to think this thing that is contrary in itself: a body and a soul that owe strictly nothing to one other, even though they are necessarily united at the level of human existence?

Nancy here devotes his complete attention to this Cartesian conundrum. Because the philosophical problems that trouble a philosopher are not simply his weak spot. The obstacles he encounters can also be the source of his greatest audacity. In this case, it is a question of clarifying the audacity demonstrated by Descartes in his correspondence with Princess Elizabeth of Bohemia, a boldness that consists in inverting the order of arguments, and starting with "a single person who has a soul and body together," so as to think the tie that unites them. As "The Extension of the Soul" shows, Descartes thereupon develops two modes of evidence, each corresponding to the two things found in the soul—the fact that it thinks and the fact that it acts and suffers with the body—each deriving from a specific relation to exteriority. Either the soul is affected by itself in doubt, or the soul is united to the body in ordinary life. But the point is that the self, in either case, finds itself somehow placed "outside itself": depending, in Nancy's terms, in the first case on "emotion" (*ex-movens*), in the second case on "extension."

For Descartes, the world, in the first place, configures interiority as extension, and the soul determines exteriority by exempting itself—during its time of doubt—from everything that renders it present to the inside of the world. Thus, thought thinking itself, or the return of the soul to itself, is not a return to an intimate self-presence but the interruption of all ties conditioning this presence, including the tie to others. In cutting themselves off from the world, the "auto" of auto-affection and the "I" of the "I am, I exist" don't regain an interiority closed in upon itself but experience themselves in the concentrated extremity of thought. The experience of doubt exceeds the soul and in the process inverts the logic of inside and outside.

The soul affects itself by withdrawing, punctually, from all that makes it present to the inside of the world, from what Descartes calls ordinary life, life lived with others and endowed with matter and extension. This is why, because of its auto-affection of self, an immaterial substance without extension, the soul is, "of all things interior, the one that's most exterior."[1] The philosopher of the *Meditations on First Philosophy* never treats self-certainty and ordinary life as the two sides of an interior opposition. Quite

the contrary. The *res cogitans* is nothing but the extremity of a withdrawal; it is simply outside extension. Or to put it more simply, self-certainty is only given in and by its exteriority to ordinary life. The double exclusion produced by doubt does not resort to any given schema of interiorization, but derives from a fiction operating solely through the effect of a disjunction.

The world is something inside which I'm "outside myself"—and outside which I momentarily position myself through the metaphysical fiction that "I'm not a body" exposed to others and to what happens to me. Nancy, in his fashion, passes through this inversion, echoing it through an ellipsis as lapidary as it is enigmatic: "The outside is inside; it is the spacing of the dis-position of the world; it is our disposition and our co-appearance."[2]

It's this disjunction between world and self, and not a reflexive division, that governs the Cartesian development of the relation uniting soul and body. Rather than ranking them in a hierarchy, the philosopher thinks of the union as something arising not from a *res*—a substance—but from a heterogeneous relation between two substances. The soul's not subordinated to the body; in being linked to it, it unites with something improper to it. In consequence, the soul conjoined to the body doesn't know according to the clear and distinct evidence of reason: it accedes to things, to others, that are there with it and that "are known only obscurely by understanding alone, or by understanding assisted by the imagination; but . . . are known very clearly by the senses." [3]

Lived knowledge is paradoxical in that it coincides with its very confusion, and further, with a confusion tending to mix body and soul. This mixing is the criterion not of the erroneous character of such knowledge but of its very existence. This knowledge designates the conjunction in which the more a person's relation to the self is effaced, the more he experiences himself "*in* himself," and in which self-presence finally stops being identified with the essence of some thing—a substance—and just becomes the presence of "someone" who feels himself here among others, who is there, among them all. Someone for whom being inside the world is synonymous with being exposed outside himself. Or, to put it otherwise: body and soul are given together in a single person, where this person sets himself apart from himself. To experience myself "in myself" is again, therefore, to find myself in a relation to exteriority, but one that this time occurs through an exposure, rather than a withdrawal.

But how does being thus set apart from oneself—in Nancy's terms, "being exposed"—constitute an evidence, an evidence that is furthermore acquired in ordinary life and conversation? Here we must not be deceived.

Someone's active and ordinary knowledge proves obscure, but only insofar as we ask in what way it confuses the principle operation of substantial reason. But the union of body and soul doesn't need to be reasoned to be experienced, and each and every person exercises discrimination every day by mixing indifferently the three registers of knowledge—thinking, imagining, feeling—according to the situation in which he is. Anyone who experiences in this way goes outside conscious intention, so given over is he to the world, to what happens to him, to what he does, to others.

From one outside to the other. Either the soul is the auto-affection of itself, an immaterial substance without extension, and is, then, of all interior things the one that's most exterior. Or else the soul transfers itself improperly in its union with a body and then ceases to be a relation to self, becoming a self exposed in accord with corporeal exteriority, and thus exposed to others, present to the world, "being world." Such is Nancy's "either/or": an incessant passage in and through exteriority.

His passage through Descartes restores all its force to the strange method thanks to which a philosopher reinvented thought: the force of a doubt that recovers its punctual character without having its exteriority removed, the force of an existence and of a knowledge whose heterogeneity he never ceased to explore, concurrently with the pursuit of ancient languages, travels, study of customs, mathematics, correspondence, war, repose. Descartes, the inventor, who doesn't think by following the line of order but discovers the order of reasons "by himself," over time. Descartes, author of a book, *The World*, that he didn't publish. Provisionally.

It's not a matter of opposing soul and body but of showing how their union passes from one exteriority to another, how it is this very passage. Thought is always overwhelmed by existence, and existence never stops being exceeded in thought. To exist is to exit the point: the point of the fiction "that I have no hands, no eyes, no flesh, no blood, as having no sense."[4] To exist is to resort—punctually—to this fiction, "that I have no hands, no eyes, no flesh, no blood, as having no sense," not in order to seal off reason in its self-identity but to accede, in a pure pulsation of the soul, to the freedom of determination peculiar to thought.

Hardly entered, already gone: what "The Extension of the Soul" enables us to read is nothing other than the fable of Descartes' escape. "Descartes himself testifies to the exteriority of the world as the exteriority of his body. Because he hardly doubts his body, he makes a fiction of doubting it, and this pretension as such attests to the truth of *res extensa*. . . . Reality is always in each instant, from place to place, each time in turn, which is exactly how the reality of the *res cogitans* attests to itself in each 'ego sum,' which is each time the 'I am' of each one in turn [*chaque fois de chacun à son tour*]."[5]

Fifty-eight Indices on the Body

1. A body's material. It's dense. It's impenetrable. Penetrate it, and you break it, puncture it, tear it.

2. A body's material. It's off to one side. Distinct from other bodies. A body begins and ends against another body. The void is itself a subtle kind of body.

3. A body isn't empty. It's full of other bodies, pieces, organs, parts, tissues, knee-caps, rings, tubes, levers, and bellows. It's also full of itself: that's all it is.

4. A body's long, large, high, and deep: all the while being bigger or smaller. A body's extended. It touches other bodies on all sides. A body's corpulent, even when thin.

5. A body's immaterial. It's a drawing, a contour, an idea.

6. The soul is the form of an organized body, says Aristotle. But the body, precisely, is what draws this form. It's the form of the form, the form of the soul.

7. The soul is extended everywhere along the body, says Descartes; it is entirely everywhere all along it, on its very surface, insinuated within it,

and slipped into it, infiltrated, impregnating, tentacular, inflating, modeling, omnipresent.

8. The soul is material, made of entirely different matter, matter that has no place, size, or weight. But it's material, very subtly. And so it drops out of sight.

9. A body's visible, the soul is not. We can easily see that a paralytic cannot move his good leg. We cannot see that a bad man cannot move his good soul: but we should take it as the effect of a paralysis of the soul. And we have to struggle against it and subdue it. Such is the foundation of ethics, my dear Nicomachos.

10. A body is also a prison for the soul. In it, the soul pays for a very serious crime whose nature is hard to discern. Which is why the body's so heavy and awkward for the soul. It has to digest, sleep, excrete, sweat, be defiled, be hurt, fall ill.

11. Teeth are the bars of a prison window. The soul escapes through the mouth in words. But words are still the body's effluvia, emanations, weightless folds in the air escaping the lungs and warmed by the body.

12. A body can become speaking, thinking, dreaming, imagining. It always senses something. It senses everything corporeal. It senses skins and stones, metals, grasses, waters, and flames. It doesn't stop sensing.

13. But it's the soul that senses. And the soul, first of all, senses the body. It senses it from all parts containing it and retaining it. If the body didn't retain it, the whole soul would escape in gossamer words, evaporating into the sky.

14. The body's like a pure spirit: it keeps completely to itself and inside itself, in a single point. Break that point, and the body dies. The point's situated between the eyes, between the ribs, in the middle of the liver, all around the skull, in the midst of the femoral artery, and in lots of other places, too. The body's a collection of spirits.

15. The body's an envelope: and so it serves to contain what it then has to develop. The development is interminable. The finite body contains the infinite, which is neither soul nor spirit, but in fact the development of the body.

16. The body's a prison, or a god. There's no in-between. Or else the in-between is mince-meat, an anatomy, an *écorché*, with none of this producing a body. The body's a cadaver, or it's glorious. The cadaver and the glorious body share shining, immobile splendor: when all is said and done, it's a statue. The body is achieved as statue.

17. Body to body, side to side or face to face, aligned or opposed, most often just mixed, tangential, and having little to do with each other. But that's how bodies, which properly exchange nothing, send one another quantities of signals, notices, winks, or signaletic gestures. A bearing, debonair or lofty, a tensing up, an appeal, a depression, a gravity, a flair. And whatever belongs to the categories of words like *youth* or *old age, work* or *boredom, force* or *awkwardness* . . . Bodies cross paths, rub up against each other, press each other. Take buses, cross streets, enter supermarkets, step into cars, wait their turn in line, sit down in movie theaters after passing in front of ten other bodies.

18. The body's simply a soul. A soul, wrinkled, fat or dry, hairy or callous, rough, supple, cracking, gracious, flatulent, iridescent, pearly, daubed with paint, wrapped in muslin or camouflaged in khaki, multicolored, covered with grease, wounds, warts. The soul is an accordion, a trumpet, the belly of a viola.

19. The nape is stiff and hearts have to be sounded. The lobes of the liver outline the cosmos. The sexes are watered.

20. Bodies are differences. Forces, therefore. Minds aren't forces: they're identities. A body's a force different from several others. A man against a tree, a dog in front of a lizard. A whale and an octopus. A mountain and a glacier. You and me.

21. A body is a difference. Since it is a difference from every other body—while minds are identical—it's never done with differing. It also differs from itself. How are we to ponder a baby and an old man next to one another?

22. Different, bodies are all somewhat deformed. A perfectly formed body is a disturbing, indiscreet body in the world of bodies, unacceptable. It's a diagram, not a body.

23. The head is detached from the body, without its having to be decapitated. The head is detached by itself, apart. The body is an ensemble,

it is articulated and composed, organized. The head consists only of holes, its empty center representing the spirit, the point, an infinite concentration in itself. Pupils, nostrils, mouth, ears are all holes, carved flights out of the body. Disregarding those other holes further down, these concentrated orifices connect with the body by means of a thin, fragile channel: the neck traversed by marrow and several vessels ready to swell or break. A thin attachment that connects, by folding, the complex body to the simple head. No muscles there, just tendons and bone with a soft, gray substance, circuits, synapses.

24. A headless body's closed in on itself. It ties its muscles together, hooks its organs up to one another. The head's simple, a combination of alveoli and liquids in a triple envelope.

25. If man is made in the image of God, then God has a body. He may even be a body, or the eminent body of them all. The body of the thought of bodies.

26. Prison or God, no in-between: a sealed envelope, or an open envelope. Cadaver or glory, recess or excess.

27. Bodies cross paths, rub up and press against each other, embrace or collide with one another: they send each other all these signals, so many signals, addresses, notices, which no defined sense can exhaust. Bodies produce a sense beyond sense. They're an extravagance of sense. Which is why a body seems to assume its sense only once it's dead, fixed. And maybe why we interpret the body as the soul's tomb. In reality, a body never stops stirring. Death freezes the movement of letting go and declining to stir. A body is the stirring of the soul.

28. A body: a smooth or wrinkled soul, fat or thin, bald or hairy, a soul with bumps or wounds, a soul dancing or plunging, a callous, humid, soul, fallen to the ground . . .

29. A body, bodies: there can't be just one body, and the body bears the difference. They are forces, placed and stretched one against the other. "Against" (in opposition, encountering, "right up against") is the major category of the body. This implies a play of differences, contrasts, resistances, graspings, penetrations, repulsions, densities, weights, and measures. My body exists against the fabric of its clothing, the vapors of the air it breathes, the brightness of lights or the brushings of shadows.

Fifty-eight Indices on the Body ■ *153*

30. Body proper: to be proper, the body has to be foreign, and therefore to find itself appropriated. The child looks at his hand, his foot, his navel. The body's the intruder that, without breaking in, can't penetrate the self-present point that the spirit is. Moreover, the latter is so utterly punctual, so closed in upon its being-to-itself-in-itself, that the body only penetrates it by extravagating or exogastrulating its own mass like a growth, a tumor outside the spirit. A malignant tumor whose spirit won't go into remission.

31. Cosmic body: bit by bit, my body touches on everything. My buttocks on my chair, my fingers on the keyboard, the chair and keyboard on the table, the table on the floor, the floor on the foundations, the foundations on the earth's central magma and shifting tectonic plates. If I go in the other direction, through the atmosphere, I reach galaxies and finally the boundless limits of the universe. A mystic body, a universal substance, and a marionette drawn by a thousand threads.

32. Eating isn't incorporating, but opening the body to the thing we devour, exhaling our insides in the tasting of fish or fig. Running unfolds those same insides with strides, fresh air on the skin, spent breath. Thinking swings tendons, and various springs, back and forth with jets of steam and forced steps over great salt lakes with no discernable horizon. There's never any incorporation, but always exits, twists, openings-out, channelings or disgorgings, crossings, balancings. Intussusception is a metaphysical chimera.

33. "This is my body" = the constant, silent assertion of my lone presence. It implies a distance: "this," here's what I put before you. It's "my body." Two questions are immediately implied: To whom does this "my" refer? And if "my" indicates "property," what is its nature? Who's proprietary, and what's the legitimacy of his property? There's no answer to "who," since it's the body just as much as the body's proprietor, and no answer to "property," since it is just as much a natural right as a right to work, or to conquest (when I cultivate and take care of my body). "My body" therefore indicates the impossibility of assigning both terms of the expression. (Who gave you your body? Only you yourself, since no program, genetic or demiurgic, would have been sufficient. But you before yourself, then? You behind your birth? And why not? Am I not always on my own back, and on the verge of reaching my body?)

34. In truth, "my body" indicates a possession, not a property. In other words, an appropriation without legitimation. I possess my body, I

treat it as I wish, I exercise a *jus uti et abutendi* over it. It, however, in its own turn, possesses me: it pulls or holds me back, offends me, stops me, pushes me, pushes me away. We're both possessed, a pair of demonic dancers.

35. The etymology of "possessing" is said to reside in the signification of "being seated on." I'm seated on my body, a child or a dwarf riding on a blind man's shoulders. My body's sitting on me, crushing me with its weight.

36. Corpus: a body is a collection of pieces, bits, members, zones, states, functions. Heads, hands and cartilage, burnings, smoothnesses, spurts, sleep, digestion, goose-bumps, excitation, breathing, digesting, re-producing, mending, saliva, synovia, twists, cramps, and beauty spots. It's a collection of collections, a *corpus corporum*, whose unity remains a question for itself. Even when taken as a body without organs, it still has a hundred organs, each of which pulls and disorganizes the whole, which can no longer manage to be totalized.

37. "This wine has body": it puts a thickness into the mouth, a consistency that adds to the flavor; it lets the tongue touch it, caress and roll it between the cheeks and against the palate. It won't settle for sliding into the stomach; it will leave the mouth coated by a film, a fine membrane or sediment of its taste and tonus. We could say: "this body has wine"; it goes to the head, it releases vapors that charm and fill the spirit, it excites and incites a touch that seeks to be charged by its contact.

38. Nothing's more singular than the sensuous, erotic, affective discharge that certain bodies produce in us (or inversely, the indifference that certain others leave us with). A certain build, a certain thinness, a certain hair color, a bearing, a spacing of the eyes, a shoulder's shape or movement, a chin, fingers, almost nothing, only an accent, a wrinkle, an irreplaceable feature . . . It's not the body's soul, but its *spirit*: its point, its signature, its smell.

39. "Body" is distinguished from "head" as well as "members," or at least "extremities." In this respect, the body is the trunk, the bearer, the column, the pillar, the built of the building. The head's reduced to a point: it doesn't really have a surface; it's made of holes, orifices, and openings, through which various kinds of messages come and go. The

extremities, likewise, are informed by an ambient milieu, where they accomplish certain operations (walking, waiting, seizing). The body remains alien to all this. It perches on itself, in itself: not decapitated, but with its shriveled head stuck onto it like a pin.

40. The body is the in-itself of the for-itself. In the relation to the self, it is a moment without relation. It's impenetrable, unpenetrated; it's silent, deaf, blind, and deprived of touch. It's massive, crude, insensitive, unfeeling. It's also the in-itself of the for-others, turned toward them but with no regard for them. It's only effective—but absolutely so.

41. The body keeps its secret, this nothing, this spirit that isn't lodged in it but spread out, expanded, extended all across it, so much so that the secret has no hiding place, no intimate fold where it might some day be discovered. The body keeps nothing: it keeps itself as secret. That's why the body dies and is borne away, concealed, into the grave. Of its passage, hardly a few indices remain.

42. The body is the unconscious: seeds of ancestors sequenced in its cells, and mineral salts consumed, and mollusks caressed, broken bits of wood, and worms feasting on its cadaver underground, or else the flame that incinerates it and the ash it yields, epitomizing it in impalpable powder, and the people, plants, and animals whose paths it crosses and with whom it rubs shoulders, and the tales from long-gone nurses, and monuments in ruins covered with lichens, and enormous turbines in factories fabricating extraordinary alloys from which its prosthetic devices will be made, and rough or lisping phonemes, with which its tongue makes spoken noises, and laws engraved on steles, and secret desires for murder or immortality. The body touches on everything with the secret tips of its bony fingers. And everything ends up making a body, down to the very *corpus* of dust assembling and dancing a vibrant dance in the thin streak of light where the last day of the world draws to a close.

43. Why indices rather than characters, signs, distinctive markings? Because the body escapes, is never sure, lets its presence be suspected but not identified. It could always just be part of another, bigger body that we take to be its house, its car or its horse, its ass or its mattress. It could be nothing more than the double of that tiny, vaporous other body that we call its soul and that escapes through its mouth when it dies. All we have at our disposal are indications, traces, imprints, and vestiges.

44. Soul, body, mind: the first is the form of the second, and the third is the force producing the first. The second is thus the expressive form of the third. The body expresses the mind, meaning that it makes it spurt out outside, squeezes its essence, draws its sweat, extracts its sparkle and tosses it all into space. A body's an explosion.

45. The body is *ours* and *proper* to us precisely to the degree that it doesn't belong to us and evades the intimacy of our proper being, if this being ever even exists, something the body, precisely, should make us seriously doubt. But to this degree, which suffers no limitation, our body isn't just ours but *us*, *ourselves*, even unto death, meaning its death and decomposition, in which we can be, and are, identically decomposed.

46. Why indices? Because there's no totality to the body, no synthetic unity. There are pieces, zones, fragments. There's one bit after another, a stomach, an eyelash, a thumb-nail, a shoulder, a breast, a nose, an upper intestine, a choledoch, a pancreas: anatomy is endless, until eventually running into an exhaustive enumeration of cells. But this doesn't yield a totality. On the contrary, we must immediately run through the whole nomenclature all over again, so as to find, if possible, a trace of the soul imprinted on every piece. But the pieces, the cells, change as the calculation enumerates in vain.

47. The body's exteriority and alterity include the unbearable: dejection, filth, the ignoble waste that is still part of it, still belongs to its substance and especially its activity, since it has to expel it, which is not one of its lesser functions. From excrement to the outgrowth of nails, hairs, or every kind of wart or purulent malignity, it has to put outside, and separate from itself, the residue or excess of its assimilatory processes, the excess of its own life. The body doesn't want to say, see, or smell this. It feels shame about it, and all kinds of daily distress and embarrassment. The soul enjoins itself to silence concerning a whole part of the body whose own form it is.

48. The body is precision: it is here, nowhere else. It's at the tip of the right big toe, it's at the base of the sternum, it's in the nipple of the breast, it's on the right, the left, above, below, deep or on the surface, diffuse or punctual. It is pain or pleasure, or just a simple mechanical transmission, like that of keys on a keyboard under the pads of my fingers. Even what's described as diffuse in one or another sensation keeps the precision of the "diffuse," which irradiates each time in a very precise way. The spirit's

precision is mathematical; the soul's is physical: it's exposed in grams and millimeters, in a fraction of ejection and with the speed of sedimentation, in a respiratory coefficient. There's nothing reductive about anatomy, contrary to the claims of spiritualists, indeed it's the soul's extreme precision.

49. The imprecision of bodies: here's a man who's about forty years old, who appears rather dry and nervous, looks rather worried, perhaps even a little shifty. He walks with a certain stiffness; he might be a professor or a doctor, or else a judge or administrator. He's not very attentive to his clothes. He has high cheekbones and a slightly rugged hue: no doubt he's of a somewhat Mediterranean stock, certainly not, in any case, Nordic. Anyway, he's of middling size. One gets the feeling he is clumsy, and one wonders whether he has any authority and determination. One also doubts that he likes himself. We could go on at length in this register, with all those indices scattered across one sole body. We'd certainly be wrong on many points, and maybe on all of them. But it is not possible to be completely wide of the mark, unless an artfully contrived disguise is able to deceive us. And this disguise will have borrowed its features from some typical and schematic reservoir of species or genus. For there are types of humans (as, indeed, there are of animals). Inextricably, these are biological or zoological, physiological, psychological, social and cultural; they come from constants of diet and education, sexuation and subjection by work, condition, history: but they impress their typology, even at the price of, and in the midst of, an infinite individual differentiation. We can never say where the singular begins and the typical ends.

50. The denial of types, individual as well as collective, is a result of the antiracist imperative we've had to adopt. A poor necessity, however, since it obliges us to efface family likenesses, those vague but insistent similarities, touching or amusing blends of the effects of genetics, fashion, social divisions, ages, from the midst of which there emerges, and with greater distinctness, what is incomparable in each person.

51. Beauty spot: this is the name for those brown or black particles, slightly prominent, that sometimes (and, for some, often) make a point, a mark, or a mole on the skin. Rather than spot the skin, they accentuate its whiteness, or at least this is what was often said in days when snow and milk served as points of comparison par excellence for women's skin. Women would then, if need be, put velvet "flies" on their cheeks and neck. Today, we prefer darker skin, sunbathed or tanned. But the beauty

spot keeps its appeal: it signals skin, sets off its expanse, and configures it, guides the eye and affects it as a mark of desire. We'd almost be inclined to call a beauty spot the seed of desire, a minuscule rise in intensity, a corpuscle whose dark tint concentrates the energy of the entire body, as does the nipple of the breast.

52. The body works in spasms, contractions and releases, folds, unfoldings, knottings and untyings, twists, somersaults, hiccups, electrical discharges, releases, contractions, quiverings, shakings, goose-bumps, erections, heavings, starts. A body that rises, falls, is emptied out, flaked, pierced, dispersed, zoned, squirts and seeps or bleeds, moistens and dries up or suppurates, grumbles, groans, gasps, creaks, and sighs.

53. The body fabricates the soul's auto-immunity, in the technical sense of this medical term: it protects the soul against itself; it prevents it from retreating entirely into its intimate spirituality. It provokes, within the soul, a rejection of the soul.

54. The body, the skin: the rest is anatomical, physiological, and medical literature. Muscles, tendons, nerves and bones, humors, glands, and organs are cognitive fictions. They are functionalist formalisms. But the truth is skin. Truth is in the skin, it makes skin: an authentic extension exposed, entirely turned outside while also enveloping the inside, a sack crammed with rumblings and musty odors. Skin touches and lets itself be touched. Skin caresses and flatters, gets wounded, flayed, and scratched. It's irritable and excitable. It absorbs sunshine, cold and heat, wind, rain; it inscribes marks from within—wrinkles, spots, warts, peelings—and marks from the outside, which are sometimes the same, or else cracks, scars, burns, slashes.

55. Polymorphous, oxymoronic body: inside/outside, matter/form, homo/heterology, auto/allonomy, growth/excrescence, mine/none . . .

56. Indexical body: someone is there, someone's hiding there, showing the tip of an ear, some man or woman, some thing or some sign, some cause or some effect, there's a kind of "there" there, a "down-there," very close, quite far . . .

57. A body touched, touching, fragile, vulnerable, always changing, fleeing, ungraspable, evanescent under a caress or a blow, a body without a husk, a poor skin stretched over the cave where our shadow floats . . .

58. Why 58 indices? Because 5 + 8 = the members of the body, arms, legs, and head, and the eight regions of the body: the back, the belly, the skull, the face, the buttocks, the genitals, the anus, the throat. Or else because 5 + 8 = 13 and 13 = 1 & 3, 1 standing for unity (one body) and 3 standing for an endlessly circulating agitation and transformation; dividing and exciting itself among the body's matter, soul and spirit . . . Or even: the arcane XIII of the tarot deck designating death, death incorporating the body in an everlasting universal body of mud and chemical cycles, of heat and stellar bursts . . .

59. *Arises therefore the fifty-ninth index, the supernumerary, the excessive—the sexual: bodies are sexed. No body is unisex, as certain clothes are nowadays said to be. A body, on the contrary, is also a sex through and through: also breasts, a penis, vulva, testicles, ovaries; bony, morphological, physiological features, a type of chromosome. The body is sexed in essence. This essence is determined as the essence of a relation to the other essence. The body is thus determined in essence as a relation, or as in relation. The body is related to the body of the other sex. In this relation, its corporeality is involved insofar as it touches through sex on its limit: it delights [jouit], meaning that the body is shaken outside itself. Each of its zones, delighting for itself, emits the same light to the outside. This is called a soul. But mostly it stays caught in the spasm, the sob, or the sigh. Finite and infinite have intersected there, have crossed paths and exchanged places for an instant. Each of the sexes can occupy the position of the finite or the infinite.*

The Intruder

There is in fact nothing so ignobly useless and superfluous as the organ called the heart, the filthiest invention that beings could have invented for pumping me with life.

—Antonin Artaud[1]

The intruder introduces himself forcefully, by surprise or by ruse, not, in any case, by right or by being admitted beforehand. Something of the stranger has to intrude, or else he loses his strangeness. If he already has the right to enter and stay, if he is awaited and received, no part of him being unexpected or unwelcome, then he is not an intruder any more, but then neither is he any longer a stranger. To exclude all intrusiveness from the stranger's coming is therefore neither logically acceptable nor ethically admissible.

If, once he is there, he remains a stranger, then for as long as this remains so—and does not simply become "naturalized"—his coming does not stop: he continues to come, and his coming does not stop intruding in some way: in other words, without right or familiarity, not according to custom, being, on the contrary, a disturbance, a trouble in the midst of intimacy.

We have to think this through, and therefore to put it into practice: the strangeness of the stranger would otherwise be reabsorbed—would be an issue no longer—before he even crossed the threshold. To welcome a stranger, moreover, is necessarily to experience his intrusion. For the most

part, we would rather not admit this: the very theme of the intruder intrudes upon our moral correctness (and is in fact a remarkable example of the *politically correct*). But it is inseparable from the stranger's truth. This moral correctness presupposes that, upon receiving the stranger, we efface his strangeness at the threshold: it aims thereby not to have received him at all. But the stranger insists and intrudes. This fact is hard to receive, and perhaps to conceive . . .

I (who, "I"? this is precisely the question, an old question: who is the subject of this utterance, ever alien to the subject of its statement, whose intruder it certainly is, though certainly also its motor, its clutch, or its heart)—I, then, received someone else's heart, about ten years ago. It was grafted into me. My own heart (you will have understood that this is the whole question of the "proper"—or else it is nothing of the sort, and then there is properly nothing to understand, no mystery, not even a question: just the mere evidence of a transplant, as the doctors prefer to call it)—my own heart, then, was useless, for reasons never explained. In order, therefore, to live, I had to receive the heart of another person.

(But what other program, then, was crossing my physiological program? Less than twenty years earlier, no one was doing grafts, and certainly not protecting against their rejection through the use of cyclosporin. Twenty years hence, to be sure, other grafts will involve other methods. Personal contingency intersects with the contingency of technological history. Earlier I would be dead, later I would survive by other means. But "I" always finds itself tightly squeezed in a wedge of technical possibilities. Hence the vain debate, as I watched it unfold, between those who wanted a metaphysical adventure and those who preferred a technical performance: certainly both are at stake, one inside the other.)

After they told me I needed a graft, any sign could fluctuate, any data be reversed. Without further reflection, certainly, without even identifying an act, a permutation. Just the physical sensation of a void already opened up in the chest, a sort of apnea where nothing, absolutely nothing, even today, could help me disentangle the organic from the symbolic and imaginary, or disentangle what was continuous from what was interrupted: it was like a single gasp, exhaled thereafter through a strange cavern already imperceptibly opened up and like the spectacle, indeed, of leaping overboard while staying up on the bridge.

If my own heart was failing me, to what degree was it "mine," my "own" organ? Was it even an organ? For some years I had already felt a fluttering, some breaks in the rhythm, really not much of anything (mechanical figures, like the "ejection fraction," whose name I found to be

pleasing): not an organ, not the dark red muscular mass loaded with tubes that I now had to suddenly imagine. Not "my heart" beating endlessly, hitherto as absent as the soles of my feet while walking.

It became strange to me, intruding by defection: almost by rejection, if not by dejection. I had this heart at the tip of my tongue, like improper food. Rather like heartburn [un haut-le-coeur], but gently. A gentle sliding separated me from myself. I was there, it was summertime, we had to wait, something broke away from me, or this thing surged up inside me, where nothing had been before: nothing but the "proper" immersion inside me of a "myself" never identified as this body, still less as this heart, suddenly watching itself. Later on, for example, when climbing stairs, feeling each release of an "extrasystole" like the falling of a pebble to the bottom of a well. How do you become a representation to yourself? And a montage of functions? And where, then, does it go, that potent, silent evidence that was holding things together so uneventfully?

My heart became my stranger: strange precisely because it was inside. The strangeness could only come from outside because it surged up first on the inside. What a void suddenly opened up in the chest or the soul— they're one and the same—as soon as I was told: "You will need a transplant" . . . Here, the mind pushes against nothing: nothing to know, nothing to understand, nothing to sense. The intrusion of a body foreign to thought. This blank will stay with me like thought itself and its contrary, at one and the same time.

A heart that only half beats is only half my heart. I was already no longer inside me. I'm already coming from somewhere else, or I'm not coming any longer at all. Something strange is disclosed "at the heart" of the most familiar—but "familiar" hardly says it: at the heart of something that never signaled itself as "heart." Up to this point, it was strange by virtue of not being even perceptible, not even being present. From now on it fails, and this strangeness binds me to myself. "I" am, because I am ill. ("Ill" is not exactly the term: not infected, just rusty, tight, blocked.) But this other, my heart, is done for. This heart, from now on intrusive, has to be extruded.

No doubt this can only happen if I want it, along with several others. "Several others": those who are close to me, but also the doctors, and, finally, myself, now doubled or multiplied more than ever before. Always for different motives, this whole world has to agree, in unison, to believe that prolonging my life is worth the effort. It isn't hard to picture the complexity of this strange group, intervening thus in the most sensitive part of "me." Let's pass over those who are close and pass over my-"self"

(which, however, as I have said, is doubled: a strange suspension of judgment makes me picture myself as dying without protest, but also without attraction . . . we feel the heart weakening, we think we are going to die, we feel that we aren't going to feel anything anymore). But the doctors—here a whole team—are far more involved than I might have supposed: they have to decide, first of all, on whether a graft is indicated, then propose it without imposing it. (In doing so, they tell me there's to be a constraining "follow-up," nothing more—and what else could they guarantee? Eight years later, and after many other problems, I will develop a cancer brought on by the treatment: but today I'm still alive; who knows what's "worth the trouble," and what trouble?)

But the doctors also have to decide, as I will learn bit by bit, on inscription in a waiting list (in my case, for example, to accede to my demand not to be scheduled before the end of summer: presuming a certain confidence in the heart's staying power), and this list presupposes some choices: they will tell me about another candidate for a graft, apparently not in any shape, however, to survive the graft's follow-up, in particular the course of medication. I also know that I have to be grafted with a type O+ heart, thereby limiting the options. A question I will never pose: How does one decide, and who decides, when a graft, suitable for more than one graftee, is available? Here we know that the demand exceeds the supply . . . From the very outset, my survival is inscribed in a complex process interwoven with strangers and strangenesses.

Upon what does everyone's agreement on the final decision depend? Upon a survival that cannot be strictly weighed from the standpoint of pure necessity: Where would we find it? What would oblige me to live on? This opens out onto many other questions: Why me? Why live on at all? What does it mean "to live on"? Is this even the appropriate term? In what way is a long life-span a good thing? At this point I am fifty years old: young only for people in an "advanced" country at the end of the twentieth century . . . Only two or three centuries ago there was nothing scandalous about dying at this age. Why can the word *scandalous* occur to me in this context today? And why, and how, for us, the "advanced" people of the year 2000, is there not a "right time" to die (just shy of eighty years, and it will not stop advancing)? At one point a doctor, having abandoned the quest for the cause of my cardiomyopathy, told me that "your heart was programmed to last for fifty years." But what is this program, which I cannot turn into either a destiny or a providence? Just a brief programmatic sequence in an overall lack of programming.

Where are exactness and justice here? Who measures them, who declares them? This whole thing will reach me from somewhere else and

from outside—just as my heart, my body, are reaching me from somewhere else, are a somewhere else "within" me.

I do not claim to scorn quantity or to declare that nowadays we know only how to measure a life-span and are indifferent to its "quality." I am ready to recognize that even in a formula such as "c'est toujours ça de pris" ["at least we've got that"] more secrets are hidden than might be supposed. Life can only drive toward life. But it also heads toward death: Why in my case did it reach this limit of the heart? Why would it not?

Isolating death from life—without leaving one intimately entwined with the other, and each intruding into the heart of the other—this we must never do.

For eight years, during these ordeals, I will so often have heard, and will so often have repeated to myself: "But then you wouldn't be here any more!" How are we to think this kind of quasi-necessity, or desirable aspect, of a presence whose absence could always, very simply, have configured otherwise the world of various others? At the cost of some suffering? Of course. But why persist in re-figuring the asymptote of an absence of suffering? An old question, but aggravated by technology, and carried, we have to admit, to a point where we are hardly prepared for it.

Since the time of Descartes, at least, modern humanity has transformed the longing for survival and immortality into an element in a general program of "mastering and possessing nature." It has thereby programmed the growing strangeness of "nature." It has revived the absolute strangeness of the twofold enigma of mortality and immortality. Whatever religion used to represent, humanity has carried to a level of technical empowerment that defers the end in every sense of the word. By prolonging the span, it extends the absence of an end: prolonging what life, with what aim? To defer death is also to exhibit it, to underscore it.

We need only remark that humanity was never ready for any phase of this question and that its unreadiness for death is nothing but death itself: its stroke and its injustice.

Thus, the multiple stranger intruding into my life (my thin and winded life, sometimes slipping into malaise on the edge of abandonment, simply stunned) is nothing other than death, or rather life/death: a suspension of the continuum of being, a scansion in which "I" has/have nothing important to do. Protest and acceptance alike are strange to the situation. But nothing would not be strange. In the first place, the means of survival are themselves completely strange: What does it mean to replace a heart? Representing the thing is beyond me. (Opening up the entire thorax, taking care of the graft-organ, circulating the blood outside the body, suturing the vessels . . . I know very well that surgeons insist on the

insignificance of this last point: the vessels in transplants are smaller. But still: transplanting imposes an image of passing through nothingness, a flight into space emptied of any propriety or intimacy, or else, conversely, an image of that space intruding upon the inside of me: feeds, clamps, sutures, and tubes.)

What, "properly," is this life whose "saving" is at stake? At least it's agreed, anyway, that this propriety does not reside anywhere within "my" body. It is not sited anywhere, nor in this organ whose symbolic reputation requires no further development.

(Someone will say: there is always the brain. And the idea of a brain transplant certainly makes it into the papers now and then. Someday, no doubt, humanity will raise it again. Meanwhile, we acknowledge that the brain does not survive without a remnant of the body. Conversely, and dropping the subject for now, it might survive with a whole system of foreign body grafts . . .)

A "proper" life, not to be found in any organ, and nothing without them. A life that not only lives on, but continues to live properly, under a strange, threefold rule: that of decision, that of an organ, and that of sequellae to the transplant.

First of all, the graft is presented as a *restitutio ad integrum*: the heart is found to be beating once again. Here, the whole dubious symbolism of the gift of the other—a secret, ghostly complicity or intimacy between the other and me—wears out very quickly. In any event, its use, still widespread when I was grafted, seems to be disappearing bit by bit from the minds of the graftees: there's already a history of representing grafts. With the aim of stimulating organ donation, a great emphasis has been placed on the solidarity, and even the fraternity, of "donors" and recipients. And no one can doubt that this gift is now a basic obligation of humanity (in both senses of the word), or that—freed from any limits other than blood-group incompatibility (and freed especially from any ethnic or sexual limits: my heart can be a black woman's heart)—that this gift institutes the possibility of a network where life/death is shared by everyone, where life is connected with death, where the incommunicable is in communication.

Sometimes, however, the other very quickly appears as stranger: not as a woman, a black, or a young man, or a Basque, but as the immunitary other, the insubstitutable other that has nonetheless been replaced. "Rejection" is its name: my immune system rejects the other's. (Which means: "I have" two systems, two immunitary identities . . .) Many suppose that rejection consists in literally spitting the heart out, vomiting it

up: indeed, the word seems to be chosen to make this plausible. That's not it, but there is certainly something unbearable about the intruder's intrusion, and it is quickly fatal if left untreated.

The possibility of rejection resides in a double strangeness: the strangeness, on the one hand, of this grafted heart, which the organism identifies and attacks as being a stranger, and, on the other hand, the strangeness of the state in which medication renders the graftee in order to protect him. It lowers the graftee's immunity, so that he can tolerate the stranger. It thereby makes him a stranger to himself, to this immunitary identity, which is akin to his physiological signature.

An intruder is in me, and I am becoming a stranger to myself. If the rejection is very strong, I need treatments to help me resist human defenses. (This is done by means of an immunoglobulin drawn from a rabbit and then assigned, as its official description specifies, to this "anti-human" use, whose surprising effects—tremblings almost convulsive—I remember very well.)

But becoming a stranger to myself does not draw me closer to the intruder. Rather, it would appear that a general law of intrusion is being revealed. There has never been just one intrusion: as soon as one is produced, it multiplies itself, is identified in its renewed internal differences.

Thus, on several occasions I will know the shingles virus, or cytomegalovirus—strangers that have been dormant within me from the very start and are suddenly raised against me by the necessary immuno-depression.

At the very least, what happens is the following: identity is equal to immunity, the one is identified with the other. To lower the one is to lower the other. Strangeness and being a stranger become common, everyday things. This gets translated through a constant exteriorization of myself: I have to be measured, checked, tested. We are flooded with warnings about the outside world (crowds, stores, swimming pools, little children, sick people). But our liveliest enemies are within: old viruses crouching all along in the shadows of immunity, having always been there, intruders for all time.

In this last instance, no possible prevention. Instead, treatments that deport to further strangenesses. They fatigue, they ruin the stomach, or there's the howling pain of shingles . . . Through it all, what "me" is pursuing what trajectory?

What a strange me!

Not because they opened me up, gaping, to change the heart. But because this gaping cannot be sealed back up. (In fact, as every X-ray shows,

the sternum is stitched with filaments of twisted steel.) I am closed open. Through the opening passes a ceaseless flux of strangeness: immuno-depressor medications, other medications meant to combat certain so-called secondary effects, effects that we do not know how to combat (the degrading of the kidneys), renewed controls, all existence set on a new register, stirred up and around. Life scanned and reported onto multiple registers, all of them recording other possibilities of death.

Thus, then, in all these accumulated and opposing ways, my self becomes my intruder.

I certainly feel it, and it's much stronger than a sensation: never has the strangeness of my own identity, which for me has always been nonetheless so vivid, touched me with such acuity. "I" clearly became the formal index of an unverifiable and impalpable change. Between me and me, there had always been some space-time: but now there is an incision's opening, and the irreconciliability of a compromised immune system.

Cancer also arrives: a lymphoma, notice of whose eventuality (certainly not a necessity: few graftees end up with it), though signaled by the cyclosporin's printed advisory, had escaped me. It comes from the lower-ing of immunity. The cancer is like the ragged, crooked, and devastating figure of the intruder. Strange to myself, with myself estranging me. How can I put this? (But the exogenous or endogenous nature of cancerous phenomena is still being debated.)

Here too, in another way, the treatment calls for a violent intrusion. It incorporates certain amounts of chemotherapeutic and radiotherapeutic strangeness. Just as the lymphoma is eating away at the body and exhaust-ing it, the treatments attack it, making it suffer in several ways—and this suffering links the intrusion to its rejection. Even morphine, easing pain, provokes another suffering—brutalization and spaciness.

The most elaborate treatment is called an "autograft" (or "stem-cell graft"): after relaunching my lymphocytic production through "growth factors," they take white blood cell samples for five days in a row (all the blood is circulated outside the body, the samples being taken as it flows). These they freeze. Then I am installed in a sterile chamber for three weeks, and they administer a very strong chemotherapy, leveling my mar-row production before relaunching it as they reinject me with the frozen stem-cells (a strange odor of garlic pervades this injection . . .). The im-mune system is extremely weakened, whence the strong fevers, mycoses, and serial disorders that arise until the moment the lymphocytes start being produced again.

You come out of the whole thing bewildered. You no longer recognize yourself: but "recognize" no longer means anything. Very soon, you are just a wavering, a strangeness suspended between poorly identified states, between pains, between impotences, between failings. Relating to the self has become a problem, a difficulty or an opacity: it happens through evil or fear, no longer anything immediate—and the mediations are tiring.

The empty identity of the "I" can no longer rely on its simple adequation (in its "I = I") as enunciated: "I suffer" implicates two I's, strangers to one another (but touching each other). The same holds for "I delight" (we could show how this is indicated by the pragmatics of either statement): in "I suffer," however, the one I rejects the other, while in "I delight" the one I exceeds the other. Two drops of water are doubtless no more, and no less, alike.

I end/s up being nothing more than a fine wire stretched from pain to pain and strangeness to strangeness. One attains a certain continuity through the intrusions, a permanent regime of intrusion: in addition to the more than daily doses of medicine and hospital check-ups, there are the dental repercussions of the radiotherapy, along with a loss of saliva, the monitoring of food, of contagious contacts, the weakening of muscles and kidneys, the shrinking of memory and strength for work, the reading of analyses, the insidious returns of mucitis, candidiasis, or polyneuritis, and a general sense of being no longer dissociable from a network of measures and observations—of chemical, institutional, and symbolic connections that do not allow themselves to be ignored, akin to those out of which ordinary life is always woven, and yet, altogether inversely, holding life expressly under the incessant warning of their presence and surveillance. I become indissociable from a polymorphous dissociation.

This has always more or less been the life of the ill and the elderly: but that's just it, I am not precisely the one or the other. What cures me is what affects or infects me; what keeps me alive is what is makes me age prematurely. My heart is twenty years younger than I, and the rest of my body is (at least) twelve years older than I. Turning young and old at one and the same time, I no longer have a proper age, or properly have an age. Likewise, though not retired, I no longer properly have a trade. Likewise, I am not what I'm here to be (husband, father, grandfather, friend) without also being under the sign of this very general condition of an intruder, of various intruders who could at any moment take my place in the relation or representation to others.

In a similar movement, the most absolutely proper "I" retreats to an infinite distance (where does it go? from what vanishing point does it still

proffer this as *my* body?) and plunges into an intimacy deeper than any interiority (the irreducible niche from which I say "I," but which I know to be as gaping as a chest that is opened over a void, or as a sliding into the morphine-induced unconsciousness of pain and fear mixed in abandonment). *Corpus meum* and *interior intimo meo*, the two being joined, in a complete configuration of the death of god, in order to say very precisely that the subject's truth is its exteriority and its excessiveness: its infinite exposition. The intruder exposes me to excess. It extrudes me, exports me, expropriates me. I am the illness and the medicine, I am the cancerous cell and the grafted organ, I am these immuno-depressive agents and their palliatives, I am these ends of steel wire that brace my sternum and this injection site permanently sewn under my clavicle, altogether as if, already and besides, I were these screws in my thigh and this plate inside my groin. I am turning into something like a science-fiction android, or else, as my youngest son said to me one day, one of the living-dead.

We are, along with the rest of my more and more numerous fellow-creatures,[2] the beginnings, in effect, of a mutation: man begins again by passing infinitely beyond man. (This is what "the death of god" has always meant, in every possible way.) Man becomes what he is: the most terrifying and the most troubling technician, as Sophocles called him twenty-five centuries ago, who denatures and remakes nature, who recreates creation, who brings it out of nothing and, perhaps, leads it back to nothing. One capable of origin and end.

The intruder is nothing but myself and man himself. None other than the same, never done with being altered, at once sharpened and exhausted, denuded and overequipped, an intruder in the world as well as in himself, a disturbing thrust of the strange, the *conatus* of an on-growing infinity.[3]

Notes

Corpus

NOTE: A small portion of "Corpus," in a quite different version, was first put together for the April 26–28, 1990, meeting of the International Association for Philosophy and Literature entitled "Bodies: Image, Writing, Technology," at the University of California, Irvine. Translated by Claudette Sartiliot, it was published in Jean-Luc Nancy, *The Birth to Presence*, trans. Brian Holmes and others (Stanford, Calif.: Stanford University Press, 1993), 189–207, and reprinted in *Thinking Bodies*, ed. Juliet Flower MacCannell and Laura Zakarin (Stanford, Calif.: Stanford University Press, 1994), 17–31, the volume drawn from the Irvine conference.

1. David Grossman, *Voir ci-dessous: Amour*, translated from the Hebrew by Judith Misrahi and Ami Barak (Paris: Seuil, 1991).
2. Gōzō Yoshimasu, *Osiris, dieu de pierre*, translated from the Japanese by Makiko Ueda and Claude Mouchard, *Po&sie*, no. 56 (Paris: Belin, 1991).

On the Soul

NOTE: This lecture was given on April 8, 1994, at the Regional School of the Fine Arts in Le Mans, after a colloquium on "The Body" organized by Servane Zanotti, the school's director. Partly improvised, the lecture was recorded and then re-transcribed by Bruno Tackels with an exemplary fidelity to the chances and accidents of improvisation: so I haven't changed any of it. The text was previously published in the acts of the colloquium, *The Weight of the Body* (Le Mans: Beaux-Arts, 1995).

The Extension of the Soul

NOTE: This text was first published in Italian in the acts of the *Fundamenta* in Venice in 2002, then in French in *Poésie*, no. 99, and in a volume with the following text by Antonia Birnbaum, in Cahiers du Portique, University of Metz, 2004.

1. René Descartes, *Meditations and Other Metaphysical Writings*, trans. Desmonde Clarke (London: Penguin, 2003), 152–54.

2. Descartes goes so far as to say that the soul, rather than being accidentally united to the body, can be said to be accidentally separated from it by death (cf. the letter of December 1641 to Regius, where we see that he tempers this affirmation because of prudence regarding theology). Or he proceeds to compare the union of the soul to the "glorified body" of the resurrection (letter to Silhon, March 1642).

3. Cf. the idea of man as accidental being, in the previously cited letter to Regius.

4. Ludwig Wittgenstein, *Tractatus Logico-Philosophicus*, 6.41.

5. On the subject of force, both what is applied to the soul and that by which the soul can give commands to the body, let me refer you to Serge Margel, *Corps et âme* (Paris: Galilée, 2004).

To Exist Is to Exit the Point

1. Jean-Luc Nancy, *Ego Sum* (Paris: Flammarion, 1979).

2. Jean-Luc Nancy, *Being Singular Plural*, trans. Robert D. Richardson and Anne E. O'Byrne (Stanford, Calif.: Stanford University Press, 2000), 13.

3. René Descartes, *Correspondance avec Elisabeth et autre lettres*, ed. and introd. Jean-Marie Beyssade and Michelle Beyssade (Paris: GF-Flammarion, 1989), 73.

4. René Descartes, *Meditations and Other Metaphysical Writings*, trans. Desmonde Clarke (London: Penguin, 2003), 152–54.

5. Nancy, *Being Singular Plural*, 19.

Fifty-eight Indices on the Body

NOTE: The first version of this text was written for *Revista de comunicação e linguagens*, no. 33 (Lisbon, 2004). It has also been published together with a text by Ginette Michaud, "Appendice" (Montreal: Nota Bene, 2004).

The Intruder

1. In *84*, no. 5–6, 1948, p. 103.

2. I rejoin certain thoughts of friends: Alex speaking in German about being *un-eins* with AIDS, to speak of an existence whose unity lies in division and discord with itself, or Giorgio speaking in Greek about a *bios* that is only *zoī*, about a form of life that would be no more than merely maintained. See Alex Garcia-Düttmann, *At Odds with Aids*, trans. Peter Gilgen and Conrad Scott-Curtis (Stanford, Calif.: Stanford University Press, 1996), and Giorgio Agamben, *Homo*

Sacer: Sovereign Power and Bare Life, trans. Daniel Heller-Roazen (Stanford, Calif.: Stanford University Press, 1998). To say nothing of Derrida's grafts, supplements and prostheses. And the memory of a drawing by Sylvie Blocher, "Jean-Luc with the heart of a woman."

3. This text was first published in response to an invitation by Abdelwahab Meddeb to participate, for his review *Dédale*, in a number that he entitled "The Advent of the Stranger," no. 9–10 (Paris: Masisonneuve and Larose, 1999).

Perspectives in Continental Philosophy Series

John D. Caputo, series editor

John D. Caputo, ed., *Deconstruction in a Nutshell: A Conversation with Jacques Derrida*.

Michael Strawser, *Both/And: Reading Kierkegaard—From Irony to Edification*.

Michael D. Barber, *Ethical Hermeneutics: Rationality in Enrique Dussel's Philosophy of Liberation*.

James H. Olthuis, ed., *Knowing Other-wise: Philosophy at the Threshold of Spirituality*.

James Swindal, *Reflection Revisited: Jürgen Habermas's Discursive Theory of Truth*.

Richard Kearney, *Poetics of Imagining: Modern and Postmodern*. Second edition.

Thomas W. Busch, *Circulating Being: From Embodiment to Incorporation—Essays on Late Existentialism*.

Edith Wyschogrod, *Emmanuel Levinas: The Problem of Ethical Metaphysics*. Second edition.

Francis J. Ambrosio, ed., *The Question of Christian Philosophy Today*.

Jeffrey Bloechl, ed., *The Face of the Other and the Trace of God: Essays on the Philosophy of Emmanuel Levinas*.

Ilse N. Bulhof and Laurens ten Kate, eds., *Flight of the Gods: Philosophical Perspectives on Negative Theology*.

Trish Glazebrook, *Heidegger's Philosophy of Science*.

Kevin Hart, *The Trespass of the Sign: Deconstruction, Theology, and Philosophy*.

Mark C. Taylor, *Journeys to Selfhood: Hegel and Kierkegaard*. Second edition.

Dominique Janicaud, Jean-François Courtine, Jean-Louis Chrétien, Michel Henry, Jean-Luc Marion, and Paul Ricœur, *Phenomenology and the "Theological Turn": The French Debate*.

Dominique Janicaud, *Phenomenology "Wide Open": After the French Debate.* Translated by Charles N. Cabral.

Ian Leask and Eoin Cassidy, eds., *Givenness and God: Questions of Jean-Luc Marion.*

Jacques Derrida, *Sovereignties in Question: The Poetics of Paul Celan.* Edited by Thomas Dutoit and Outi Pasanen.

William Desmond, *Is There a Sabbath for Thought? Between Religion and Philosophy.*

Bruce Ellis Benson and Norman Wirzba, eds. *The Phenomoenology of Prayer.*

S. Clark Buckner and Matthew Statler, eds. *Styles of Piety: Practicing Philosophy after the Death of God.*

Kevin Hart and Barbara Wall, eds. *The Experience of God: A Postmodern Response.*

John Panteleimon Manoussakis, *After God: Richard Kearney and the Religious Turn in Continental Philosophy.*

John Martis, *Philippe Lacoue-Labarthe: Representation and the Loss of the Subject.*

Jean-Luc Nancy, *The Ground of the Image.*

Edith Wyschogrod, *Crossover Queries: Dwelling with Negatives, Embodying Philosophy's Others.*

Gerald Bruns, *On the Anarchy of Poetry and Philosophy: A Guide for the Unruly.*

Brian Treanor, *Aspects of Alterity: Levinas, Marcel, and the Contemporary Debate.*

Simon Morgan Wortham, *Counter-Institutions: Jacques Derrida and the Question of the University.*

Leonard Lawlor, *The Implications of Immanence: Toward a New Concept of Life.*

Clayton Crockett, *Interstices of the Sublime: Theology and Psychoanalytic Theory.*

Bettina Bergo, Joseph Cohen, and Raphael Zagury-Orly, eds., *Judeities: Questions for Jacques Derrida.* Translated by Bettina Bergo, and Michael B. Smith.

Jean-Luc Marion, *On the Ego and on God: Further Cartesian Questions.* Translated by Christina M. Gschwandtner.

Jean-Luc Nancy, *Philosophical Chronicles.* Translated by Franson Manjali.

Jean-Luc Nancy, *Dis-Enclosure: The Deconstruction of Christianity.* Translated by Bettina Bergo, Gabriel Malenfant, and Michael B. Smith.

Andrea Hurst, *Derrida Vis-à-vis Lacan: Interweaving Deconstruction and Psychoanalysis.*

Jean-Luc Nancy, *Noli me tangere: On the Raising of the Body.* Translated by Sarah Clift, Pascale-Anne Brault, and Michael Naas.

Jacques Derrida, *The Animal That Therefore I Am.* Edited by Marie-Louise Mallet, translated by David Wills.

Jean-Luc Marion, *The Visible and the Revealed.* Translated by Christina M. Gschwandtner and others.

Michel Henry, *Material Phenomenology.* Translated by Scott Davidson.